LISTENER SUPPORTED

The Culture and History of
Public Radio

JACK W. MITCHELL

Westport, Connecticut
London

Library of Congress Cataloging-in-Publication Data

Mitchell, Jack W., 1941–
   Listener supported : the culture and history of public radio / Jack W. Mitchell.
     p. cm.
   Includes bibliographical references and index.
   ISBN 0–275–98352–8 (alk. paper)
   1. Public radio—United States—History. 2. Radio programs, Public
service—United States—History. 3. National Public Radio (U.S.)—History.
4. Public radio—United States—Public opinion. 5. Public opinion—United
States. I. Title: Culture and history of Public Radio. II. Title.
HE8697.95.U6M58   2005
384.54'0973—dc22   2004022506

British Library Cataloguing in Publication Data is available.

Library of Congress Catalog Card Number: 2004022506
ISBN: 0–275–98352–8

First published in 2005

Praeger Publishers, 88 Post Road West, Westport, CT 06881
An imprint of Greenwood Publishing Group, Inc.
www.praeger.com

Printed in the United States of America

The paper used in this book complies with the
Permanent Paper Standard issued by the National
Information Standards Organization (Z39.48–1984).

10 9 8 7 6 5 4 3 2

Contents

PART THREE
Critics

Acknowledgment

Although the title page does not show it, this book has a coauthor. Public radio has been important in the life of my wife Bonnie because it has been so important in mine. Only in retrospect have I realized how much her sacrifices and self-reliance allowed me to participate in public radio's story as actively as I did. She felt the frustrations even more than I did during the difficult times in this story. She enjoyed little of the recognition that came to me as the story worked out to a mostly happy conclusion.

Bonnie Barnett Mitchell is coauthor in a more literal sense as well. What started out as help in editing my manuscript evolved into a partnership that was virtually equal. She challenged the reasoning throughout the book and shamed me into extensive rewrites. She simplified and clarified virtually every paragraph in my draft. If the book reads easily, the reader can thank Bonnie. Any direct active-voice sentence, any metaphor, any felicitous turn of phrase reflects her intervention. Any clumsy, klutzy phrase, or sentence that remains survived only because of my failure to accept her advice.

Any contribution I might have made to the development of public radio would not have been possible without Bonnie's sacrifice and support. This book would not have been written without her inspiration. It would not be as strong as I hope it is without her very active participation.

Introduction

A couple of years ago, the editor of *Current*, the newspaper of public radio and television, called to ask if I had a copy of National Public Radio's founding document, *National Public Radio Purposes*. He was working with the National Public Broadcasting Archives to post key historical documents on a web site, and the archivists could not find a copy. I replied that I had a copy, but asked why he had not just asked NPR. He said he had asked, but they could not seem to find one!

NPR without a copy of its *Purposes* struck me as incredible as a preacher without a Bible or the U.S. Supreme Court justices without a copy of the Constitution. The *Purposes* document officially defined NPR's mission and unofficially summarized the mission of all public radio. It reflected lengthy and spirited discussions by NPR's founding board of directors and the particular views of the document's principal author, William Siemering, who became NPR's first program director. This document attempted to define how "public" radio would differ from its parent, "educational" radio. While some dismissed them as pie in the sky, the *Purposes* generated a sense of renewal among those who had labored in the often frustrating field of educational radio and attracted a new generation of idealistic practitioners in the early 1970s. The *Purposes* were the subject of formal discussions and heated bull sessions. Loved by some, hated by others, they provided the starting point in public radio's evolution. They were powerful enough to dominate the debate over their implementation during public radio's early years that culminated in a schism in 1976 that literally tore NPR asunder.

Amazingly, a quarter century later, NPR could not find a copy of this incendiary document. Perhaps the *Purposes* lost relevance because NPR had evolved so far from its beginnings as to leave them nothing more than quaint historic footnotes unworthy of file space at NPR's headquarter's in Washington—or in the archives established to preserve public broadcasting's history. Perhaps the *Purposes* had become so much a part of the very fabric of the organization that NPR did not need a copy of the original text. Reality, I believe, blends both explanations. Although public radio has evolved beyond recognition from its origins, in fundamental ways it has not changed at all. This book explores that dichotomy.

I acknowledge that this book is personal and that its personal nature may represent either its strength or its weakness. By happenstance of birth place (Michigan) and year (1941), I landed in the right place at the right time to play a part in launching public radio. I witnessed the last days of educational radio and the first twenty-five years of public radio. I was a graduate student at the University of Michigan and a newsperson at its radio station, WUOM, in the years immediately before the Public Broadcasting Act of 1967, which created public television and, almost as an afterthought, public radio. My combination of experience and interest in educational radio and my relative youth influenced the newly created Corporation for Public Broadcasting to make an investment in me in the future of this new concept that would be called public radio. Consequently, the CPB sent me to Britain to work at and study BBC radio for a year. Upon returning to the United States, I became the first employee of National Public Radio. I started work in CPB's building at 888 Sixteenth Street NW in Washington on August 15, 1970. As the first person there, of course, I enjoyed many opportunities to do "first" things. I did the first NPR newscast, wrote its first strategic plan, wrote its first standards and practices document, and served as the first permanent producer of NPR's seminal program, *All Things Considered.* I left NPR in 1976 and spent the next twenty-one years as manager of WHA Radio in Madison, Wisconsin, which evolved into Wisconsin Public Radio, second only to Minnesota Public Radio in size and budget. In charge in Madison, I was better able to shape public radio as I envisioned it than I had been at the far more complex NPR. While in Wisconsin, I spent twelve years on the board of directors of NPR, three of those as chairman. I got to see public radio from inside and outside the Beltway.

A participant sees events up close, often too close to keep everything in focus. As a participant, I admit that I may look so closely at particular trees as to miss the forest. And as a participant, I understandably liked some people better than others, saw some as friends and some as foes, some as colleagues and some as rivals. Participation must color my story as seen from the inside. However, for the past six years, I have served as a professor at the University or Wisconsin's Journalism School trying to explain public broadcasting to undergraduates. This experience—along with the simple passage of time—has helped me put those events and people in better perspective. From a distance of years, heroes seem less heroic and villains less villainous. Specific events seem less calamitous or transforming when viewed with all the other events stretching over a period of forty years since I took my first job in educational radio in 1964. My perception of my individual importance has also diminished as more and more individuals have left their mark through the years. Nonetheless, beware of my biases.

I have been aware for a long time of the pitfalls of a participant in events writing a history of them. Only more recently, however, have I realized that this book is personal—and therefore distorted—in a somewhat different sense. As I have discussed some of the ideas in this book with others, I have heard variations on the theme "I've never heard of it" in reaction to something I had regarded as centrally important. At first such reactions shook my confidence. Then I realized that everyone in the field brings a somewhat different background and vision to public radio, and probably no one else sees it exactly as I do. To include all views of public radio's evolution would produce a book too long in length and too short on coherence, so I will present public radio as I saw it and see it. I will stick to facts but emphasize the ones that best make sense of this institution from my perspective. Reader beware.

The first section of the book is particularly idiosyncratic. I first drafted it on the assumption that I was summarizing the major ideas that shaped public radio. By the second draft, I understood that I was really summarizing the ideas that shaped *my* perception of public radio's mission and purpose. I hope my perception is worth sharing with you. In 1997, the Corporation for Public Broadcasting awarded me its Edward R. Murrow Award for lifetime contributions to public radio. The letter nominating me for that honor said, "Jack shaped both important institutions and important principles that give our field its distinctive character, mission, and role in American life." It argued that public radio is distinguished by its values, and the values of public radio are my values.[1] If true, two dynamics provide the explanation. Because of the accident of time and place, I was in a position to help shape the values of public radio. I was there in the beginning and involvement for more than thirty years in various venues kept me immersed in the discussion of public radio's goals longer than most other people. And because I spent more than thirty years in public radio, its values also helped shape mine.

In a sense, this book began in the spring of 1969, a bit more than a year after Congress passed the Public Broadcasting Act of 1967 and two years before *All Things Considered* debuted in 1971. It was a wonderful time for dreaming and philosophizing, coming in that exciting period between knowledge that public radio would happen and the harsh reality of actually producing programs. I was doing research in the basement of the University of Wisconsin's Memorial Library, when I came across a thin volume titled *Proceedings of the First National Newspaper Conference*. The year was 1912; the location, the University of Wisconsin. The convener was Charles Van Hise, the president of the University of Wisconsin and leader, along with his friend, Senator Robert La Follette, of the progressive movement in Wisconsin. The theme was the commercialization of newspapers and the need for alternatives to newspapers operated for profit. As I read the transcripts of the discussions, I was struck by their similarity to the arguments being made for public radio and television in 1969. Critics in 1912 were arguing that unfettered commercial competition distorts the marketplace of ideas and that alternatives driven by public service were needed to right the balance. Further investigation into progressive critiques of "commercialism in journalism" convinced me that, consciously or unconsciously, turn-of-the-twentieth-century progressive ideas provided the rationale for public broadcasting and should guide its editorial vision. Many years later, research into the values of public radio's listeners completed the circle for me. Public radio's listeners are very much like turn-of-the-century progressives. Public radio reflects the attitudes of these progressives and a century later appeals primarily to their twenty-first-century equivalents. Public radio has a symbiotic relationship with its listeners, who, like early twentieth-century progressives, are well educated and societally conscious and who feel so connected to their medium that they are willing to support it financially. I discuss this relationship in the first chapter.

If public radio reflects progressive values by its very existence in defiance of the economic marketplace—even if not in its content—it should surprise no one that the latter-day opponents of public radio are conservatives. Whether public radio's programs are fair and balanced is irrelevant. Conservatives take issue with its very existence, which runs counter to their faith in free markets. Public radio also attracts criticism from the left, of course, but that criticism does not question the fundamental premises of an anticommercial, antimarket broadcast system, only its performance, often portrayed as insufficiently different from commercial media. Thus, the last two chapters, "Critics on the Right" and "Critics on the Left," return to the arguments in the first chapters of the book.

The middle chapters explore the other ideas that influenced my view of public radio's role and the evolution of these ideas when placed into practice. Three organizations for which I worked prior to the start of NPR immersed me in the idea of public service discussed in chapter two. The BBC gave me an appreciation of public service broadcasting in its purest form, as educator of a nation. WHA Radio at the University of Wisconsin in Madison introduced me to the American mutation of the BBC's public service philosophy. The concept was similar, but the product was not. WHA was by far the largest and many would say the best of old-line AM educational radio. WUOM Radio at the University of Michigan in Ann Arbor showed me the latter-day version of American educational radio, the FM variety, that essentially presented what it regarded as quality programming for its own sake regardless of the likes and needs of potential audiences. My Ann Arbor experience also put me in the prime position to watch the machinations of my boss, Ed Burrows, and his two former employees, Jerrold Sandler and Dean Costen, to sneak the words "and radio" into the Public Television Act of 1967.

Other key ideas that influenced my views of public radio were less direct. I never worked in a Pacifica radio station or any of its "community radio" counterparts, but I understood their rationale and the ways in which they resembled and differed from more mainstream educational radio. The movement for public television was similarly distanced from my direct experience, but, again, I understood the Carnegie Report that recommended federal funding for public television and the books that laid out the premise of public television. I was too young and too far away (in England) to take part in the discussions or to help draft any documents that led to public radio, but I read and re-read them all as I tried to sort out for myself what this public radio thing ought to be.

While the first part of the book consists primarily of ideas that influenced my thinking about public radio, the second part looks at their implementation. A mere understudy in the first part, I am an actor in the second. I had a lot to do with the development of NPR's first program, *All Things Considered*. I served in advisory roles or as a board member (or chairman) during the critical developmental years. I helped guide NPR out of its financial crisis in 1983. I balanced my involvement at the national level with twenty-one years at the helm of Wisconsin Public Radio. WPR boomed during those years, as did public radio across the country. In the last years of my tenure at WPR, I instituted the call-in talk-based "Ideas Network," which network combined authoritative guests in the tradition of educational radio, a wide range of opinions characteristic of the Pacifica stations, and public participation in the democratic egalitarian spirit of the *National Public Radio Purposes*. It summed up for me what public radio was all about. The pages that follow will explain why.

PART ONE

Dreams

CHAPTER 1

The Progressives

Our country's most highly educated people enjoy comfortable lifestyles, even though few are fabulously wealthy. They are our educators, our mainline clergy, our writers, our artists, our high-tech workers, our social service providers, and our professionals. They work in government. They volunteer their time and talents for political and social causes. They care about their communities, the environment, and the well-being of our planet and its inhabitants.

Today, at the turn of the twenty-first century, 13 million such individuals wake up each week to *Morning Edition* on their local public radio station and 22 million tune in to public radio at least once during the week.[1] They may not always like the news *Morning Edition* reports in the era of George W. Bush, but they respect the way public radio reports it. They like the way public radio deals seriously with important issues and the way public radio treats its listeners as intelligent, curious, and fair minded. They like the way public radio treats issues as problems to solve or as opportunities for improvement. They like the way public radio provides information to enlighten rather than to shock, frighten, reassure, or, in a perverse way, to entertain them. They also appreciate *Morning Edition*'s breadth, the way it ventures into topics that do not meet the standard definition of "news" but might fascinate highly educated teachers, professors, clergy, writers, artists, professionals, public servants, and involved citizens.

Before radio, at the turn of the twentieth century, such individuals were called "progressives." They could not wake up to *Morning Edition*; instead, they read newspapers. They may not have liked the news reported in the era of William McKinley any more than *Morning Edition* listeners like the news today, but they did not like the way most newspapers reported it either. They lived in the era of sensationalistic "yellow journalism" that prized scandal and entertainment and eschewed accuracy and perspective. Their frustration with "yellow journalism" generated the intellectual underpinnings for the public radio that their turn-of-the-twenty-first-century counterparts enjoy.

Media reform did not head the agenda of the early twentieth-century progressive movement, however. Progressives ranked economic reform and political reform above media reform, but the three areas depended on one another and were, in a sense, inseparable. The progressives shared with most Americans and with the founders of the Republic a faith in free markets, for both economics and ideas. Like Jefferson, they envisioned a society premised on open opportunity rather than on entrenched economic, political, or ideological power. Like Lincoln, they envisioned government of the people, by the people, and for the people. They defined "people" as folks like the progressives themselves—responsible, informed, and civic minded.

The progressives accepted Adam Smith's vision of a free-market economy, an "invisible hand" that would allocate resources in the most rational way if all were free to make their own economic choices and to pursue their economic self-interest in the open marketplace. They accepted the Founding Fathers' extension of the free-market concept to ideas, in which a similar invisible hand would lead to an approximation of truth if all were free to express their ideas and to hear the ideas of others. They believed democratic process would translate the resulting perception of truth into wisest political decisions.

Progressives at the turn of the twentieth century may have accepted these beliefs, but they saw that economic reality bore little resemblance to the Adam Smith's invisible hand. As every sports fan knows, competition yields winners and losers. Economic competition yields winners and losers too, but losers on the economic playing field do not get a fresh start with the next game or the next season. The winners in the economic competition cement their victories and grow larger and more powerful each year until "competition" becomes more theoretical than real. No new player could expect to compete in key industries like banking, railroads, petroleum, and steel. Established winners in those industries—Rockefeller, Carnegie, Morgan, and Harriman—were unassailable. They formed trusts—interlocking corporations—that entrenched their power and wealth and crushed any potential competitor.

Although most Americans perceived economic reality, the better-educated, more comfortable, more community-involved progressives were more likely to comprehend the implications, to become alarmed, and to initiate a reaction. They wanted their children, who had the advantages of education and a solid middle-class background, to compete fairly on America's economic playing field. An entrenched plutocracy would render such competition impossible. The progressives, therefore, attacked the trusts in a desperate attempt to restore competition that Americans believed formed the basis for a democratic and essentially egalitarian society. The progressives gave us terms like "trust-busting" and pushed the Federal government to pass "antitrust" laws, designed to break up large trusts that dominated key industries and to open these industries to real competition.

Where trust-busting failed or proved impractical, progressives advocated regulation of business by the federal government or public ownership of key services such as water, sewer, electricity, or mass transportation. Regulation resulted in government agencies such as the Interstate Commerce Commission, the Federal Trade Commission, and the Food and Drug Administration. Public ownership resulted in local and state governments acquiring and operating basic utilities such as water and sewage and transportation systems.

All three remedies for the problem of economic concentration required government action, to break up the trusts, to regulate them, or to own them. Of course, such government intervention in the economy ran counter to the doctrine of Adam Smith, but the progressives regarded doctrinal purity as less important than stopping the economically powerful from exploiting Americans in general and well-educated, upper-middle-class individuals such as themselves in particular. Progressives realized that totally unrestrained markets ultimately snuffed out competition and negated democracy, and were willing to compromise, or even abandon, their free market ideology to sustain both competition and democracy.

The progressives' concerns about economic concentration quickly expanded to concerns about the very government they hoped would bust the trusts. They found the government less eager to act than they would have liked and concluded that government was controlled by the same economic forces that ruled the economy. These economic forces installed political bosses, who could manipulate the great mass of urban workers—mostly immigrants. Poor, uneducated, and unfamiliar with democratic principles, these struggling laborers' votes could be bought with a turkey on Thanksgiving or a drink on election day. Progressives concluded that to reform business they had to reform government. And they did.

The progressive movement can take credit for a long and varied list of structural and procedural reforms from the direct election of U.S. senators by voters (rather than by corrupt state legislatures) to the creation of a professional civil service. The progressives, however, took a bipolar approach to governmental reform. They pushed for reforms that made government more democratic and gave more power to voters, but they also pushed for reforms that sought to make government less political, less democratic, and more professional. Their democratic reforms included the ability of voters to recall officials and the ability to bypass officials through binding referenda that made or overturned laws through direct democracy. In addition to a career civil service, their professional reforms included giving power to nonpolitical, professional city managers and nonpartisan city commissioners. While seemingly contradictory, the progressive reforms remained consistent in their final goal. All reforms sought to insure good government by breaking the power of corrupt political bosses and the wealthy plutocrats whom they served. Of course, such good government gave more influence to the civic-minded, educated middle class and less to the ruthless, profit-obsessed captains of industry and the uneducated, poor laborers they manipulated.

While the progressives' agenda focused on government and economic reform, it had to include media reform. If democracy is to function, free speech and a free press are necessary. Indeed, Jefferson himself once opined that, if forced to chose, he would prefer a free press without government to a government without a free press. And, of course, the First Amendment to the Constitution emphasizes the importance of a free press to democracy by prohibiting Congress—and by extension, any government—from limiting that freedom. The Founding Fathers saw a free press as central to our democratic system.

Like the Founding Fathers, progressives prized a free press, but were not convinced that the country had one at the turn of the twentieth century. While the Founding Fathers had feared government censorship, the progressives feared a press controlled by plutocracy, which would use it to manipulate and sedate a mass working class audience. Their boogeymen were the same ones they feared in government and economics. Who controlled the press? A relatively small number of wealthy men. Who advertised in the press? Big businesses and trusts.

To whom did the press pander? Working-class people who could not tell truth from lies, who preferred news involving sex and crime to news about Congress, who preferred a comic strip about the adventures of "The Yellow Kid"—hence the name "yellow journalism"—to exposés about trusts and earnest proposals for reform. Again, the middle-class progressives perceived themselves as caught between the power of plutocracy and the ignorance of the working class. They needed to assert their own interests to assure that the press reflected their values and promoted their reforms in government and economics.[2]

Progressives discovered, however, that media reform was even more difficult than economic or governmental reform because of that pesky First Amendment to the Constitution that told Congress to leave its hands off the media. Progressives could not use government to impose standards on the press. They could not use government to break up media trusts, nor could they use government to regulate them. While the progressives wanted to achieve the First Amendment's goal—a free and active marketplace of ideas—that same amendment limited their ability to do so. They could—and did—urge voluntary compliance with higher standards. They could also urge—and some did—creation of noncommercial, not-for-profit alternatives to commercial media. If for-profit media would not meet their standards of fairness, seriousness, and openness to reform, the progressives could create not-for-profit alternatives, unfettered by the corrupting profit motive. The goal of a true marketplace of ideas was free discussion in the pursuit of truth; the goal of commercial media was profitability.

The editor of *The Independent,* a progressive magazine, crusaded for more than a decade against the corrupting influence of "commercialism" in journalism.[3] "The ordinary commercial press," he argued at that First National Newspaper Conference in 1912 in Madison, failed to provide quick, reliable, and complete information so people could make informed judgements and take informed action about public issues. Nor, he said, did commercial papers provide "competent discussion of pending issues from different points of view." And, he concluded, they never can, because "it does not PAY to be as thorough or impartial as the ideal paper should be. A self-supporting journal must be sensational. It must give undue prominence to spectacular events and crowd out quieter but more important movements." He proposed that every community should have profit-oriented commercial newspapers, privately-endowed nonprofit newspapers, and government-supported newspapers. Those government-supported newspapers would resemble state-supported "public" universities, committed to research (investigation), teaching (reporting), and public service.[4]

Progressives in Los Angeles experimented with a not-for-profit newspaper in 1911. At the newspaper reform conference in Madison, that paper's editor explained the project in the context of the broader progressive movement, which, he said, was trying to replicate the direct democracy of a New England town meeting in a large twentieth-century city. He lauded the initiative and the referendum reforms giving citizens a direct voice in government but added, "We have made no adequate provision for public presentation of facts and the discussion thereof."[5] He proposed municipally owned newspapers "giving news without bias and making definite provision for the presentation of arguments of the contending sides." He also offered a statement of principles for a "public paper" that previews goals that the Progressive era may never have achieved but which public radio would pursue later in the twentieth century:

> The publicly owned daily newspaper, covering the entire field of journalism, must be a very high grade paper if it is to be of value. Its news must be accurate, its arguments fair, and its style interesting. It must not present the weaknesses of mankind as worthy, nor the vices of mankind as amusing, nor the virtues of mankind as stupid. It must not rely on scandal and vice, the improprieties of the state, and pictures of perfect women as the means of interesting readers.[6, 7]

As with the dichotomy of restoring competition through trust-busting or through government regulation and of reforming government through greater citizen participation or through more professionalism, progressives' proposals to reform the media were somewhat dichotomous. The progressives sought a more professional journalism, emphasizing accuracy and proportionality in reporting the news, providing citizens with reliable information, distinguishing between fact and error, truth and falsehood. They also sought debate among conflicting points of view, approximating the New England town meeting in which each citizen enjoys a roughly equal opportunity to state his or her views, no matter how ill-informed, no matter how unsupported, and assuming that open debate generates an approximation of truth and good decisions.

Both progressive approaches to media reform resoundingly rejected the commercial profit motive. Progressives were sure that wealthy individuals or corporations should not enrich themselves by imposing their worldview on the public nor by pandering to the tastes and wants of their readers. "Public papers," they believed, should deliver what democratic society needs—reliable, accurate, proportionate facts and/or a venue for a wide range of individuals to express their opinion about those facts.

The progressive movement died before seeing its media reforms implemented on a large scale. It succumbed to the disillusionment following World War I that promised global reform that would make the world "safe for democracy," coupled with the disillusionment following Prohibition, the progressives' last great effort to impose middle-class Protestant values on working-class Americans. Even when the progressive movement was buried, its ideas continued to trouble social critics. In 1922, four years after World War I ended, the most significant critique of the relationship of media and democracy came from author, journalist, and political philosopher Walter Lippmann. A disillusioned soldier in the late progressive movement and an advisor to President Woodrow Wilson, Lippmann wrote *Public Opinion*, in which he ripped those progressives who thought the media should be more democratic, a printed version of the New England town meeting.[8] He argued the case for a more professional mass media that would form public opinion rather than reflect it. Lippmann argued that public opinion leadership should not come from a self-interested business elite but that disinterested "objective" social scientists should identify social problems and propose solutions, for which the media should "manufacture consent" by educating or manipulating public opinion.[9]

Lippmann rejected as naive the underlying premise of classic democracy: that individual citizens are informed and rational and able to reach good conclusions by pooling their wisdom and interests. Even if the average citizen could act rationally, Lippmann believed, he could not possibly enjoy the expertise of, for example, an economist about economics or a criminologist about crime, nor could he understand the political situation in Russia as well as a diplomat or international expert. He believed that the contemporary industrialized world was simply too complicated for anyone to comprehend all of it and for all but a few experts to understand even a part of it. The media, Lippmann concluded, needed to convey to the public the best thinking of experts.

Idealistic progressives and committed democrats might hate his analysis, but Lippmann believed they needed to accept it if they were to achieve their goals of stopping vested interests from exploiting public ignorance and to institute policies that serve the public interest. The media ideal, according to Lippmann, was not a broad marketplace of ideas, good and bad, informed and ignorant, true and false, but an instrument of mass education—not a mirror but a molder of society. Lippmann saw a well-educated elite using the "objective" techniques of science to identify the best solutions to society's most serious problems and the media educating and leading citizens to understand those problems and accept the solutions.

Few questioned the power of Lippmann's analysis, but few former progressives could bring themselves to accept it enthusiastically. The progressive ideology had divided between advocacy of regulated markets and professionalized government, sometime identified as the New Nationalism, and advocacy of prepared to restore free markets and democratize government, sometimes identified as the New Freedom.[10] The most prestigious advocate of more, not less, democracy in media was progressive philosopher John Dewey, who argued that democratic processes were more valuable than "the best" decisions. Perhaps experts were better able than lay people to find an objectively "best" solution to a problem, but pragmatist Dewey thought that any problem might have a range of solutions, any of which might "work." Dewey thought the process of devising a solution would educate citizens and generate popular support and legitimacy for it. Citizens, Dewey believed, even if less informed and less rational than the founders of the Republic had assumed, could have sufficient information and rationality to reach acceptable conclusions. He advocated placing our faith in democracy and urged the media to foster that democracy.[11]

Lippmann and Dewey agreed more than they differed, however. Neither wanted the media to reflect the interests of the commercial plutocracy. Neither wanted the media to pander to the lowest standards of a mass audience. Each expected the media to facilitate good government. Lippmann would have the media facilitate through leadership, opinion formation, even manipulation; Dewey, through fostering debate and the democratic process in addressing important issues. Such was the intellectual atmosphere in which radio took shape in the 1920s in America, in Britain, and throughout the world.

Such is the legacy that gave us public radio.

CHAPTER 2

Pioneers

In the 1920s the better-educated, upper-middle classes in Britain and America believed that newspapers and magazines exerted extraordinary power over those who read them. They had seen how the massive propaganda efforts of the recently concluded world war used the power of the mass media to manipulate and indoctrinate. Such indoctrination made Britons and Americans hate the "Huns" with sufficient passion to endure the most horrific war in history and to accept millions of deaths and casualties, both psychological and physical, that would maim a generation.

The power of the war propaganda particularly startled observers in the United States. American citizens had elected a president who pledged to keep them out of war just months before he took them into one. They had treasured the ocean that separated North America from Europe and the isolation from the Old World it made possible. Their ranks included a large, proud, and self-aware German population, some of whom still read German newspapers and used German in their worship, as well as a large contingent of Irish Americans who hated the British, yet Americans entered a war against the Germans to aid the British. If propaganda could convince such a nation to support this war, observers saw it as capable of doing just about anything.

The educated, upper-middle class need only look to the newly professionalized and energized advertising and public relations industries to confirm that the smart money believed the media could shape buying habits and public attitudes. Even when not consciously selling products, the mass media by their very nature shaped attitudes. They drew "the pictures in our heads," to use the phrase Walter Lippmann coined

11

early in that decade.[1] Citizens made decisions based on these pictures the media put in their heads rather than on reality. Indeed, the pictures in their heads became reality. Those citizens who carried on the banner of progressivism asked if the media could so effectively sell war and sell soap, could they not—should they not—sell positive values? If, by their very nature, media shaped perceptions, could responsible citizens ignore the content of those media? If the media were so powerful, could the educated upper-middle class let the profit motive determine their content, particularly since it distrusted the motives of the media owners and the tastes of the mass audience? These citizens concluded that using the media for positive ends was not so much an opportunity as an obligation.

Of course, these progressive heirs pondered the new medium called radio. They saw it as potentially more powerful than print media. Since even illiterates could listen to the radio, they reasoned, it might become the favored medium of the most primitive members of the mass audience. Those who could not read or who preferred not to read only had access to the pictures and the cartoons in newspapers, but the radio was fully accessible to them. In addition, the good citizens worried that those who controlled radio would exert even more power than those who controlled print because technology limited the number of broadcast outlets. Only a handful of organizations could operate radio stations without interfering with one another in the limited broadcast spectrum. With only a few radio outlets possible in each community, they reasoned, their owners might exercise extraordinary influence, frightening levels of influence, for good or for bad. They wanted broadcasters to seek societal good rather than profit alone, to promote high moral and artistic standards, to support the democratic process, and to serve audiences unlikely to generate the highest possible revenue.

Broadcasting that fulfills all these requirements is known as "public service." Public-service broadcasting sees the scarcity of viable broadcast frequencies as a rationale for imposing on broadcasters obligations "to serve the public interest, convenience, and necessity" insisting that broadcasters choose what is good for society over profits. Traditionally, critics have distinguished market-based broadcasting and public-service broadcasting as the difference between giving people what they want and giving people what they need. That paternalistic construction is not quite right. Market-based broadcasting gives the *individual* what he or she wants, whereas public service broadcasting gives the *collective so-*

ciety what it wants, or, more precisely, what the educated upper-middle class thinks society needs.

In the 1920s and 1930s, governments everywhere endorsed public service broadcasting. They differed only in how they pursued those public service goals. The United States decided that a commercially supported system could meet those goals. Britain and most of the rest of the world saw public service and commercialism as incompatible. Over the decades from the 1920s to the 1950s, at least five individuals or groups advocated different approaches to public service broadcasting. In Britain, a Victorian visionary defined the British approach. In America, a socially responsible political leader articulated the American version. Some American educators, however, rejected their nation's version and advocated emulating the British, while a San Francisco pacifist proposed his own unique approach to pursuing public service goals. Finally, television's arrival dictated a new and more narrow way for radio to achieve public service, as the curator of quality programs.

The Victorian

"What a curse it is to have outstanding comprehensive ability and intelligence, combined with a desire to use them to maximum purpose."[2] Such was the modest lament of John Reith, later Lord Reith, the founding head of the British Broadcasting Corporation (BBC). The "zealous, high-minded, deeply-religious, authoritarian, driven, un-clubbable, difficult, battle-scarred, lonely, self-absorbed, inwardly-tormented but remarkable and visionary Scot"[3] defined the mission of the BBC, the epitome of the public service broadcaster.[4]

Reith opposed control of radio by either government or business. His BBC would stand as an independent not-for-profit institution dedicated to public service. He insisted that the BBC operate without advertising and that listeners pay for radio programming directly through a mandatory annual license on the use of receivers, similar to the annual automobile license fee familiar to Americans.

Even more important, however, Reith believed that the BBC could do its job effectively only as a monopoly. Surely, Britain could have found room on the radio dial for several competitive services. Frequencies were scarce, of course, but not so scarce as to prevent any alternatives to the BBC. The decision to allow just one radio service suggests that something other than "scarcity" drove the public service philosophy in Britain. While the technological limit on the number of broadcasters provided a rationale for imposing the public service philosophy, the real motivation was to offer no alternative to programs that were good for society. Reith's dour, puritanical understanding of human weakness led him to conclude that, given the choice between programs designed to please the listener and programs designed to shape a good society, few would choose the latter and that, therefore, broadcasters should not provide a choice.

Reith defined public service as a blend of information, education, and entertainment. He provided programs for persons of all ages, regions, and tastes, arguing that the "mass" audience is really a collection of distinct audiences. He presented programs for minority tastes rather than some amorphous majority taste. He wanted the BBC to serve each audience and to build a sense of nationhood by introducing each to the cultures of the others. He would broadcast a quiz show followed by a lecture, a dance band followed by a symphony, or a soap opera followed by Shakespeare. He used his radio monopoly as compulsory mass education. By scheduling the dance band before the symphony, he introduced audiences for popular entertainment to what he regarded as more substantive programming, broadening horizons and raising standards for the working class and the nation as a whole.

Reith made the BBC central to civic life in Britain. His news operation maintained impeccable standards and a studied neutrality. It broadcast regularly from Parliament. He provided platforms for opposing political views, carefully balanced between contending parties and factions. He broadcast events that contributed to a sense of national unity, everything from a coronation to a World Cup soccer match. He insisted on broadcasting a church service each morning and a Sunday schedule devoid of entertainment. He sought to create better citizens, better human beings.

The Commerce Secretary

Surprisingly, a public service philosophy similar to Reith's initially guided early broadcasting in the United States. Radio in America did not begin as a for-profit business. Rather, it grew out of the work of physicists and engineers, many of them based at universities and all of them concerned with the technical aspects of the medium. At first, if they thought about practical applications at all, they probably thought in terms of point-to-point communication, ship to shore, for example. Those who worked at universities with extension missions were first to see radio as a way to reach a dispersed audience of farmers with agricultural information, markets, and weather reports. The physicist primarily responsible for radio at the University of Wisconsin expanded this agricultural extension idea to a broader philosophy of university outreach. He saw radio as a means to carry "the university atmosphere"—programming representing the values and standards of the university—to all corners of the state.[5, 6]

Some 200 universities, labor unions, and religious groups were broadcasting to one degree or another before the contemporary commercial system took hold. By the 1930s, however, the commercial system had squeezed out all but a handful of them. The first profit-oriented broadcasters did not recognize the potential of commercial advertising. They assumed they would make money in radio from selling receivers. They saw programming as simply providing their customers with a reason to buy a receiver. It hardly mattered whether that programming came from a not-for-profit public service organization, an independent profit-oriented corporation, or the receiver manufacturers themselves. When broadcasters finally saw the profit potential in commercial advertising, they argued that commercial sponsorship need not conflict with public service.

The person primarily responsible for American broadcast policy, Secretary of Commerce Herbert Hoover, also saw little conflict between public service and profit. In fact, he wrote a book, *American Individualism*,[7] which proclaimed public service the most reliable way to profitability in business. He argued that wise business leaders pursued their enlightened self-interest rather than their narrow self-interest and that enlightened self-interest required serving the public interest. According to Hoover, businesses that took a long-term view knew that educated, responsible, and comfortable citizens made the best consumers and were the ticket to making money. Such businesses would promote good citizenship and the prosperity of individuals and their communities. This long-term thinking, Hoover reasoned, distinguished American individualism from the short-sighted individualism that sought immediate maximization of profit. In Hoover's view, for-profit commercial broadcasters not only *could* but *would* provide public service because, by doing so, they would promote the healthy society that would insure their long-term profitability. Hoover's philosophy gave legitimacy to the arguments of the commercial giants who would dominate radio and eventually television in the United States.

By the time Congress wrote the basic law that governs broadcasting, the Communications Act of 1934, for-profit commercial broadcasters had established themselves as the dominant force in American radio. It was clear during the law's formulation that America would never have a BBC-style not-for-profit public service monopoly, but hope remained that it could have a noncommercial system *parallel* to the commercial system, if Congress chose to reserve frequencies for noncommercial use. A coalition of university broadcasters—the folks who started radio—and labor unions, socially involved religious groups, and holdovers from the progressive movement of two decades earlier, such as democratic philosopher John Dewey, banded together to lobby Congress.[8] They argued that profitable commercial broadcasters would overwhelm not-for-profit broadcasters if federal law failed to guarantee the noncommercial sector 25 percent of all broadcast channels. They argued, too, that, contrary to Hoover's beliefs, commercialism would inevitably overwhelm public service in any broadcast organization operated for profit and, therefore, broadcast public service would survive only if certain frequencies were protected for noncommercial, not-for-profit public service broadcasters.[9]

These advocates for protected not-for-profit frequencies defined public service broadly. Their definition resembled the BBC's.[10] Since a monopoly like Reith's BBC was impossible, however, they did not argue that they could impose higher standards on society but that they at least could offer a choice for those interested in public service programming.

Ironically, those arguing against setting aside frequencies for public service channels also made Reithian arguments. Those in the Hoover camp wanted educational and other public service institutions to work with commercial broadcasters to sprinkle "good for you" programming between their commercial entertainment shows, a strategy far more likely to reach large numbers of people than ghettoizing such material on separate noncommercial channels.[11]

In the end, the set-aside frequency advocates lost to the Hooverites and, for a while at least, commercial broadcasters carried through with their promise to include public service programming in their schedules. Over time, however, such programming moved to less- and less-desirable time periods and shrank until, for all practical purposes, it disappeared. Profit prevailed, just as the advocates of reserved noncommercial public service frequencies predicted. Those advocates were correct, too, in predicting that without reserved channels, most noncommercial radio stations would disappear. As radio prospered through the 1930s, the Federal Communications Commission gave desirable frequencies that public service broadcasters occupied to commercial broadcasters, arguing that the commercial broadcasters would serve more people and deliver public service programming more effectively. Some universities sold their increasingly valuable stations to commercial broadcasters, and a few chose to operate their stations commercially as a source of income for their institutions.

The Educators

Only 10 percent of the original 200 noncommercial broadcasters survived the 1930s. The city of New York operated a noncommercial station, but the rest were in universities, almost exclusively state land-grant institutions in the Midwest and Pacific Northwest. Land-grant institutions carried an obligation to serve not just enrolled students but the general public. The archetypal land-grant university, Wisconsin, declared the boundaries of the university the borders of the state. With that slogan, known as "The Wisconsin Idea," the university promised to assist individuals in every community in the state, to help communities and state government address social, economic, and political problems, to help protect natural resources, to contribute to cultural life, and to offer adult education courses wherever they were needed. First among all its "extension" activities, however, stood the promise to assist agriculture and improve the quality of rural life. "Cooperative Extension"— linking university research with a network of "county extension agents" —provided crop and livestock advice to farmers, home economics information to their wives, and 4-H activities to their children.

The Wisconsin Idea's promises shaped the programming of the university's pioneer radio station, WHA, and characterized the programming of the small band of AM radio stations that survived in the 1930s, '40s, and '50s as the last refuge for the public service broadcast philosophy in the United States. Each morning a truck pulled up outside the old university heating plant, called Radio Hall, to drop off bags of mail from listeners reacting to programs heard on WHA and the ten other state stations that carried its programming throughout Wisconsin. By the hundreds, listeners requested recipes featured on the *Homemakers* program or agriculture and gardening bulletins offered on the noontime *Farm Show*. Schoolchildren from around the state sent their drawings to the *Let's Draw* program, while their teachers requested "teacher's guides" to *School of the Air* programs broadcast for classroom use. Listeners asked for the title of the book being read on *Chapter a Day*, reading lists for *College of the Air*, and music selections for classical music programs. They wrote letters they hoped to hear read on *Dear Sirs*, a most literate "letters to the editor" feature. While falling far short of the BBC in their impact, the university stations that survived the 1930s played a significant role in the lives of their listeners.

Following the BBC concept of public service broadcasting, these university radio stations offered a diversity of programs to "educate" a broad swath of the population. They defined education as broadly as did Reith. They started with practical programs for farmers, rural homemakers, and their children, then added classical music, drama, and other cultural programming. Most tapped their universities' faculties for talks on a variety of topics, particularly those relating to public policy issues. They invited political leaders to express their views. They offered programs on topics from astronomy to zoology and dispensed practical advice on everything from backyard agronomy to Zen meditation. Some rounded out their diverse program menu with popular entertainment, an integral part of the public service model of both Reith and Hoover. They gave listeners information, education, and entertainment in a single program schedule.

As commercial radio dominance grew, most of these stations narrowed their focus from providing "education for all" to the negative goal of filling the gaps left by commercial radio. This narrowed focus represented a critical change. Both the commercial and the educational broadcasters themselves began to define educational stations as the place for programming commercial broadcasters would find unprofitable, programming that Hoover's public service philosophy argued the commercial broadcasters would want to carry.

By assuming responsibility for unprofitable programming, university broadcasters gave themselves a strong rationale for their continued existence in a commercially dominated broadcast system. At the same time, they put themselves at risk. In the remote possibility that commercial broadcasting did all it had promised to do, their alternative role would disappear. Equally troubling, the "alternative" philosophy left educational broadcasters with no guidance for deciding which unprofitable needs to satisfy. Should they seek to serve the urban poor, the

Spanish speaking, the cowboys, the poets, the opera lovers, the polka folk, or any of the multitude of potential listeners unserved by commercial radio? As a negative definition, "alternative" provided educational radio with little guidance.

While describing themselves as "alternatives" to commercial radio stations, however, these university stations implicitly followed a very positive mission that had nothing to do with what commercial broadcasters did. They extended the strengths and the values of their universities. They offered programs that fit those strengths and values and rejected those that did not. This distinction proved key to educational (public) radio's subsequent development. "Alternative" could not work as a mission. Academic values could and did.

Academic values in state universities were secular. They rejected doctrines and demanded evidence. They made sense of specific events by placing them in historic, scientific, or philosophic context. These institutions saw themselves as the source of honest information, honest analysis, and honest, but always tentative, solutions. So did the radio stations they operated. These institutions supplied a haven for dissent and open discussion. So did their radio stations. These institutions fostered high culture. So did their radio stations. Just like Reith's BBC, American university radio stations sought to "educate" the mass audience on important issues, but unlike the BBC, they did not reach a mass audience; they reached only those who wanted education.

The Pacifist

While John Reith, the austere, guilt-ridden Scotsman with Victorian values, personified the public-service philosophy of both the BBC and American educational radio, an equally austere, tormented American[12] with pacific values personified a different version of public-service broadcasting, what became known as "community radio." Lewis Hill fathered the Pacifica radio stations as surely as Reith fathered the BBC, and neither Pacifica nor the BBC has ever fully escaped the influence of their respective sires. The ideas of both Hill and Reith reflected the progressive criticism of commercial media. Both understood that the profit motive subverts the search for truth and compromises quality, but they viewed the world differently, Reith as a member of the establishment and Hill as a dissident outsider.

Reith saw human beings as needing guidance from those who, by experience, by training, or by birth, have a superior understanding of issues and culture. He regarded the accepted values of his society as positive and sought to promulgate and reinforce them.

Hill spent his life at odds with the dominant values of his society. He had the courage to declare himself a conscientious objector during World War II, that "good," and overwhelmingly popular, war that united the country as have few other events in history. His decision put him, the son of a comfortable middle-class Oklahoma family, in conscientious-objector camps in California during the war years. In the camps, he met men who strengthened his commitment to pacifism. At the end of the war, he went to San Francisco, a city that welcomed those with lifestyles and philosophies outside the American norm. It was by San Francisco Bay that Hill founded the Pacifica Foundation and its first radio station, KPFA. Hill and his confederates set out to promote peaceful resolution of differences among people and among nations. They saw a radio station as the first step in building a comprehensive peace-promoting organization to facilitate communication among people and, hence, a more pacific world.

Prior to arriving in San Francisco, Hill worked for two organizations in Washington, DC. His experiences in those organizations contributed to his philosophy of radio.[13]

Hill served on the staff of the American Civil Liberties Union, the champion of free speech, free press, and peaceful assembly, an organization that often stood on the "liberal" side in civil liberties conflicts. Orthodoxies, after all, never encourage free speech, which really means dissenting speech. Those liberals of the eighteenth century who defied the orthodoxies of King and Church proclaimed a right to dissent and proved the primary beneficiaries of that right. As in all centuries, dissent in the twentieth century came from the unorthodox, who were primarily on the left. Along with his pacifism, Lewis Hill took his allegiance to civil liberties to the radio station he founded and proclaimed the station a bastion of free speech and dissenting opinion. He found little contradiction between "pacifism" and "free speech" as the core principles of his radio station, since pacifism was far from mainstream thought, particularly in the oppressive cold war environment of the late 1940s and early 1950s, when Pacifica began.[14]

The second Washington, DC, organization influenced Lewis Hill was a commercial radio station where he worked as an announcer. Hill came to realize that no one speaks sincerely in commercial broadcasting. In entertainment and news, performers and newscasters read scripts that someone else wrote. Good actors could play roles with conviction. Good newscasters could read the news with authority. Certainly, some contributed to their scripts, and their individual styles influenced how the scripts were written, but by and large, radio entertainment and information meant individuals reading the words of others as if they were their own. In fact, Hill pointed to the audition process that required prospective announcers to read meaningless gibberish with sincerity, enthusiasm, pathos, or any other designated emotion. Those who gave the best performance became the voices on the radio; they were selected, Hill observed, precisely for their ability to deceive. An earnest communicator with something important to say need not apply. This phenomenon reached its epitome in the commercials. The message and the script came directly from the advertising agency. No one even pretended that the announcer reading the copy or the singers warbling the jingle cared an iota about the product they were selling or believed anything they said or sang.[15]

Hill's experiences underscored the concept for his radio station. The conscientious objector wanted a voice for pacifism, a pulpit from which to promote peaceful approaches to conflicts in the community, the nation, the world, a place for people to listen to and understand one another. Hence, he named his foundation "Pacifica" and chose as the call letters of his first station KPFA. The supportive ACLU staff member created a place where anyone might express his or her views without fear of censorship or reprisal, and the disillusioned commercial radio announcer created a place where people expressed their true beliefs, played music they personally loved, and performed the music, the poetry, the drama, and the essays they had created as a personal artistic expression rather than to serve a commercial market.

The three goals supported each other. A free-speech environment facilitates genuine artistic expression and sincere political statements. Genuine artistic expression will likely differ from music or drama with a commercial goal and thus appeal to unconventional tastes. Sincere political statements will likely differ from opinions public relations professionals manufacture. Sincere communication and free speech went hand-in-hand with Hill's commitment to pacifism. Nonviolence and opposition to war were unpopular beliefs, but they were sincerely held and exemplified the viewpoints a free-speech philosophy encouraged. Most media of Hill's day did not give antiwar views serious consideration—particularly when they were most needed, at times of threatened conflict. Threats, perceived or real, generate tidal waves of national unity that drown dissent. More fundamentally, however, Hill believed that the path to peace rests in communication and understanding and that the very existence of a free forum for all points of view would generate understanding and reduce the likelihood of conflict and violence. His Pacifica would promote a more peaceful world not just by presenting pacifist ideas but by providing a place for honest expression of a full range of sincerely held beliefs.

Pacifica historian Matthew Lasar believes this "dialogue" rationale motivated Hill above all else and characterized the earliest efforts of KPFA.[16] When it went on the air in 1949, KPFA sought to generate discussions among individuals and groups with widely differing views, to reach mutual understanding and respect, and perhaps even to achieve agreement or compromise. It saw dialogue as the alternative to hatred and violence. Naive, perhaps, but a clear and noble mission.

KPFA's initial commitment to dialogue morphed quickly into First Amendment or free-speech radio. Dialogue and free speech are not identical. Dialogue implies listening as well as speaking; free speech implies no obligation to listen to other points of view. Respectful dialogue gave way to uncensored expressions of opinions, particularly those not heard regularly in commercial media. KPFA remained open to all points of view, of course, but those in the mainstream had no need to use it.[17]

Hill's radical philosophy did not translate into a radical-sounding radio station in the 1950s. His station sounded erudite and academic, not particularly different from certain programming on the BBC or from programming that emerged on educational radio's FM stations at about that time. Lasar coined the phrase "hybrid highbrow" to describe the sound.[18] Hybrid highbrow included a lot of classical music, particularly new or seldom-heard compositions; liberal amounts of jazz and folk music; "talk" features emphasizing lectures, discussions, and interviews with academics, writers, and public intellectuals; and both classic and contemporary poetry and drama. Pacifica dumped this hybrid highbrow sound in the 1960s. It left the concert hall, the lecture hall, and the seminar room and hit the streets. Mass movements against the Vietnam War and for civil rights were bringing unprecedented levels of interest to the free speech—the dissenting speech—that Pacifica had promulgated at its start, when few cared or paid much attention. Protests against the Vietnam War reignited Pacifica's pacifist origins, except that the 1960s version of pacifism sounded militant and angry in contrast to the dignified and somewhat academic objectors to World War II and to the cold war. Pacifica covered antiwar marches and demonstrations that reflected a major social movement, and it did so at a time when FM radio began to find an audience which, within a decade, would surpass that of AM radio. By the mid-'60s, the FM band was available to more people, and Pacifica presented voices that a sizable number wanted to hear.

Nonetheless, the Pacifica radio stations broadcast largely to the converted. Those with strong antiwar feelings turned to Pacifica to hear views that agreed with their own, reinforcing those views and building a sense of community among the like-minded. The stations (now five of them, in Berkeley, New York, Los Angeles, Houston, and Washington, DC) did little to foster dialogue among persons with different points of view, but became, instead, the strident voice of a single point of view. That point of view may have deserved an outlet that presented it as a respectable option to mainstream thinking, but it did not reflect a return of Hill's original concept of respectful dialogue as a path to peace.

In a similar way, the civil rights movement of the 1960s changed the sound of Pacifica radio. That movement changed the definition of "unheard voices" from the well-modulated words of the politically and artistically sophisticated and academically inclined—Lasar's hybrid highbrows—to the angry cries of blacks, ethnic minorities, women, and gays. Free speech for the individual dissenter—usually white and male—became free speech for divergent groups, who gained access to the airwaves as representatives of their race, heritage, gender, or sexual orientation rather than because of their individual artistry or erudition. The prepositions "by," "for," and "about" each "identity" group came to define this type of programming. Programming "by" and "about" an identity group fit Hill's vision of sincere expression, presumably for the edification of nonmembers of that group. The preposition "for," on the other hand, suggested an inward looking philosophy rather than an evangelical purpose. Identity groups reinforced their sense of community through these broadcasts, but they did not necessarily increase understanding outside their group.

In its original incarnation, Hill's radio station sought to transform the world, resisting war and conflicts of all kind. Hill wanted to make a positive impact on society just as surely as John Reith sought to uplift the British population. By retreating to a free-speech rationale, however, Pacifica shifted from dialogue between those with conflicting points of view to programming that reinforced divisions.

The Curators

Whatever its merits, Pacifica's programming of the 1960s abandoned its founder's dreams of a transformed world in favor of a more pragmatic mission. It put a diversity of voices on the air for their own sake rather than because of their impact. Similarly, American educational radio in the 1950s and 1960s retreated to airing programming for its own sake rather than for its impact on listeners. Airing programming for its own sake seemed a much more manageable goal than mass education, especially since large audiences had moved to television and educational radio stations had moved to the new FM band that few could receive. Besides these practical reasons for its retreat to programming for its own sake, educational radio could once again look to the BBC for a philosophical rationale. The American educators had emulated Reith's philosophy when they started their old-line AM stations. They now moved with a clear conscience to a different philosophy, because the BBC had given it respectability.

Lord Reith would not have approved of the emerging philosophy, and only his forced departure from the BBC at the start of World War II cleared its way. Under Reith's less-rigid successors, the BBC retained the public-service goals of information, education, and entertainment, but interpreted them more loosely, offering listeners choices. The monopoly continued in the sense that the BBC remained the sole broadcast entity, but it broadcast different programming on different stations.

The first option the BBC introduced was the Light Service. This frankly "popular" option featured more entertainment to help buoy spirits through the stress of wartime. The program mix on the Reithian original station became the Home Service; the Light Service menu contained more cake and less spinach than the Home Service. Nonetheless, the Light Service did not offer a total escape from Reithian tradition. Reith's successor as head of the BBC reiterated raising standards as a prime purpose of the organization, and although the Light Service emphasized entertainment, it included information, education, and cultural uplift. Mass education now came with electives.

At the conclusion of the war, the BBC introduced a third choice, a high-end alternative to the Home and Light Services. It was this Third Programme that attracted the attention of American educational broadcasters and gave them the philosophical underpinnings to justify airing programs for their own sake. The BBC's Third Programme cared little about audience preferences. It provided "the best" in culture and ideas as determined by artists, intellectuals, and academics. The most "intelligent" broadcast service ever created, the Third Programme made no compromises with popularity. It made the "best" available for those who wanted it, no matter how few their numbers. More like a graduate seminar than mass education, the Third Programme departed from Reith's vision of mandatory uplift as much as the Light Service did. While the Third Programme set a standard, it did not seek to impose it on society. Instead it fed the tastes of cultural minorities.[19]

The Third Programme, therefore, provided an acceptable role model for the new generation of American educational stations emerging on the FM band, where lack of listeners was a fact of life. In contrast to its 1934 rejection of reserved AM frequencies for educational radio, the government set aside one fifth of the FM radio band for noncommercial stations. Many colleges and universities that had given up their AM stations or never had them now moved into the wide-open territory of FM, a broadcast band largely ignored by commercial broadcasters and set manufacturers, who were busy starting television stations and selling television sets. For the first twenty years of their history, FM educational radio stations went virtually unheard, and programmed accordingly. No broad mass education mission for these stations. No farm or home economics advice. They emulated the Third Programme and broadcast esoteric programming for its own sake and for the inadvertent delight of a small number of interested listeners who owned FM radios.[20]

Like the Third Programme, both the Pacifica stations and the FM university stations aired what the broadcasters deemed worthy, not what audiences wanted or what society needed. Like the Third Programme, these stations served as a venue for eminent artists, academics, and intellectuals. They believed they provided a public service, even if to only a tiny portion of the public.

Some university radio stations, however, did not emulate the Third Programme but adopted a more narrow definition of education. A few saw their relatively low power stations taking to the air in the 1950s and 1960s as laboratories for student training. They did not expect to reach many listeners, to mold a better society, or to create better citizens. Other FM educational radio stations followed the example of the pioneer AM stations, who provided some programs each school day for classroom use under the rubric "School of the Air." These stations focused on K–12 education and were started by school systems in several cities to beam instructional programming to their schools. These stations that did not emulate the Third Programme provided public service only by the most narrow of definitions.

By the 1940s and 1950s, institutions sought public funds to support their radio stations by citing "quality for the sake of quality," or the value of in-school instruction or student training. The vocabulary of broad public service, of education for all, fell by the wayside as no longer plausible in the post–World War II environment. The frequencies reserved for noncommercial stations sat on an FM band that few listeners knew existed. FM radio shared its infancy with the birth of television, which eclipsed radio, commercial and educational, as the truly mass medium. If the broad, more Reithian vision of public-service broadcasting had a chance, it was in television, to which educators with a broad public-service mission turned their attention, leaving radio to justify its existence as a source for student training, for instruction, for programming that few wanted to hear, or for programming for its own sake.

CHAPTER 3

Public *Radio*

In the 1950s and 1960s, those who had a broad vision of public service broadcasting looked to television instead of radio to realize their vision, and looked to stations in Boston and New York rather than Midwest land-grant colleges, for leadership. The character of these new broadcast institutions reflected their Boston–New York locations. They arose in the realm of elite private schools that had neither a legal nor mission obligation to provide public service. Harvard, Princeton, and Yale did not list operating a radio station in their mission statements. However, their graduates and members of their academic communities were precisely the sort of individuals who envied Britain for its BBC and wanted to create something similar in this country. Some dabbled a bit in radio, but they focused on educational television as the medium to transform life in American society.

These new broadcasting leaders started "community licensed" television stations that operated outside university bureaucracies but were still imbued by higher education. In addition to being graduates or officials in elite eastern academic institutions, these leaders were well connected to corporate, foundation, or family money. These people could move and shake their communities and the nation. They promised to make things happen in educational television.

Author's Note: I observed the events in this chapter from the University of Michigan radio station, where I worked from 1964 through 1967. My boss was Ed Burrows, who happily related his adventures to his young and very interested staff member. The tale as I tell it is essentially the tale as I heard it from Burrows.

WGBH in Boston was the pioneer and model for these new stations. Created by money from old Boston families like the Lowells, WGBH combined the leadership of the premier educational institutions in the Boston area like Harvard and MIT. WGBH, was an independent not-for-profit station, not owned by an educational institution, but an equal partner with educational institutions. In structure, governance, and funding, it resembled the museums, the symphony orchestras, and similar free-standing educational and cultural institutions private philanthropy supported. These community licensed stations were the creatures of the Eastern—sometimes liberal—establishment and symbol of private philanthropy used for the public good. The Ford Foundation provided the leadership and much of the money to spread the concept across the country. Free from the bureaucratic and political constraints of large state universities, WGBH and those stations that copied it in cities across the country developed public-service broadcast organizations central to the civic and cultural fabric of their communities.

Like the BBC, these new community licensees represented the social and cultural values of an educated civic elite. They represented something of a *nobless oblige*: the responsibility of the educated, the prosperous, and the privileged to look after the less-fortunate majority. Although these community licensees sometimes operated both radio and television stations, they focused on television. Since radio did not have the potential for a mass audience, they saw TV as the medium to reach large audiences with cultural and public affairs programming not provided by commercial broadcasters. Their radio stations, such as WGBH-FM, presented high-end "alternative" programs not unlike those of the university FM stations not devoted to instruction. The stations broadcast many hours of classical music, interspersed with drama and talks, and sounded every bit as aloof and academic as their university-based counterparts. Like the Third Programme, these stations broadcast material for its inherent quality (as they defined it) rather than to educate or elevate the populace, most of whose members barely knew the stations existed, let alone listened to them. These educational radio stations provided a quiet refuge for the highly educated but made no missionary effort to reach the less educated.

Educational radio sank to its nadir in 1960s. It had demonstrated that it could not deliver on its promises to transform society. Reformers and their money turned to television. When the primary source of philanthropic income for educational broadcasting, the Ford Foundation, cut all its funding for radio in 1963, it seemed to have signed educational radio's death warrant. The foundation, which had made educational broadcasting its cause, decided educational television, not radio, was the means to make a major impact on society. It decided that it was wasting resources on radio that might otherwise build a powerful television system. Other sources of money and the most talented, or at least the most ambitious, broadcasters followed the Ford Foundation lead and migrated to television. The only question after 1963 was how long it would take educational radio to expire.

But even the mighty Ford Foundation could not afford the money necessary to make educational television a sustaining influence on American life. Like most foundations, Ford liked to use its resources to start activities but then chafed at funding them indefinitely. Ford had invested hundreds of millions of dollars in getting educational television up and going, but in the mid-1960s, it decided it was time to pull back. Educational television needed to find a new source of revenue to survive and grow. It looked to the only organization that had more money than the Ford Foundation, the federal government.

Educational television faced this challenge at a fortuitous time. President Lyndon Baines Johnson was promising to use the full resources of the federal treasury to build a Great Society. He sought equal rights for minorities, the end of poverty, and security for the elderly. At the top of Johnson's agenda, however, was education. He saw it as the key to building all other aspects of his Great Society. He valued education at all levels: colleges, universities, K–12, preschool (think Head Start), and continuing education for adults. Promoters of the Great Society were willing to back educational television because it was the perfect medium to educate the population from toddlers to adults.

Ford, Carnegie, and other foundations had connections and influence in the Kennedy–Johnson administrations, as did the Boston educational establishment, the source of much of the vision and energy that had taken educational television as far as it had. Not surprisingly, the Johnson administration, at the behest of these groups, indicated it would look favorably on a recommendation for federal funding of educational television if that recommendation came from a privately funded commission comprised of distinguished Americans. Educational television became the last major initiative of the Great Society before the Vietnam War overwhelmed the President and the treasury of the United States.

The Carnegie Corporation (Foundation) agreed to pay for the commission, earning the right to attach its name to its report and recommendations. The Carnegie Commission's membership—major figures in education and business, along with an artist or two—took a year to hear testimony and delivered its report to President Johnson in December 1966. That commission's report comes closer than any other document to spelling out the purposes of public broadcasting, synonymous, at the time, with public television. It provided the basis for the Public Broadcasting Act of 1967, which established and provided federal funding for the Corporation for Public Broadcasting. The commission gave us the name "public broadcasting," calling to mind the broad mandate of Reithian public-service broadcasting and separating it from the more narrow moniker of "educational" or "instructional" broadcasting. Public broadcasting, like public-service broadcasting, was to educate, to socialize, to democratize, to culturally uplift an entire society. These goals fit the vision of a Great Society.

The commission report implied that the media were all-powerful, the very implication that generated both fear and hope in the minds of the turn-of-the-century progressives and the BBC's Lord Reith. The commission declared everything on television, commercial as well as public, as "educative." Television, the commission said, "continues to educate us long after we have left the classroom. It replenishes our store of information, stimulates our perceptions, challenges our standards, and affects our judgment. In the sum of what it presents, television is as profoundly educative as life itself is educative, and perhaps all the more so because there is no formal syllabus to which we can refer so that we may see what we have learned."[1]

Commission members were too politically savvy to argue, as the progressives would have, that commercial television "educates" us using the wrong values, those of consumption and corporate profit. Commercial broadcasters were—and continue to be—among the most powerful political forces in our country. Indeed, President Johnson had made his personal fortune as a commercial television station operator in Austin, Texas. Politically, the commission could not advocate public television as anticommercial television nor suggest that it would question the core assumptions of capitalism. Commercial broadcasters and the public officials who represented them would not accept such proposals, nor, likely, would most Americans.

The commission realized, however, that to justify federal tax support, public television had to offer something that commercial television did not. It chose "diversity" as the central rationale for public television. Commercial television served a "mass" audience; public television would serve the many subaudiences within that mass audience. The year, remember, was 1966, when only three commercial television networks sought the same broad mass audience. Fox, WB, UPN, and PAX were still in the future. Cable existed in 1966, but only to improve reception in areas remote from television transmitters. But, the commission pointed out, "America is geographically diverse, ethnically diverse, widely diverse in its interests. American society has been proud to be open and pluralistic, repeatedly enriched by the tides of immigration and the flow of social thought. Our varying regions, our varying religious and national and racial groups, our varying needs and social and intellectual interests are the fabric of the American tradition. . . . Television should serve more fully both the mass audience and the many separate audiences that constitute in their aggregate our American society."[2]

The commission proposed that commercial television take care of the mass audience, while public television would serve the separate audiences. It presumed that every individual would from time to time be a member of a minority audience. Public television would air country music for the country music fan, opera for opera fans, gardening tips for the gardener, wildlife explorations for the outdoors man, sewing instruction for the seamstress, and Lithuanian culture for the citizen of Lithuanian descent. "The utilization of a great technology for great purposes, the appeal to excellence in the service of diversity—these finally became the concepts that gave shape to the work of the Commission. In the deepest sense, these are the objectives of our recommendations," the commission concluded.[3]

From its conception in the era of Reith and Hoover, public-service broadcasting embraced service to unserved minorities, and the Carnegie promise of quality in the service of diversity fell neatly into the public-service tradition. That tradition shines through even more starkly in the promise to bring to viewers "scientists and students of our society" from universities across the land. It also promised to present the work of our greatest artists in many genres, again showcasing "the best" of our diverse society, thereby implementing the public-service tradition of uplift and diversity. In a sense, the commission followed the example of the BBC, which proclaimed an obligation to serve a variety of tastes and interests with quality programming. The BBC, however, did not and does not concede broadly popular programming to the commercial networks.

Besides the public service tradition of education and uplift, the

Great Society and 1960s rhetoric lauded participatory democracy. The Pacifica philosophy of free speech and public participation fit the spirit of the times at least as well as Reithian tradition, and the Carnegie Commission Report recognized that fact. The commision, therefore, asked that public television not just provide programming targeted at minority audiences but a platform for "unheard voices." It did not specify that those voices represent pacifists, as had Lewis Hill, nor dissidents, nor those who questioned the capitalist system. Rather than a venue for alternative political views unwelcome in commercial broadcasting, the commission proposed providing a voice for unheard artists and subgroups in the population—they envisioned the poor and the black—who had something they wanted to say to the larger community.

The commission wisely realized that a meaningful forum with real participation most easily happens locally and called for a television system built on "the bedrock of localism." This approach was more in harmony with the community radio of Pacifica's philosophy than with the monolithic, authoritative, high-quality "national service" of the BBC or the Ford-funded programming of educational television. Both the internal politics of public television and the interests of commercial broadcasters and states'-rights senators encouraged support for local stations over a strong "fourth" national network. The commission put a positive spin on the politically correct position as it pointed to "the whole living, meaningful world of civic affairs at something less than the national level."[4] Cities, it said, had grown too large to hold in-person town meetings of the New England model, "but part of what the town meeting accomplished is certainly within the reach of educational television. And the matter is all the more important in an era when cities are suddenly confronted with an unending series of new problems that cannot be met by administrative arrangements alone: problems that demand the engagement of each individual citizen, who must be both informed and moved to act."[5]

With the words "moved to act," the Carnegie Commission took educational television out of its ivory tower and into the world of social activism. In doing so, it mirrored the social activism taking place on university campuses across the country, as universities became the locus of protest and reforms, if not the sponsors of them. In pushing educational television toward more involvement in the community and in fostering active participation, Carnegie was not pushing public broadcasting away from its roots in higher education as much as it was reflecting what was happening in higher education. Public television would not lead protest nor seek reforms, but it would provide an environment and an apparatus for protesters and reformers to use.

In the end, however, the authors of the Carnegie Report were less enamored of protest and action than civilized discussion that followed the academic rules of evidence, logic, and an openness to persuasion. Through a civilized exchange of ideas, the commission said, "Americans will know themselves, their communities, and their world in richer ways." Viewers, said the commission, "will gain a fuller awareness of the wonder and the variety of the arts, the sciences, scholarship, and craftsmanship, and of the many roads along which the products of man's mind and man's hands can be encountered."[6]

The Carnegie Commission proposed that public television promise both diversity and excellence, "the best" that America offered in the arts and ideas. At the same time, it reflected the vast diversity of tastes, voices, and opinions, some of which, by definition, would comprise something less than "the best." The Carnegie Commission preferred not to acknowledge any conflict between the diverse and the best but promised instead "excellence within diversity . . . a civilized voice in a civilized community."[7]

"Radio" never appeared in the Carnegie Commission Report, a television document through and through. Few cared. Most of the major public-broadcasting organizations included both television and radio, with television the dominant focus in all of them. These organizations were quite content to ignore radio to achieve national tax support for their dominant television enterprises. Radio stations unattached to television stations tended to be so small, understaffed, and underfunded that they had no extra time or resources to devote to building their futures. They were barely surviving their present. Certainly, no impetus for change came from their few listeners; they liked what they heard. They had no reason to fight for a new vision for "public" radio when they were quite content with the "educational" radio that served their tastes and interests so nicely. The public who did not listen to educational radio definitely had no reason to care, particularly when public television was promising so much.

There were a very few crusty old guys who did care, however. Some were radio guys who, even though they worked at universities pursuing television, just were not interested in the visual medium. Others were from institutions with a significant broadcast operation that for one reason or another had not gotten into television. The most notable such institution was the University of Michigan, which ran one of the larger

FM radio operations in the country but never built a television station in Ann Arbor. The University of Michigan broadcast operation would wither if public broadcasting were defined as television, and that station's leadership organized a guerilla operation to slip the words "and radio" into the public television act recommended by the Carnegie Commission. They would adopt a stealth strategy that involved misrepresentation, temper tantrums, and an inside connection in the Johnson administration. Their below-the-radar campaign was anything but noble. If it was successful, however, it would allow public radio to begin with virtually a clean slate and no public expectations.

One of the people who cared was the manager of the University of Michigan radio station, Ed Burrows. As chairman of the radio division board of the joint radio-TV professional organization, the National Association of Educational Broadcasters, he led the way. Using a federal grant intended for a different purpose, his radio board decided to hire what amounted to a radio lobbyist at the NAEB office in Washington. Burrows made his Michigan program director Jerrold Sandler that lobbyist, a position for which Sandler's gregarious personality suited him well. Then the radio board engineered Burrows' election as chairman of the overall board of the NAEB, a move totally unexpected, and deeply resented, by the television forces. That vote made Ed Burrows, an unabashed advocate of educational radio, the official chief spokesperson for television as it lobbied for federal funding.

In Washington, Sandler fought a losing battle within the NAEB office. His powerful television counterpart, Scott Fletcher, worked relentlessly to secure federal monies for educational television and to engineer the transition from the funds Fletcher had administered as a Ford Foundation executive to federal funds. Answering Sandler's pleas to include radio, Fletcher promised his support for bringing radio along at some time in the future. One day, Fletcher went to Sandler's office and said, "Jerry, you know I love radio." He assured Sandler that some of his best friends were in radio.

Sandler replied, "Scotty, I know that, and I believe you, and I'll always love you for it, but we have a problem on our hands. We are being totally neglected in this. You know better than I that you can't put it aside for a later time. The future is now."

Fletcher responded that the issue was decided. The act would be the Public Television Act and the corporation, the Corporation for Public Television. To bring radio in at that point, he concluded, would "change the scenario."

"So be it," Sandler replied.

"But you can't change the scenario."

"Why not?" Sandler persisted.

"Because it's been written that way; it's got to be that way," Fletcher answered.

"Well, it's very simple," Sandler explained. "You change it to the Corporation for Public *Broadcasting*, and you change it to the Public *Broadcasting* Act."

"Well, the word *broadcasting* doesn't have the right sound. It's not television."

"You're damn right, it's not television," Sandler replied.[8]

The efforts of Burrows and Sandler would have proven futile, however, were it not for a third member of the University of Michigan radio staff, its former chief engineer, Dean Costen. An active Democrat in Ann Arbor, the radio station engineer went to Washington at the start of the Kennedy administration as an assistant to a Michigan dean who had been appointed an assistant secretary of health, education, and welfare. Costen stayed on after the former dean returned to academia and, in 1966, was a deputy undersecretary of HEW, responsible for drafting and shepherding through Congress all administration legislation relating to education—including educational television.

When the administration's public television legislation based on the Carnegie recommendations emerged from Costen's office in the winter of 1967, careful readers found the words "and radio" following the word "television" nearly everywhere it appeared in the document. No public discussion preceded the insertion of these two little words. No political movement demanded their inclusion. Costen simply complied quietly with the request of his former boss (Burrows) and his former colleague (Sandler). The proposed legislation was called the Public Television Bill and it created a Corporation for Public Television, but the fine print extended federal tax support to educational radio as well.[9]

Needless to say, the public broadcasting leadership, which had deliberately written off radio as a waste of money better spent on television, was less than happy with this unanticipated development and successfully used its influence to undo Costen's sleight of hand. On the Saturday morning before the White House would send the education message and the Public Television Bill to Congress, the telephone rang in Sandler's home just outside of Washington. Sandler answered in his downstairs study and found himself talking to a journalist with the unlikely name of Tack Nail, the editor of *Television Digest*, a trade publication. Despite his cartoon name, Tack Nail had Sandler's respect, and the two had developed a close reporter–source relationship. Two days before this phone call, Nail had told Sandler that his other sources said the president's bill would include radio. Sandler, who already knew about the inclusion through his relationship with Dean Costen, provided Nail with some specifics.

In that Saturday morning call, however, Nail delivered new information from his sources. Something had happened. Radio was out of the Public Television Bill. Had the television forces pressured the White House? Had the White House staff acted on its own? Had someone just made a mistake? Whatever had happened, Nail reported to Sandler that the happy truth of two days ago was truth no longer, and the message, minus radio, would go to Congress on Monday.

While he assumed that Nail's information was correct, Sandler still could not believe what he was hearing. "But, Tack," he protested, "I just spoke with the White House yesterday, and I spoke with Dean Costen of HEW." "Jerry, that was yesterday," Nail insisted, "That was Friday. Today is Saturday, and you are no longer in the act."[10]

Still incredulous, Sandler called Costen at home and related Nail's report. He asked Costen to check it out. Costen did not report back until 5:30 Sunday morning, almost twenty-four hours later; Sandler heard the voice of a very tired Dean Costen at the other end of the phone line. Costen had worked all day Saturday and throughout the night with Doug Cater, the President's assistant in charge of the public television legislation at the White House, because, in fact, radio *had* been taken out, and they had to put it back. So crudely did they do the job that the finished document clearly shows where they taped the insertions into the original draft and then photocopied the pages. The typeface of the inserts doesn't even match that of the document.[11]

So, via some midnight oil and Scotch tape, radio got into the President's draft of what was still the Public Television Bill creating the Corporation for Public Television. The television forces were not happy, and just as radio had suddenly disappeared from Costen's draft of the bill, there was no guarantee that it would not disappear in the Senate's or in the House of Representatives' drafts. Indeed, the Senate was working off a draft version of the bill that did not contain Costen's last-minute insertions.

Sandler called his radio board members, telling them, "When you come to Washington next, each one of you is going to be assigned a certain number of senators and a certain number of congressmen. You're going to fulfill a certain number of calls. You're going to have a quota, and you're going to have a call-in system, into the office. You're going to work your butts off but we're going to cover that Congress." The six radio board members were not sure exactly what to do or how to do it, but committed themselves to blanket the Capitol with visits, calls, and follow-up letters.[12]

Jack Burke, manager of the educational radio station at Kansas State University in Manhattan, Kansas, had replaced Burrows as radio chair of the NAEB. He recalled the effort as a series of calculated risks by the radio forces, essentially working at cross-purposes from its parent organization. "You just knew you were going to catch hell at the next NAEB board meeting, and probably before that. Some of the television people . . . would give Sandler a tough time, and Jerry Sandler was the workhorse in this thing. He really was the architect of public radio as we know it today."[13]

Prior to the Senate hearings, the radio dissidents compromised with the television-dominated NAEB leadership. All would support the President's version of the bill, which now included "and radio," and no one would ask for any changes. The television forces agreed not to try to delete radio again, and radio accepted the ancillary nature of its inclusion in what was still the Public Television Bill creating a Corporation for Public Television.[14] The insurgent nature of the radio effort is best illustrated by the words and tone of a confidential report Burke wrote from his office in Kansas. He wrote of the final NAEB board meeting before going to Congress to testify for the bill:

> These funny looking fellas all gathered around this big table and nervously drank water and smoked cigarettes. Friday night was spent in careful love making with TV and radio both getting what they wanted and giving up a few points relative to bill 1160 and our testimony. We agreed that in our testimony, neither [the radio insurgents] or NAEB would push for a change in title of bill or corporation. Ed [Burrows] got to lead off testimony and we got to present a pot pile of witnesses.[15]

But the public radio men did not intend to keep their promise. Burke continued in his report: "I propose to keep up the effort to have 'Public Broadcasting' replace 'Public Television' in the bill. This change is more than academic I feel."[16]

That was Friday night. The atmosphere had changed by Saturday morning. According to Burke's confidential report, that morning's session of the NAEB Executive Committee was

> something to remember. Our budget and irresponsible spending was the main topic. . . . [The TV forces] . . . made it an around the barn attack on radio. We lost and the executive committee passed a motion stating: "No division can exceed its total budget without the approval of the officers of the Association and the Executive Committee. Within a budget, no line item can be exceeded by more than 15 percent without similar approval."
>
> This is designed to stop us from the Herman Land association. Since we have already spent our money, we should be able to live with this.[17]

"Herman Land" was the consultant Sandler hired to write radio's version of the Carnegie report, ultimately titled, *The Hidden Medium: Educational Radio, A Status Report.*" Sandler made the agreement with Land with the expectation that the Ford Foundation would pay the $25 thousand cost. Ford, however, had no intention of helping the radio insurgency even with this relatively small amount. The Ford rejection did not prompt Sandler to tell Land the deal was off or to stop his work, however. He simply dumped Land's bills on his parent organization, the NAEB, which, in turn, handed them to its sugar daddy, the Ford Foundation. In the end, radio got its case statement to present to Congress.

The Hidden Medium walked a delicate line between pessimism in describing the sorry state of educational radio in 1967—"under-financed, under-staffed, under-equipped, under-promoted, and under-researched"—and optimism in cataloging the seemingly indispensable services educational radio provided to communities scattered across the country. The report concluded that radio would deliver those indispensable services far more effectively, if its problems of financing, staffing, equipment, promotion, and research were addressed.[18]

Given the subsequent development of public radio, some of the statistics in *The Hidden Medium* provide interesting benchmarks. Noncommercial radio stations numbered 326 in April 1967, 220 licensed to colleges and universities. Only thirteen were operated by independent "educational organizations" not affiliated with a college/university, school system, library, or municipal or state government. Over a third of the 326 operated with only ten watts of power, one tenth the power of a 100-watt light bulb, barely enough to reach more than a couple of square miles. Half the stations had budgets of less than $20 thousand per year. Only one in seven had annual budgets of $100 thousand or more. Most of the stations had no full-time staff, but rather were the part-time responsibility of those with other duties such as teaching.[19] Listening, the report said, "is greatest in the evening hours, rising from seven to nine, and 'peaking' at ten PM." If accurate, this statement showed that educational radio competed with television for audiences rather than with commercial radio. By the 1960s, commercial radio drew its biggest audiences in the morning and its smallest in the evening, when listeners turned into television viewers. The hidebound world of educational radio had not adapted to the reality of television, assuming that listeners still sat down in the evening to listen to their favorite "programs." Few people actually did that, of course, which may explain in part why so few people listened to educational radio.

The Hidden Medium described educational radio's listeners as "generally above average in education and income, and . . . older than average audiences listening to the popular music-and-news stations."[20] Above-average income is linked to above-average education, of course, and the university home of educational radio—the values of the university—made educational radio's programming appeal primarily to those with university educations. Public radio would never shake this problem—if it is indeed a problem, as so many within and without public radio say it is. Indeed, when the next section of the report talked about the promises of public radio, it promised to serve listeners with precisely the opposite characteristics, a promise perhaps made sincerely but never pursued sincerely.

Not surprisingly, *The Hidden Medium* declared classical music the primary reason listeners tuned to educational radio, although it eagerly noted that "the interest in other programming keeps growing."[21] Perhaps so, but in the 1950s and 1960s educational radio drew most of its listeners with classical music, and, like its upscale audience, classical music was something of an embarrassment which public radio tried to ignore in order to make its case for federal funding. Its advocates had to sell educational radio on the basis of programming, existing or promised, that served needs more in line with the Johnsonian vision of a Great Society. The older, well-educated, classical music listeners might be part of the Great Society, of course, but they were hardly its foremost concern. The Great Society wanted to help out those at the bottom, to open opportunities to those lacking them, and to integrate these individuals into the broader society. While educational broadcasters realized whom their listeners were and whom they were not, one would never know it from the list of promises made in the name of educational radio, if Congress would only give it the money.

The Hidden Medium began its list of promised programming with public and community affairs, including addressing problems of poverty and minority groups, and promoting lively discussion of local issues. Next it promised programming for the socially disadvantaged like the aged and the blind. It answered the question of why radio stations that served older, well-educated, classical music listeners would consider redirecting their missions and serving audiences so different than they already served. In the turbulent 1960s, it said, "Universities were no longer limited to providing 'cultural enrichment' for the privileged minority," and university radio stations, therefore, should broaden their missions to serve the needs "of the total society."[22]

Not until its third promise did *The Hidden Medium* suggest something close to what educational radio actually did. It promised in-depth reporting and analysis of the news, followed by general educational programming for adults in fields ranging from politics to economics to science to classical history. Indeed, educational radio did those things, and public radio would do them in the future, but in 1967 they did not rival classical music as an audience draw. Such erudite programming did not even pretend to attract the poor, minorities, and the less educated. Nonetheless, such informative and educational matter made a stronger public-service case than classical music for the enjoyment of college-educated listeners while they read books in the evening, when normal people were watching television. Only at the end of the list of promises did the report mention "cultural enrichment," with the caveat that "educational stations are far more than classical jukeboxes."[23] "Far more" might have been a bit strong, but educational stations were more than their primary programming draw and might become "far more" should the Congress provide the resources.

In April 1967, the Senate Commerce Committee approved the President's public television bill and passed it on to the full Senate and the House of Representatives, where it sailed through with barely a dissent. "And radio" remained in the approved language, which should have pleased the radio insurgents. In the approval process, however, the Senate committee agreed to change the name of the legislation from the Public Television Act to the Public Broadcasting Act and to change the name of the proposed Corporation for Public Television to the Corporation for Public Broadcasting. Senator Robert Griffin of Michigan raised the issue during Sandler's testimony before the committee, suggesting that such a name change would be "more accurate." Sandler agreed that "public broadcasting" would be a more accurate name, but stopped short of endorsing it.[24] The radio and television forces, after all, had agreed not to ask for a name change in exchange for leaving public radio in the bill. Burke, in his confidential memo to his board, had suggested that they continue to push for the change in spite of the agreement, but Sandler declared afterward that neither he nor any or his people had ever talked with Senator Griffin about such a change. In the literal sense, he was right. He would have had more difficulty, however, if someone had asked if Ed Burrows, the NAEB board chairman, had talked to Senator Griffin's *staff* about making the change.

The public radio guerrillas could not believe their good fortune. They had had no right to win over the television juggernaut, and few of them had believed they really would. To them, the fight had been mainly a game played for the fun of it, the most exciting escapade of their professional lives. Concluded Burke: "You know, the snotty nosed kid that has to wait for his turn at bat. No one wanted us in the act. That's pure and simple. . . . Then we entered a whole new ball game. It was exciting. We saw some possibility of getting in. . . . We said, 'God damn it, this is important. We're going to do it.' "[25]

Indeed, they did it. Their improbable victory made possible National Public Radio and all of the local stations that compose public radio today. Their improbable victory also cost the small band of insurgents any role in public radio's future. They offended the very people who would run public broadcasting. They were angered by the defeat and, more importantly, the less-than-honorable way it was achieved. None of those who went to battle for radio earned leadership roles in the new public radio system that emerged from their efforts. Not Jack Burke of Kansas State University. Not Will Lewis of Boston University. Not Marjorie Newman of Florida State University. Not Myron Curry of the University of North Dakota. Not Burt Harrison of Washington State University. Not Martin Busch of the University of South Dakota. Not Jack Summerfield of the Riverside Church in New York. Not Al Fredette of the State Medical College of New York. And certainly not Ed Burrows nor Jerry Sandler, each of whom applied for positions at the new National Public Radio, Sandler many times. Neither was ever hired. Instead, the task of developing public radio would fall to radio managers who sat on the sidelines as Sandler and company waged war, to those who sided with television, and to those, like your author, who were too young to have played any significant role one way or the other.

Shortly after passage of the Public Broadcasting Act of 1967, Sandler was on his way out as radio staff at the NAEB. He was not surprised:

> I was warned by a very wise man named Herman Land . . . that to the extent we were successful in our efforts as underdogs to get the act changed, to the extent that we succeeded, that I personally should be prepared to be *persona non grata* among members of the establishment. I said I thought I understood that, and he said, "Well, I think you really ought to think hard about that. Are you prepared for that? It may have some very serious consequences for you."[26]

In 1976, I was hired to head WHA and the Wisconsin State Radio Network. The runner-up candidate was Ed Burrows. In 1990, Wisconsin conducted a national search for a new program director. I set up a five-person search and screen committee to go through applications and recommend four or five finalists for interviews. After the committee made its selections, I leafed through the unsuccessful applications. One was Jerrold Sandler's. He was working at a public television station in Moline, Illinois. Only one person on that search committee would have had any idea who Jerrold Sandler was or what he had done for public radio twenty-three years earlier or would have understood why this public television guy would want a job in public radio. His radio experience was not recent enough to consider him for an interview.

Rather than an invitation to interview, the committee sent Jerrold Sandler of Moline, Illinois, along with all the other unsuccessful applicants, a form letter thanking him for his interest in public radio.

He died in Moline in 1995.

CHAPTER 4

Purposes

Radio's inclusion in the public television legislation in 1967 was, in the words of Scott Fletcher, "not part of the scenario." Radio ended up in the legislation not through public demand nor even with public knowledge. Its fluky inclusion resulted from the efforts of a few individuals who wanted to outmaneuver a bunch of arrogant television people more than they were able to outline a realistic vision for radio. *The Hidden Medium* was a pragmatic document that said what was needed to get radio into the television legislation but did not lay out a concrete plan for public radio. Moreover, once these individuals attained victory, they were banished. The new Corporation for Public Broadcasting ended up with a mandate to develop public radio in this country, but it had no particular knowledge of the medium nor interest in it. No stations or individuals, as in television, stood ready to lead. No constituency demanded action. No expectations existed. The slate was blank.

Incredibly, the leader of television's effort to keep radio out of the public broadcasting act responded to CPB's dilemma by proposing that he and his colleagues develop and operate what they called "The National Public Radio System." Hartford Gunn was the president of WGBH in Boston, the mastermind of public television's Carnegie ef-

---

Author's note: I observed the events in this chapter from the vantage point of London, where I worked at the BBC courtesy of a fellowship from the Corporation for Public Broadcasting. I participated in none of the events, but I followed them carefully, expecting to work for the new public radio network upon my return.

fort, and would soon become the first president of PBS. He proposed a public radio system built around WGBH-FM and five to eight other major metropolitan area stations on the East and West Coasts. He suggested stations that were mostly operated by public television stations with little interest in radio. He proposed that, although all of the country's public radio stations would carry the network's programming, their coalition of public-television-operated stations in Boston and other major markets would produce the programming and would control "The National Public Radio System." With the exception of WHA Radio in Madison, Wisconsin, by far the largest educational radio operation in the country, the coalition excluded stations outside of major metropolitan areas and stations owned and operated by universities.

While this proposal came from the wrong person and involved the wrong stations, it had much to recommend it. Gunn and his colleagues recognized that, in many communities, the new public radio service would need to compete for listeners with up to fifty commercial stations. According to Gunn, "If the audience is to find it at all, this service must have a clearly definable character or sound. . . . This programming would have to be offered daily in large blocks of time over stations that reach influential populations in large cities."[1] Gunn's proposal implied, but never said, that the "definable character or sound" would appeal to a narrow slice of the population.

Although Gunn's concept departed from the lofty promises in *The Hidden Medium* to serve the disadvantaged, the minorities, and the residents of rural America, it realistically assessed the requirements to affect a crowded radio marketplace. Public radio would need to have a consistent sound, to focus on the largest markets, and to escape university bureaucracies. Gunn rightly recognized that music sounds the same on a public or a commercial station, but his proposed "sound" of intelligent talk was distinctive and would stand out in a crowd of commercial babble. This sound could define public radio. Gunn saw that public radio could not become a nationally recognized medium unless it became as important to Manhattan, New York, as it was to Manhattan, Kansas. Also, Gunn accurately perceived the stifling effect university bureaucracies had on public broadcasting, given that universities usually ranked broadcasting near the bottom of their priorities. Universities may have invented the American style of educational radio and provided it a home, but that home was as often stultifying as it was nurturing.

However, even if Gunn were correct in wanting to exclude university stations from future public radio leadership, his proposal was highly impolitic. It reflected the Bostonian's contempt for those Midwest land-grant state university stations at the heart of educational radio, and blatantly shunned the handful of university stations that had pulled off the insurrection that sneaked public radio into his public television legislation. Whatever its merits, Gunn's plan could go nowhere given the politics of educational or public radio.

Nonetheless, Gunn's programming ideas were well defined and reflected an understanding of contemporary format radio and of the audiences of educational radio. Gunn proposed a plan for a public radio network service "of tightly-formatted, in-depth national and international news and public affairs, with the emphasis on analysis, commentary, criticism, and good talk."[2] The ingredients Gunn listed were already part of educational radio, but he proposed greatly increasing their quality and quantity. Ultimately, they would become the essential ingredients of National Public Radio. In 1968, however, news and public affairs paled in comparison to classical music's ability to attract listeners to educational radio, but Gunn was right that news and public affairs would appeal to educational radio's existing audience—mature, affluent, and, most important, educated. Gunn did not propose to produce radically new kinds of programs, nor did he propose to reach out to new and different audiences. He simply proposed to do what was already being done, but to do it with more professionalism and, he presumed, more impact.

However, Gunn's emphasis on a consistent sound or "formatting" departed from current educational radio practices. In 1969, educational radio stations thought in terms of program schedules, stringing a series of separate, unrelated programs together, one after another, just as commercial radio did prior to television and just as television does today. Gunn saw a "format" as one continuous program, a "sound" that listeners could expect and recognize. Gunn's public radio "sound" could compete with commercial radio stations that had adopted formatting with the arrival of television. As realistic as Gunn was about content, his proposal glossed over the difficulty of relying on several different producing stations to forge a consistent sound.

Realistic or flawed, Gunn's concept for the National Public Radio System was doomed. Broadcasters at Midwest university stations, who dominated educational radio, would never turn over their enterprise to the arrogant gentleman from Boston, no matter how realistic or flawed his proposal.

A Gunn protégé in Boston, and later at PBS in Washington, also understood the importance of formatting but was more politic. Sam Holt's family interests included commercial radio stations, and he loved and understood the medium. The new Corporation for Public Broadcasting, charged by Congress with developing public radio, turned to this man, who loved and understood the medium, for guidance. The Corporation commissioned Holt to conduct a major study of educational radio's predicament and to recommend a strategy to deal with it.

Holt's *Public Radio Study* made a number of recommendations to CPB that would prove critical to the development of public radio.[3] One urged CPB to pump significant money into local public radio stations to help them wean themselves from their parent universities and to help them identify with a national system. When CPB instituted such grants, however, it limited them to stations with enough resources and enough commitment to warrant an investment of national money. CPB set very reasonable criteria, yet only 73 of the 425 educational radio stations operating at the time met them. Only seventy-three stations had power of 250 watts or more, an adequately-equipped control room and studio, three full-time professional broadcasters on staff, a minimum operational schedule of eight hours per day, six days per week for forty-eight weeks of the year with half the broadcast hours devoted to educational, informational, and cultural programs for a public audience.[4] Another Holt recommendation was for CPB to establish its own "radio activities office" to give visibility to the invisible medium within the television-obsessed organization.

Holt recognized the political and practical folly of placing the system in the hands of a select group of stations as Gunn had proposed. He suggested, instead, that CPB fund a new, independent organization in Washington. His proposed organization would lead its member stations and answer to them through a station-elected board of directors. Holt recommended that the new organization produce public affairs programming, which he saw as the program category on which public radio could build its reputation. CPB acted on this recommendation and founded National Public Radio in Washington to produce the national program service and provide leadership for public radio stations. No other decision was more momentous for the eventual success of public radio in America. By way of contrast, the Public Broadcasting Service, created by CPB for television, followed the strategy its first president, Hartford Gunn, had proposed for public radio. Its program production divided among WGBH and a half dozen other major stations. Unlike NPR, PBS was specifically prohibited from producing programs. As a result, public television never became more than a collection of separate programs and series. It had no unified quality to set it apart from the collections of programs eventually offered on cable channels such as Discovery.

While Sam Holt's recommendations to CPB were clearly important, his *Public Radio Study* was most perceptive in its analysis of the strengths and potential of public radio as a unique medium rather than as public television without pictures. Like Gunn's proposal (which Holt probably had a hand in writing), Holt's study recognized that educational radio needed a format, a distinctive sound, to compete with commercial radio stations. The *Public Radio Study* further observed that, even among the largest commercial stations, formats did not aim at a mass audience but at narrowly targeted ones. A barrage of individual programs could lob one program at farmers, one at opera fans, and one at news junkies; a format had to choose its target. No commercial radio station expected to reach more than a fraction of the total audience in a market with fifty competitors, and Holt urged noncommercial radio to forgo a something-for-everyone philosophy.

Public television, under the Carnegie Commission recommendations, had to take the barrage approach to serve the various audiences underserved by commercial television. At one time or another, a public television station might have a program to interest just about everyone: kids, the elderly, the Spanish speaking, inner-city residents, rural residents, hunters, homemakers, and Wall Street financiers. Audiences for a public television station could change from hour to hour. People watched programs, not channels. The concept of a "favorite" channel did not exist in television, commercial or public. Radio had been that way, too, before television came along. It had to change to survive, and it did. Each station sought to appeal to one demographic all day long. It chose to "own" a slice of the population and concede the rest to other stations. Commercial radio made this move from broadcasting to narrowcasting in the late 1950s and 1960s. Unlike television, contemporary radio became extremely personal. Individuals developed a close relationship with a "favorite" radio station and seldom tuned to more than one or two others.[5] Public radio would need to follow suit in the 1970s, said Gunn implicitly and Holt explicitly.

Like commercial radio stations, public radio stations would need to get comfortable with the idea that they would serve only a segment of the population. Holt argued, "As fractionation becomes more severe in commercial radio, there is a growing acceptance of the argument that a small audience is perfectly tolerable, so long as it can be defined and made loyal. The time may have come when educational radio can accept without apology or rationalization a limited audience, so long as it knows who it is and can develop feedback from it to measure its desires and needs."⁶ Such thinking was heretical in 1969. Mainstream thinking was represented better by *The Hidden Medium* which had promised to serve many audiences, particularly the underserved. The Public Broadcasting Act made no distinction between radio and television in its stated goal of providing quality programming for diverse audiences. The concept of serving multiple audiences was sacrosanct and applied to both television and radio whether or not it was appropriate for both. Few were willing to question its application to radio. Holt was an exception. While something of a political embarrassment at the time, his would become the strategy for changing public radio from the "hidden medium" to what he described as the "emerging medium."

Gunn had proposed a service that would do a better job of providing programming to our society's hypereducated, the same audience educational radio already served. His protégé Holt then proposed that public radio need not feel guilty about serving a small slice of society, since serving small audiences is the nature of radio. Gunn and Holt expressed realistic views, but they were hardly compatible with the views in the Carnegie Commission report or in *The Hidden Medium*. Those two documents would forever hover over public radio as well as public television, not so much as a guide to action but as a public mantra. While Holt absolved public radio from guilt over serving only a defined segment of the public, he did not stop public radio broadcasters from experiencing it, or from, on occasion, openly expressing it.

While most veterans of educational radio could not really imagine serving any audience beyond that narrow one espoused by Gunn and Holt, few other than Gunn and Holt dared express those views out loud. They stood in the midst of the Great Society's effort to help the least privileged in society; how could they justify catering to the well educated and most privileged? While they could make a case for the government to support their radio service in the same way it supported museums and other cultural institutions available to all but of primary interest to society's most privileged, they felt guilty doing it. So the emerging leaders of the new public radio proclaimed that they would not just update educational radio but take a totally new approach to the medium. While any revolutionary idea ran against their instincts, their habits, and perhaps their better judgment, few would argue for anything less than a medium that would help the entire nation, every segment of society. They set out to do what Lord Reith at the BBC in Britain had set out to do and what the pioneer educational radio stations in America had set out to do: bring the values and expertise of higher education to the entire population.

The person who best expressed that new spirit was a thin, stooped man in his late thirties with a blond beard that compensated for his thinning blond hair. Nurtured in the Wisconsin tradition of educational radio, William Siemering literally grew up in the shadow of WHA Radio: The house of his boyhood sat under the station's transmission towers. He developed an evangelistic approach to continuing education for adults as a result of his exposure to the Chautauqua tent shows that brought drama, music, lectures and inspiration to rural America from the late 1800s through the first third of the 1900s. For a half-dozen summers, Siemering's parents signed on as Chautauqua actors and toured small towns in the Midwest. Some said radio killed the Chautauqua shows, but Siemering said *educational* radio kept the Chautauqua tradition alive. He liked to point out that the first dictionary definition of "broadcast" is "a throwing at large of seed. . . . To scatter widely." As farmers broadcast seeds, uncertain about where they would land and which would grow, so did Chautauqua broadcast seeds of culture and ideas throughout the rural Midwest with the faith that some would take root and grow. Siemering believed the educational radio stations of Wisconsin and other land grant universities carried both meanings of "broadcasting."

When Siemering entered the University of Wisconsin, he became a member of the WHA student staff, performing both technical and on-air duties, while training for a career as a high school counselor. In 1962, the State University of New York—Buffalo chose a University of Wisconsin faculty member for a top administrative post. That faculty member wanted to create a radio station in Buffalo just like the WHA that he had grown to love in Madison. The manager of WHA suggested he hire Bill Siemering. Bill shuffled off to Buffalo, happy to tackle the problems of society instead of the comparatively trivial problems of high school students.

The State University of New York—Buffalo in the 1960s, however, was not the University of Wisconsin at the turn of the century. Siemering molded its radio station, WBFO, as much to fit Buffalo's environment as to implement The Wisconsin Idea he had brought with him. He sought to do for contemporary urban residents what the traditional land-grant university stations had done for rural ones. As in Wisconsin, the Buffalo station had to reflect a broader commitment on the part of its parent institution, and SUNY—Buffalo in the 1960s sought an involvement in its community much as Wisconsin had at the turn of the century. Siemering liked to quote the chancellor of the state university system of New York, Samuel B. Gould, whom, the *New York Times* reported in 1967, urged universities to "stop standing on the sidelines" as "the United States is faced with the greatest peril of its history."[7] Gould wanted to tap "the greatest collection of intelligence, ability and creativity in the country" by involving the university in the difficult issues of the day. Siemering embraced Gould's philosophy and applied it to his radio station.

WBFO did play classical music and, most often, sounded like other educational radio stations. It attracted attention, however, by tackling the two issues that dominated the thinking of the campus and the times, race relations and the war in Vietnam.

To foster understanding between the races and to provide a voice for Buffalo's minority community, Siemering set up a storefront studio in Buffalo's ghetto and provided air time for volunteer broadcasters. Proclaiming that "the communication most whites have heard from the black community is the sound of a brick shattering a plate glass window," he set out to provide an outlet for minorities to communicate directly their frustrations, grievances, and problems and for whites "to learn of the daily life and problems of the non-white and not just of the incendiary issues in a time of crisis."[8]

When the inevitable student strike to protest the Vietnam War hit the SUNY campus and 300 police moved in, Siemering and WBFO's student staff provided live coverage and, more importantly, made the station the forum for discussion of the issues surrounding the strike. "Truth," Siemering explained, "was reflected through different perceptions of reality, and we broadcast a full spectrum of opinion. Amid tear gas in the building and some administration objections, we stayed on the air . . . as a beacon of light amid the chaos."[9] Siemering's emphasis on ordinary people expressing themselves to the entire community, "primary sources," was a departure from the traditional educational radio he had learned at WHA and from traditional journalism. Traditional educational radio gave the authoritative role of selecting and organizing material for the listener to an educator. Traditional journalism assigned that authoritative role to a journalist. Public affairs programming on educational radio featured academics, office holders, candidates, and spokes-

persons for organized interests. Siemering added to that mix the unfil-
tered views of people without credentials, or, as he might prefer to put
it, people whose credentials came from their own experience. His addition reflected the skepticism about authority that characterized the
campus movements of the '60s and early '70s.

Siemering's views resembled the BBC founder Lord Reith's "public
service" ideology adapted by American educational radio less than they
did those of Pacifica founder Lewis Hill. Public-service ideology had authority figures "educate" an audience. If it failed to attract an audience,
public service nonetheless promulgated "the best" programs for their
own sake. Hill's ideology, on the other hand, was democratic. He valued
authenticity over authority. Artists performed their own works for their
own sake, not as part of an effort to educate the audience. In its earliest incarnation, Pacifica Radio sought understanding among peoples as
the antidote to conflict. It advocated free speech and diversity and listening respectfully to all voices. Pacifica Radio meant dialogue radio. Hill
and his colleagues quickly learned, however, that most people have little
interest in the differing views of others. Indeed, most people have little
interest in expressing their views to those with differing ones. While Pacifica Radio never abandoned its belief in dialogue, in reality it became a
platform for voices excluded from mainstream media, particularly voices
on the left. Siemering's views bore an uncanny resemblance to Hill's at
their inception, when they were most idealistic and most naive.

At WBFO, Siemering used his experience covering antiwar demonstrations and running his store-front studio to create a new daily program that was as free of structure as it was free in content. He set aside
four full hours—not fifteen-minute, half-hour, nor hour-long program
segments—each afternoon to broadcast "live" radio, allowing time for
ideas to grow and events to happen. His four unstructured hours allowed form to follow substance. *That*, he said, was "radio." Hence his
title: *This Is Radio*.

Siemering's application to the new Corporation for Public Broadcasting for money to support *This Is Radio* clearly stated his concept.
His application described an America in which an increasingly com-
partmentalized population selected information sources that reinforced
its existing beliefs. Public broadcasting, he said, should provide an information source in which diverse groups could put their faith. He chas-
tised both sides in the Vietnam War debate for avoiding meaningful
discussion. One side waved the flag while the other, the students,
"groomed and dressed in a manner which is blatantly offensive to many,

chanting 'One, two, three, four, we don't want your fucking war,' are not issuing an open invitation to meaningful dialogue." He argued that both sides feared that "discourse would modify, or in the eyes of some, weaken or compromise a position which has all the righteousness of a fundamentalist religion."[10]

Siemering's CPB application declared that *This Is Radio* would promote the exchange of ideas between people with different values, between the flag-wavers and the students. His program would seek to make institutions more responsive to people, to share a university's wealth of knowledge in a context meaningful to people, and above all, to sound flexible and engaging enough to maintain credibility with large numbers of diverse people. Siemering contrasted his vision with "the traditional journalistic filtering of ideas which many feel results in distortion." He pointed out that WBFO's antiwar demonstration coverage, had not merely provided access for a variety of viewpoints, but had clarified issues by selecting articulate spokesmen and providing a quiet setting and, through good discussion-leader techniques, defined problems, questioned, restated, and summarized. It treated discussion participants with what psychologist Carl Rogers described as "unconditional positive regard": "We assumed they had a respectable point of view; our attitude was more like that of a counselor trying to have an individual share his perception of reality than an interrogating journalist." He proposed that combining live reports of news events, interviews with people in the news, "persons of differing political life-style patterns," and carefully selected music would create "a sense of joy, as well as the dynamic tempo of the community." He concluded his proposal by harkening back to the involved university of his native Wisconsin: "Universities are on a front of turbulent air masses; they cannot avoid this position, and must be actively engaged in sharing its resources with the community, and listening closely to what the outside community is saying. Other institutions must show greater responsiveness to the people, and that includes the institution of public radio."[11]

Sadly, *This Is Radio* never realized Siemering's vision on a daily basis. His grant application expressed a vision not grounded in reality. Just providing air time to allow wonderful things to happen did not guarantee their happening. Nonetheless, by the spring of 1969, Bill Siemering had emerged as one of the few fresh thinkers in educational radio. If public radio needed to differ from educational radio, Siemering at least had expressed a fresh and vibrant vision. That vision, and his ability to express it, led to his selection as one of nine educational radio station managers who would compose the founding board of directors of National Public Radio.

That founding board would operate in total obscurity, have no constituency, and face no expectations. It could make public radio anything it wanted. Siemering's eight fellow board members had read his rationale for *This Is Radio* when they gathered for their first meeting just before Christmas in 1969, and they decided other members should put ideas they might have in writing to share. What they shared were ideas remarkably similar to Siemering's.

In at least one case, a manager who had devoted his whole career to making radio a highly crafted, carefully enunciated art found himself preaching what he had not previously practiced. WHA's Karl Schmidt defined a future NPR as a place where:

- People talk with people.
- People listen to people.
- Unities as well as dimensions are explored.
- Awareness of a shared humanity is emphasized.
- Rhetoric is de-escalated.
- Language is enriched.
- Openness is risked.
- The lives of people are our only concern.

According to Schmidt, NPR would not present conventional reporter-mediated journalism nor producer-driven radio nor traditional academically based educational radio. He called for programming that allowed real people to share ideas and experiences. He proposed establishing a decentralized organization to facilitate direct access by people from all regions and ideologies: "Only in this way can a national service, a true *vox populi*, be established, and that, I submit, must be the cornerstone of program policy."[12]

Joe Gwathmey of KUT at the University of Texas was a generation younger than Schmidt. He wrote two pages of "gut level feelings" that paralleled precisely the thinking of Siemering and Schmidt.[13] He listed six assumptions:

1. That our society is in the midst of a revolution.
2. That the revolution is rooted in a reexamination of values.
3. That artificial barriers to understanding are common in our society.

4. That these barriers prevent us from making rational choices as we deal with the revolution.
5. That a means of eliminating barriers is needed.
6. That NPR is probably not the means—but might be.

Bill Siemering could have written any of those six points, except for the pessimistic number six. Gwathmey went on to say that conventional media tell us what people do, but not what they think, feel or value. He expressed doubts about people's willingness to strive for understanding and about radio offering the best means to achieve understanding, but he concluded that public radio was obliged to try. Gwathmey proposed forsaking conventional journalism to give direct expression to diverse points of view. He wanted NPR to allow people to express what they "*think* is happening, not just what coolly objective reporters say is happening." The vision in Austin was very similar to the vision in Buffalo and Madison.

Bernard Mayes, a BBC expatriate managing KQED-FM in San Francisco, echoed the cry for *vox populi,* the voice of real people. Mayes wrote that "the BBC is as authoritarian in its outlook as our own commercial radio is exploitive. NPR will have the lucky chance to make the invention available, at last, to the public."[14] He wanted an NPR different from conventional journalism, from commercial radio, from traditional educational radio—even from the authoritarian BBC. Mayes predicted the replacement of the lowest common denominator "mass audience" with a collection of minority audiences, a situation that already existed, according to Sam Holt's *Public Radio Study.* Mayes departed from Holt on a critical point, however. Whereas Holt told public radio to accept the reality that any one radio station—even a public radio station—could serve just one minority audience, Mayes declared it should defy commercial patterns and attempt to serve many. Serving many was possible, he said, because minorities are interested in the views of other minorities. Like Siemering, Gwathmey, and Schmidt—and Pacifica's Lewis Hill—Mayes saw public radio giving voice to diverse groups and fostering understanding among groups. They all assumed that groups would listen to one another. Each would solve the old conflict between "giving the public what it wants" (commercial broadcasting) and "giving the public what it needs" (public service broadcasting) by "giving the public the microphone." They would solve the old conflict between serving a specific target audience (Sam Holt's prescription) and serving the entire population (Lord Reith's goal) by serving a series of minority audiences broad-minded enough to want to hear the programming for other minority audiences with divergent views and tastes.

The board assigned to Siemering the task of assembling a consensus statement of National Public Radio's purposes. His task was hardly difficult since most of his fellow board members had expressed views congruent with his own. Indeed, his consensus document began with a restatement of his *This Is Radio* concept. The opening paragraph is often cited as the essence of NPR's philosophy:

> National Public Radio will serve the individual; it will promote personal growth; it will regard the individual differences among men with respect and joy rather than derision and hate; it will celebrate the human experience as infinitely varied rather than vacuous and banal; it will encourage a sense of active constructive participation, rather than apathetic helplessness.[15]

Underneath the seeming consensus for a public radio dramatically different from educational radio, however, remained a counterinstinct to simply improve on educational radio's traditional programming. In a sense, the dramatic new vision was such a departure and was so idealistic that even those who espoused it could not quite imagine its implementation. While they could support the new vision enthusiastically, they really did not want to lose the programs and audiences to which each had devoted his career. The final document, therefore, included other, more predictable elements reflecting board members' interests in radio production as an art form, in drama and music, in excellent broadcast journalism, in universities as the source for expert opinion, and in high technical standards—in other words, goals associated with the public-service tradition of the BBC and educational radio.[16]

In fact, not one of the seven top priorities for the new network listed in the consensus document directly reflects the rhetoric of Siemering's proposal for *This Is Radio* or of the written submissions of board members. Instead, the document promised a "daily product, which is consistent and reflects the highest standards of broadcast journalism," a somewhat surprising first priority for an organization whose board members spoke of giving voice to real people rather than "cooly objective journalists." Its second priority was similarly journalistic, promising coverage of public events and special public affairs programming outside the "daily product." Its third priority was cultural programming, not surprising for educational radio but somewhat incongruous with the idea of public radio as a public forum. Also from a tradition of educational radio came its fourth priority, to provide access to the intellectual and cultural resources of universities. In a nod to the more democratic instincts expressed by board members, however, the fourth priority added access to the intellectual and cultural resources of urban areas and rural areas. The final three priorities listed provision of programs for special needs such as adult education, K–12 in-school broadcasts, program exchanges with foreign broadcasters, and programming "specifically intended to develop the art and technical potential of radio."[17]

Siemering's statement of purpose was far less focused than Hartford Gunn's proposal for "The National Public Radio System," nor did it acknowledge the challenge of competing for audiences in the world of contemporary commercial radio as had Sam Holt's *Public Radio Study*. Siemering's statement of purpose would have NPR do a better job doing all the same things educational radio already did, plus tackle a whole new agenda for giving access to "real people." He concluded his statement of purpose for the new organization with a list of attributes that would characterize NPR programming:

> The total service should be trustworthy, enhance intellectual development, expand knowledge, deepen aural aesthetic enjoyment, increase the pleasure of living in a pluralistic society and result in a service to listeners which makes them more responsive, informed human beings and intelligent responsible citizens of their communities and the world.[18]

Could such noble sentiments translate into successful radio programming? Could the new network's programming differ that much from educational radio's? Did the practitioners of educational radio guiding the enterprise really want it to differ that much? In the winter of 1970, there were no answers. In fact, the American public neither knew nor cared about the enterprise that so excited Siemering and his fellow board members. No newspaper other than the CPB's own house organ even reported the incorporation of National Public Radio on March 3, 1970.[19] Nevertheless, Siemering had sketched a compelling portrait of NPR. Its completion would require many brush strokes.

PART TWO

Reality

CHAPTER 5

All Things Considered

F inding effective leadership would prove difficult for a group of pa-
thetically weak radio stations gathered suddenly under the umbrella
of federal largess only because of subterfuge and dumb luck. Few educational radio station managers had the background, instincts, or desire to broaden their horizons from their local campuses to the nation.
Almost by definition, managers who had chosen careers in educational
radio lacked the drive necessary for national leadership. The individuals who had the *chutzpah* to get radio added to the public television act
were pariahs. The television-dominated public broadcasting leadership
would allow them no future role.

The television leadership did respect one "radio guy" who was also
one of their own. Don Quayle had managed both an educational radio
station at a land-grant university (Ohio State) and Hartford Gunn's east
coast "community" station, WGBH-FM, Boston. He also had briefly
headed a network service for educational radio stations strung between
Washington, DC, and New England. That network ran on Ford Foundation funds, and, when Ford cut off radio funding, Quayle jumped to
educational television to work on another Ford-funded project. He then
became a key executive of the newly formed Corporation for Public
Broadcasting. Quayle, therefore, knew radio in both its university and
its community incarnations, he knew radio networking, and he knew
the broader world of educational broadcasting. He really had wanted

Author's Note: I participated in the events in this chapter as NPR's first employee
and as the first permanent producer of *All Things Considered*.

the presidency of PBS, but when that went to Hartford Gunn, he read-
ily settled for the presidency of National Public Radio.

In the circus of public broadcasting, however, Quayle's attention remained on the center ring of television; he could not muster as much
enthusiasm for the public radio sideshow. Even after he assumed the
NPR presidency, Quayle spoke with more energy and knowledge of public television than public radio. Nonetheless, Don Quayle was as qualified a leader as public radio was likely to attract and probably a better
one than it deserved, whether or not his heart was in the job. A non-
practicing Mormon from Utah and the father of five children, the thirty-
nine-year-old Quayle took a paternal approach to his mostly young staff.
He treated staff members with warmth and kindness not generally expected of a CEO. Perhaps because of his Mormon background, he had
a very traditional attitude toward gender roles; he believed men should
act like men and women should act like women. Those attracted to National Public Radio as staff or listener were already questioning this
macho attitude that much of society would disavow in the next decade.

President Quayle surrounded himself with buddies from educational
television, most of whom seemed a bit embarrassed by stooping to jobs
in radio. The new director of promotion was one who actually had a
genuine interest in radio. He came from a similar job in educational
television, but had been a child actor in the closing days of network
radio drama and envisioned this new thing called public radio as a way
to recapture radio's role in American living rooms before television com-
pletely supplanted it. Of course, his idea was totally misguided, and it
dampened his enthusiasm for promoting what public radio was actually
trying to do in the early 1970s. The others on Quayle's team thought
in public television terms and never quite grasped public radio's potential either.

While Quayle knew from the day he assumed the NPR presidency
in September of 1970 exactly whom he wanted to fill most of the top
executive jobs at the new NPR, he had no firm idea about who should
fill the position that mattered most, director of programming. Almost
by default, he gave the job to Bill Siemering, public radio's man with a
vision, but seemed to doubt his choice from the moment he made it.
While Quayle acknowledged that Siemering had a fresh vision for public radio, he, like most public radio veterans, really thought public radio
should simply do a better job of what educational radio already did. No
surprise that NPR's first program offering under Quayle's presidency
was a series of recorded concerts by the Los Angeles Philharmonic, pre-

cisely the type of "orchestra series" that populated the schedules of most educational stations. With "recorded in concert series" from the symphony orchestras of Boston, New York, Philadelphia, and Chicago already on the air, Quayle's addition of Los Angeles hardly signaled a bold new direction for public radio.

Into this environment stepped Bill Siemering, promising "to celebrate the human experience," to quote just one high-minded, but less than specific, promise made in the statement of NPR purposes. In contrast to Quayle and his television buddies, Siemering was the "sensitive male" that society would celebrate in the next decade as the necessary counterpart to the "liberated woman." Quayle's pals were sure he had made a major mistake hiring Siemering and ridiculed the organization's program director more than they supported him. Their disdain increased as Siemering began to assemble his programming staff. Accustomed to working with idealistic, energetic, but green, college students at Buffalo, Siemering surrounded himself at NPR with young people right out of college or just a few years beyond. Siemering chose his staff based on rambling personal interviews rather than on résumés. He wanted individuals excited about the NPR purposes he had penned and anxious to join him in celebrating the human experience.

Long before affirmative action became the law of the land, Siemering set out to assemble a staff representative of the nation. That meant white, black, Hispanic, Asian, and as many women as men. Many he hired had little or no broadcast experience. Their lack of experience did not bother Siemering. His work with college students and ghetto residents had convinced him that anyone could easily learn radio techniques. Siemering cared more about a job candidate's authenticity and sense of purpose. He did not care that some staff members sounded less than professional on the air. After all, the NPR purposes he wrote promised to speak with many voices, to celebrate "the human experience as infinitely varied rather than vacuous and banal."[1] The purposes promised to "increase the pleasure of living in a pluralistic society and regard the individual differences among men with respect and joy rather than derision and hate." NPR board members said they wanted something more human than "cooly objective journalists."[2] Siemering's staff choices reflected his philosophy and, he had every reason to believe, the emerging philosophy of public radio.

The Ford Foundation tested Siemering's philosophy not long after he arrived at NPR. The foundation, which had cut off all funding to educational radio and had opposed its inclusion in the Public Television Act, offered to open its purse to public radio on one condition: Foundation officials told Quayle that they would provide NPR with funds to employ broadcast journalist Edward P. Morgan for five years as host of NPR's proposed magazine program. Morgan was ABC Radio's answer to CBS's Edward R. Murrow. His style mimicked that of Murrow—steady, authoritative, a bit pompous. His left-of-center commentaries fit Ford Foundation values and the values of most people who worked in or listened to educational radio. Moreover, Morgan had anchored public television's first major live national broadcast series, *PBL*, the *Public Broadcasting Laboratory*. Ford had funded the series for two years before PBS got going. PBL had been an exciting experiment. It did not fear controversy. It waded into the most divisive problems of the time, race and Vietnam. It debunked the claims of commercial advertising. It took chances. It tried to demonstrate all that public television might do for the country. It even attempted the kind of people-talking-to-people approach of Siemering's *This Is Radio*.

From the Ford Foundation's point of view, Edward P. Morgan was exactly what public radio needed to give it instant recognition and instant credibility. Morgan was somebody. From Siemering's point of view, however, instant recognition presented a problem. If NPR hired Morgan, it would take on Morgan's identity, the positive and the negative. Siemering did not want one person to define NPR, even if that person had a career and reputation as solid as Morgan's. Siemering did not address the obvious conflict between Morgan's ponderous and authoritative style and the lively, populist image he had for the program that would become *All Things Considered*. Morgan might represent the best tradition of radio journalism's golden age, but Siemering did not want to merely revive that golden age. He wanted to usher in a new and different age. Exactly what he wanted was less clear than what he did not want, but Morgan did not fit. Quayle dutifully passed on to Ford the decision of his program director, shutting the door to financial support from that foundation for many years to come.

Siemering did not want to buy the instant credibility of Morgan. He wanted a new identify to emerge organically out of his ideas and his anonymous young staffers who embraced them. He brought three staff members from his station in Buffalo. Two had worked as student volunteers at the station. They were capable, enthusiastic young men fiercely loyal to Siemering's approach to radio. The third, Mike Waters, had been WBFO's full-time news director, an interesting position given his lack of interest in current events. Waters' warmth, empathy, and off-center take on life mattered more to Siemering than the conventions of journalism. Waters might bungle an interview with a public figure, but his descriptions of a sunset were pure poetry. Waters came to symbolize Siemering's vision for NPR in the minds of both his supporters and detractors.

Siemering hired several young refugees from commercial radio. He chose two who had worked for UPI Audio, a shlocky spot-news service for commercial radio stations that epitomized precisely the kind of journalism NPR eschewed. Siemering hired them much as a church embraces repentant sinners, although each subsequently violated Siemering's creed from time to time. Siemering picked two other journalists from a rat-a-tat-tat all-news station, another negative role model for the new NPR. Unfortunately, neither quite understood that Siemering hired them because they seemed to renounce their past rather than to tap into their commercial experience. Quayle, on the other hand, approved these hires because they sounded "professional."

Siemering also hired another commercial radio refugee, but of a rather different sort. He had worked for FM underground rock stations and had developed a compelling style that used sounds to capture raw emotions, then integrated them into breathless dramatic narratives. In a sense, his stories were the radio equivalent of a television news report, in which "sound" assumed the function of "pictures" in video reporting. Siemering had written about advancing the art of sound, and this reporter actually knew how to apply that art to radio journalism. Sound-rich journalism became part of the NPR style, but the public radio career of the journalist who introduced it to NPR lasted but a few months. He stormed out of NPR and into a career as a television reporter, complaining that NPR relied too heavily on the style of "educational radio and the BBC" rather than on his emotion-laden, in-your-face sound of reality style. Some staff members felt ambivalent about his departure. They recognized that his approach was more compelling than anyone else's, but they had also criticized television's obsession with pictures as limiting its ability to handle abstract issues and ideas. While he did produce captivating radio, this reporter's reliance on sound limited him just as surely as pictures limited television. Also contributing to this reporter's speedy departure was his realization that, contrary to his hopes, NPR would not crusade against the Vietnam War and for social injustice. Neither would commercial television, of course, but commercial television had never suggested that it might.

While Siemering made most hiring decisions, Don Quayle brought in three experienced educational radio staff members. One was an older, very traditional, classical music announcer, whom he had befriended back at Ohio State's WOSU. He hardly represented the break with the past Siemering promised. Another was Susan Stamberg, a woman about thirty who had worked for Quayle's short-lived network of East Coast educational radio stations. She had a one-year-old son and wanted a few hours a day of part-time work. Stamberg and Siemering quickly bonded, and she became a loyal disciple. Then there was me. Quayle had also hired me before Siemering arrived on the basis of my CPB fellowship in London.

Quayle also introduced Siemering to two cast-offs from commercial network television, neither as widely known as Edward P. Morgan. Josh Darsa from CBS Television revered the memory of Edward R. Murrow and meticulously emulated his style. His studiously resonant voice articulated carefully-constructed sentences with dirge-like slowness. His every word sounded momentous. Darsa's style fit Siemering's new populist enterprise no better than did that of Morgan. Quayle was relieved, however, to have someone on staff whose resume and style said "professional."

Robert Conley, the other cast-off, also had professional credentials that included years as a foreign correspondent for NBC Television and the ultimate establishment news source, the *New York Times*. His résumé no doubt impressed Quayle, but what he said pleased Siemering. Unlike Darsa, Conley repented of his entire professional background. Conley urged NPR to reject the ways of NBC and the *New York Times*. He regarded NPR as the antithesis of those two reputable organizations. It would break new ground and establish totally different standards of excellence. Conley could quote the words Siemering had written and augment them with his own, expressing democratic dreams, always sweeping in scope and scant on details. Siemering chose Robert Conley, not Edward P. Morgan, to personify National Public Radio.

Conley's greatest contribution to NPR may have been introducing Quayle and Siemering to Cleve Mathews. A veteran editor at the *New York Times*, Mathews had once been Conley's supervisor. He was supposed to move back to New York from the *Times'* Washington bureau, but he and his wife preferred life in Washington. He saw a position at NPR as a way to stay. Quayle saw hiring him as a way to attain the journalistic credibility he sought. Quayle liked Mathews credentials, but Siemering liked the man. Siemering's interview revealed Mathews as a thoroughly decent, humble, nice guy, perhaps too nice for the competitive world of the *New York Times* but ideal for the network of nice people Siemering envisioned. Mathews had no broadcast experience, however, but he shared that limitation with many of Siemering's "unqualified" hires. With the title of news editor, Mathews joined Siemering, and Conley to complete the triumvirate about to lead a disparate staff in making radio programs out of poetic purposes.

NPR's founding board said public radio's first national program should have a daily presence, a topical focus—perhaps news—and embody in one magazine-style program all of what Siemering had laid out in the NPR purposes document. He had written that the network would start with "an identifiable daily product which is consistent and reflects the highest standards of broadcast journalism."[3] The words "identifiable daily product" reflected the consensus view that public radio needed its functional equivalent of *Sesame Street*, a program that would attract attention and provide an identity. Siemering said the daily product had to be big. It had to air every day and offer a "well paced, flexible . . . service primarily for a general audience." It had to put public radio on the map.[4]

Siemering was ambiguous in defining "the highest standards of broadcast journalism." Indeed, some questioned whether Siemering was proposing a news program at all, when he said the proposed blockbuster "*may* contain *some* hard news, but the primary emphasis would be on interpretation, investigative reporting on public affairs, the world of ideas and the arts."[5] Siemering sidestepped the ambiguity by saying NPR defined news differently than did commercial broadcasters. He defined this "news" program as focusing on the "why, how, and who" rather than on the "what, where, and when" of the day's events. He also sought a range of subject matter broader than the range of stories that made up Walter Cronkite's *CBS Evening News*.

Siemering also wanted the program to draw its expertise from a range of sources beyond those "cooly objective journalists." The program "may" (Siemering was never so definite as to say the program "would") include "views of the world from poets, men and women of ideas and interpretive comments from scholars."[6] Interpretive views of scholars had long been the stuff of educational radio, but Siemering promised that NPR would do a more thorough and better job of tapping this resource at the universities that owned and operated most educational radio stations. NPR would draw on its member stations to make available to the nation "for the first time the intellectual resources of colleges and universities."[7] Siemering's list of potential experts seemed at least as close to educational radio traditions as to the reporting and analysis of Edward R. Murrow and "his boys," generally accepted as defining the "highest standards of broadcast journalism." Siemering made "diversity" the cornerstone of the proposed identifiable daily product before that word became the mantra of the academic world. He proposed that this blockbuster daily product, while designed for a general audience, would not "substitute superficial blandness for genuine diversity of regions, values, and cultural and ethnic minorities which comprise American society; it would speak with many voices and many dialects."[8]

Siemering's plan for what became *All Things Considered* was not so much the blueprint for a radio program as it was a set of values that might contribute to a better, more humane society. His emphasis on values and his call to action lured, excited, and energized many of those who came to work for the new network. Like a magnet, the resulting flagship program attracted those who shared Siemering's values and repelled those who did not. In time, those listeners pulled to NPR by the magnet of Siemering's values formed the particularly desirable "market" of public radio. Of course, creating a market was never his intention:

> National Public Radio will not regard its audience as a "market" or in terms of its disposable income, but as curious, complex individuals who are looking for some understanding, meaning and joy in the human experience.[9]

Siemering provided the philosophy for *All Things Considered*, but Quayle made the first critical decisions, in part because Siemering was so reluctant to make them. First, Quayle settled on doing a ninety-minute program to air at 5:00 PM Eastern Time. He deemed one hour too traditional, too much like a "program," and two hours more than the staff could handle. Hence, he settled on ninety minutes. Quayle knew that morning is radio prime time and the most logical time for public radio's flagship program, but he also knew that a third of NPR member stations were not on the air during radio prime time. He might have induced them to sign on in the morning, when radio listening is highest, by offering NPR's major program at that time, but, instead, he used the number of stations not broadcasting in the morning as justification for doing it in the afternoon. He picked 5:00 to allow the staff to put in a normal work day culminating in a ninety-minute broadcast.

Besides, Quayle was used to "going home" magazine programs at 5:00; both his radio station at Ohio State and his short-lived Eastern Radio Network had broadcast one.

A Quayle protégé also came up with the program's title after Siemering and the "creative" people he hired failed to. For several weeks, Siemering collected title suggestions, posting a list to which staff members were invited to add their ideas. He started the list with his own suggestion, *This Is Radio*. I added *Give Us this Day*, which I explained was not a conventional news title, but was still topical and newsy—and had a spiritual quality about it. My suggestion generated groans instead of cheers but did inspire the next entry on the list, *Our Daily Bread*. The day before the scheduled press release announcing the new program, engineering and operations head George Geesey provided a list of suggestions including *All Things Considered*, which, all agreed, was better than anything on Siemering's list. Geesey's title conveyed the range of our interests, "all things," and the thoughtfulness of our treatment, "considered." The phrase also conveyed the program's reluctance to reach unqualified conclusions. Siemering's programming staff could not argue with the title's appropriateness, even as they cringed at the source. Geesey was the antithesis of Siemering—structured, rigid, and, above all, rigorously professional.

Not surprisingly, public radio's much-anticipated identifiable daily product, now called *All Things Considered*, got off to an uncertain start. The first edition of the program, May 3, 1971, started late and ended early.[10] Subsequent editions improved only slightly. For the first two months, Conley acted as host and executive producer. Hoping to break the bad habits of commercial broadcast news, Conley hosted without a script, speaking extemporaneously and not always accurately or appropriately. The rest of the staff hardly felt his presence as executive producer. For all practical purposes, no one was in charge. Program content and style changed daily as various staff members threw their ideas into the gaping hole that confronted them each afternoon at 5:00. Siemering could not quite explain how to translate his ideas into a radio program. His detractors suggested that such translation was impossible.

Quayle ordered a change.[11] Conley became "senior correspondent" and Mike Waters moved into the host's chair. Siemering described Waters' style as placing "a picture frame" unobtrusively around the work of individual reporters and producers. Waters did not disdain scripts as Conley had, but he did not read them literally. Perhaps dyslexic, he read with great difficulty. Instead, he grasped the essential content of the script and expressed it in his own words on the air. Waters never sounded like he was reading because, in fact, he was not. The result was magical in terms of radio communication, although less than fully reliable in terms of content.

Conley's reassignment ended whatever pretense remained that he actually ran the program. Mathews took control as best he could, but the task took a particular toll on this good man not yet comfortable with the medium, forced to work without the resources necessary to do the job as he thought it needed to be done, and too conscientious to accept a product of which he could not be proud. Nine months after its birth, *All Things Considered* was almost as undeveloped as the day it was born. Mathews wanted out and Quayle ordered Siemering to designate someone as producer of the program, who would have total authority and responsibility under Mathews's broad guidance. Siemering selected me.

I decided that *All Things Considered* must have a consistent approach to news; it should no longer vacillate almost daily between reporting the day's events and ignoring them. I opted for dependable but limited news reporting. In its first nine months, *ATC* included at least one, sometimes more, hard newscasts, similar to the five-minute news summaries heard on commercial radio. The newscasts "floated" in the free-form program. They changed in length and location as the program took shape each day. In the name of journalistic convention and reliability, I placed a major newscast right at the top of the program, just after 5:00, with a second summary an hour later shortly after 6:00. Conley complained that the decision smacked of radio news on the hour and the structure of the *Today Show* on TV, and he was right.

I further followed journalistic convention by placing our longer treatment of news stories immediately after the newscasts at 5:00 and 6:00, with stories flowing in descending order of "newsiness." Depending on the day, the 5:00 and 6:00 half hours might contain mostly news-related content or not, but I could assure listeners that whatever news-related features *ATC* offered would immediately follow the two news summaries. The middle half hour, 5:30 to 6:00, would always deal with more "timeless" matters. Applying any type of consistent structure to *ATC* violated Siemering's idea of "organic" radio. My application of a structure so conventional as to lead with "the news" was an egregious violation. Siemering accepted *ATC*'s new structure with as much grace as his critics did with relief.

I decided next to defy journalistic convention. I chose to use two hosts instead of one and made one of the two a woman, Susan Stamberg. I heard from Quayle almost as soon as I announced my choice. Quayle first protested that we could not afford two hosts and then that co-hosting was not a good use of Stamberg's talents.[12] I assumed that his objections reflected the prejudices of the male buddies with whom he had surrounded himself as well as of the traditionalists who managed most public radio stations. My nomination of Susan Stamberg came at a time when women did not anchor news programs. In addition, Stamberg had a pronounced New York accent, "too New York," said at least one Midwest station manager, a comment I interpreted to mean "too Jewish." My choice, however, delighted Siemering. After all, he had written that NPR would speak with many voices, many accents, many regions. Surely, a female who sounded like she came from where she did—the Bronx by way of Barnard College—fit his philosophy exactly, even if it did prove a bit off-putting in public radio's Midwest heartland, his home as well as mine.

I had a more important reason for picking Stamberg than Siemering's "many voices, many accents" philosophy. Siermering and I both knew that Stamberg, more than anyone else on the staff, could turn his dictum to "celebrate the human experience" into reality. An enthusiastic "people person," Stamberg found something fascinating in just about every person she met. She cared more deeply about art and literature than she did about "the news." She would approach news from the point of view of the interested, intelligent, but relatively uninformed layperson, which pretty much described my image of the public radio listener. I felt, and still do, that the best way to build a program with a particular sensibility is to build it around a person who embodies that sensibility. An insightful and idiosyncratic interviewer, a very strong writer of radio copy, and a vivacious interpreter of that copy, Stamberg embodied the values I thought we wanted *ATC* to have with a unique personal style that would leap out of the radio and say "Listen to me! This is important! This is interesting!"

Susan Stamberg's style would dominate *All Things Considered* for the next fifteen years, but that personality was too strong to fly solo. The program needed a solid, calming counterpoint. Besides, Stamberg simply insisted that she would work only four hours a day so she could get home in time to prepare dinner for her husband and young son. Her insistence placed a severe limitation on her ability to host a five-day-a-week program from 5:00 till 6:30 PM. That family life was her real priority, however, made her the kind of "real person" NPR's founding board said it wanted instead of a disembodied voice or "cooly objective jour-nalist."[13] We worked out a schedule that, unbeknownst to listeners, al-lowed her to leave after the first half hour of the program. We dropped taped segments into the second and third half hours of the program, during which only her co-host was live in the studio to deal with break-ing stories and the unexpected.

Mike Waters was solo host for the program when I added Stamberg, and he continued as co-host for two more years. His voice and style complemented hers well. He was as laid back as she was energetic. He was as marvelous a monologist as she was a conversationalist. They shared, however, a relatively low level of interest in news. Stamberg turned her relative lack of knowledge into an asset by asking the naive questions a lay person might ask. Waters turned his relative lack of knowledge into tension that produced severe digestive problems. There-fore, when we added a weekend edition of *All Things Considered*, I moved Waters to that less demanding assignment.

I replaced Waters in the weekday program with a surly young man named Bob Edwards, who had performed flawlessly reading the news-casts during *All Things Considered*. His deep calm voice and methodi-cal delivery provided the same counterpoint to Stamberg that Waters had, but unlike Waters, Edwards regarded himself as a journalist, and he could read almost anything put in front of him without missing a beat. He was little better than Waters at conducting coherent inter-views—too self-absorbed to really listen to what the other person had to say—but that mattered little because Stamberg was so good at them. And just enough of his cynical humor poked through now and then to make Bob Edwards a human being. Edwards was, however, clearly the second banana, a status that rankled until he moved to *Morning Edition* in 1979.

Adding Susan Stamberg to *All Things Considered* changed more than just the sound of the program. She made it possible to provide rel-atively consistent quality with very limited resources. As Siemering's neutral, unobtrusive "picture frame," Waters depended on other re-porters, producers, and station contributors to generate all of the pic-tures that he framed. NPR had too few reporters and the stations too few resources to generate consistently good pictures. Stamberg gave us flexibility. She could put pictures in the frame. She could use a simple telephone to talk with anyone anywhere. She could interview NPR re-porters about the stories they covered, providing a more human inter-action than is possible through a piece of edited tape—and more quickly and inexpensively. She could interview reporters from other news organizations, greatly expanding the range of coverage beyond the few stories our own reporters could cover. She could call "real people" throughout America to inquire about their lives and their views. Her real people interviews allowed us to pursue the kind of community building Siemering advocated without depending on local stations to do the interviews. Too often a local station's inept interviewing and packaging squeezed the humanity out of such human interest reports. Stamberg could interview experts on any topic on any campus without depending on the availability or capability of local station personnel.

While common at the BBC in Britain and the CBC in Canada at the time and ubiquitous on television cable news today, the active host interacting with reporters, experts, and news-makers defied the conventions of American broadcasting in 1972. Our interactive host generated quality material quickly and inexpensively, a necessity in those days of highly limited resources. Beyond necessity, however, Stamberg's work allowed *All Things Considered* to develop a distinctive personality, a "news" program that sounded human rather than mechanical, intelligent rather than authoritative. I felt we would have committed fraud had we taken an authoritative tone. Our small, young staff knew little more about the topics we discussed than most of our listeners. Like our listeners, we were intelligent, interested, and curious people; unlike our listeners, we enjoyed the mandate to pursue information on their behalf. We did not know many answers, but we recognized which questions needed answers and who might answer them. Stamberg and those who followed her example pursued interesting questions and found numerous potential answers, but never the definitive one. Ambiguity did not bother us. It provided an opportunity to seek clarity. And it left something to talk about the next day.

The approach I adopted out of necessity I soon embraced as a virtue. It also led to some unorthodox journalistic decisions. I made little attempt to cover breaking news widely covered by other media. I would tell our sometimes frustrated reporters that I saw no point in being just another microphone at a press conference. I assumed our listeners would learn about widely reported events from some other source. I used our reporters and our hosts, instead, to probe the background of events and assemble various interpretations of them. Years later, when NPR had greatly increased its resources and modified this approach, *All Things Considered* host Robert Siegal disparaged "the good old days" as covering news "a day late and calling it analysis." Siegal was right in the sense that *ATC* did tend to provide more coverage the day after an event than the day of the event. His insult was unfair, however, in suggesting that the early *ATC* staff merely "called" our reports analysis. The analysis may not always have been good, but the reports gave listeners background, viewpoints, and interpretation from a variety of perspectives— often scholarly, sometimes journalistic, sometimes real people with no credentials other than experience.

Our coverage of the most contentious issue of the day, the war in Vietnam, illustrates our skill at making a virtue out of necessity. While we could not afford to place reporters in Saigon, I argued that we would not want to even if we could. Information flowed out of Vietnam every night on the evening news. NPR reporters covering the same briefings were not likely to add anything unique. Besides, we were convinced that most of what was said in Saigon consisted of lies anyway. We could not provide fresh information about what was happening in Vietnam, but we could cover and foster the debate in this country *about* Vietnam. In fact, I came to regard that function as the most important service public radio could provide, offering a place for Americans to discuss the implications of the facts others reported and to debate what they should do about them.

Siemering and I wanted to create a national call-in discussion program that would allow citizens, scholars, journalists, and advocates of various positions to argue their positions in the respectful tones Siemering advocated in his proposal for *This Is Radio.* Quayle vetoed our idea. He had heard from the influential engineering staff, for whom he had more regard than he did for Siemering, that telephone quality was unacceptable for a network of mostly high-fidelity FM stations. Acting on their belief, the engineers did not include the capability to do telephone call-ins when designing the "state of the art" facilities they were building for NPR. Quayle heard, too, from the more traditional journalists, who argued that public radio's role was to uncover and explain facts rather than to preside over a discussion that shared ignorance. Quayle did have one very legitimate argument for saying no to a national call-in program: lack of money. He knew NPR could barely put out ninety minutes a day of *All Things Considered,* and he would not stretch those resources to establish any new program. The call-in program would not happen, but we tried to bring to *All Things Considered* the attitude of open discussion in those early years.

This attitude of open discussion probably contributed to the impression that National Public Radio spoke for the left in American politics, particularly regarding the Vietnam War. Those of us who made the editorial decisions every day felt we did so evenhandedly, although we all personally opposed the war. We offered opinions and interpretations that spanned the spectrum, including those that strongly favored the war. It is fair to say, however, that we presented a larger proportion of antiwar sentiments than most other media. We did so in part because we saw ourselves as an alternative to mainstream media. We also represented the thinking of America's campuses, where scholars and the communities in general questioned the war.

To the NPR staff, America's policies in Vietnam remained open, debatable questions. In our worldview, support for the war constituted one of several respectable positions on the issue. It was not the only patriotic position. Our open-minded approach mirrored the attitude of the academic world from which public radio had grown, on whose campuses most of our stations sat, and from which we drew many of our listeners. Our attitude probably did not seem reasonable and responsible to most Americans, who overwhelming reelected Richard Nixon as president over George McGovern in 1972, eighteen months after *All Things Considered* took to the air. While the new name "public" radio was supposed to mark a shift from "educational" radio, National Public Radio and its member stations could not escape the academic world, nor did we want to. We reflected the values of higher education, and, we would discover some years later, we appealed most strongly to people who shared those values.

CHAPTER 6

All Things Reconsidered

Quayle invited Siemering to his home on a Sunday morning in December of 1972 in order to fire him as director of programming. Ironically, he did so about the time that *All Things Considered* achieved a measure of consistency and acceptance and just a few months before NPR's first Peabody Award declared *All Things Considered* a program worthy of national respect. Siemering had assumed that *ATC's* success would move Quayle to let him keep the job he cherished. Instead, Quayle may have concluded that he no longer needed a visionary or, more likely, that *All Things Considered* succeeded in spite of Siemering rather than because of him. He might have been right in terms of Siemering's day-to-day contributions to the program, but he was wrong in discounting the importance of Siemering's lofty statements and laid back presence. They gave permission to those of us on the front lines to innovate and defy convention. Whatever Quayle's reason, he axed Siemering and dealt a blow to many on the staff who venerated him. Six months later, Quayle, too, was gone. He became vice president at the Corporation for Public Broadcasting, in charge of passing out money to both public radio and public television. His selection was a sound one from the point of view of CPB and public broadcasting in

---

Author's Note: I participated in the events described in the first part of this chapter as producer of *All Things Considered*, executive producer, and NPR's director of informational programming. I viewed events in the second part of the chapter from Madison, Wisconsin, where I managed WHA Radio for Ron Bornstein, the principal actor in the renewal of National Public Radio and whose perspective this account reflects.

general, but it proved less sound for NPR. While these two key figures in NPR's start-up were gone by the summer of 1973, the ambiguities of their respective legacies would hang over the organization for four more years. At that point, NPR would fall apart and have to begin again.

Quayle successfully urged the NPR board to replace him with his boyhood friend and closest confidant, Lee Frischknecht, a more faithful Utah Mormon than Quayle, a more rational person than Quayle, but a less adept politician. By dint of personality and facility of tongue, Quayle could blur the inconsistencies between NPR's conflicting aspirations, between those aspirations and realities, between Siemering's philosophy and the practicality of radio programming, between the disparate interests of NPR staff and NPR member stations. Frischknecht, by contrast, sought to erase the inconsistencies between aspirations, between aspirations and realities, between philosophy and practicality, and between the disparate interests of NPR staff and member stations. Quayle could blur fundamental conflicts and hold together disparate points of view. His were the skills of a great politician. Frischknecht sought to eliminate fundamental contradictions. His were the instincts of the academic.

First among the conflicts Quayle obscured and Frischknecht clarified was that between cultural programming—mostly classical music—and informational programming. The NPR purposes promised to do both, but with its focus on *All Things Considered*, NPR delivered only one. Classical music had long been the primary audience draw for most educational radio stations. Those who managed and staffed educational radio stations often chose that career because they personally loved classical music. Sandler and Burrows had downplayed classical music in seeking federal funding for educational radio, but for most people, educational radio meant classical music. Even if NPR had regarded classical music as public radio's most important service, the network could not establish a distinctive a sound with music. The classical repertoire existed. NPR could package it, but for most classical music listeners, the best packaging is the least packaging. Classical music did not offer NPR a way to build a reputation. NPR could not make a unique impact with classical music programming the way it could with news and information.

Reasonable as NPR's priorities were, many in public radio regarded them as an attack on classical music, on the arts, on "quality" radio. Bill Kling, president of Minnesota Public Radio and perennial critic of

NPR, publicly demanded "parity" for cultural programming. Station managers and staff members supported Kling's demand in numbers which, if not large, were most certainly loud. Lee Frischknecht listened to the complaints and felt compelled to respond, but could offer no response that did not take resources away from *All Things Considered*, the one program that gave NPR its public identity, the one program that made public radio different from educational radio.

Frischknecht faced a similar dilemma over the balance between high-quality journalism and Siemering's "human experience" within *All Things Considered*. Most counted me as a defender of Siemering's philosophy, but I recognized that, as it developed, *All Things Considered* fostered the expectation that it would provide both high-quality journalism and explorations of the human experience. I wanted to do both well. If our news was to emphasize investigation and analysis, as the NPR purposes said it would, I felt we needed reporters capable of doing investigation and analysis, and I did not feel we had very many of them. When the Watergate scandal flooded us in 1972 and 1973, I engaged Robert Zelnick, a hard-driving freelance reporter, an ex-Marine with a law degree, to do interpretative/investigative reports on Watergate and other complex issues. While he was not exactly Woodward and Bernstein, Zelnick kept us on top of the story and, at times, ahead of the story. However, he generated considerable criticism. Staff reporters resented him because I was paying him more as a freelancer than they were making. Some objected to his dense, lawyerlike, print writing style. He had the voice of a print reporter as well. Great content. Terrible presentation. Because the issues of the day had him portraying President Nixon as a liar and a threat to our liberties, station managers and some listeners labeled him an anti-Nixon liberal. On that, they were half right. He was anti-Nixon, but far from a liberal (as his later career would demonstrate).[1] Zelnick raked and analyzed muck, and in this case the muck happened to emanate from the White House.

In the summer of 1974, when Mathews left NPR, I was fully in charge of the NPR news and information operation. I hired Zelnick as news editor and told him to upgrade our reporting. He hired another hard-driving print reporter named Nina Totenberg with a nose for embarrassing information. She followed Zelnick's lead and engendered the same criticisms regarding her radio skills and the perception of liberal bias. More than any other NPR reporter, before or since, Totenberg broke stories that reverberated through the media. Feisty and often out-

rageous, Totenberg enjoyed her notoriety, and, because her well-publicized
journalistic coups tended to embarrass Republicans, she came to symbolize NPR's "liberal" reputation.[2]

Totenberg exploded on the national scene in April 1977, three years
after she joined the staff. She became the first reporter in history to
cover the deliberations of Supreme Court justices before they announced a decision. She caused twitters throughout Washington and
the legal community when she denied that her source was Justice Pot-
ter Stewart, explaining that "Potsy and I are just friends."[3] Subsequently,
she was the first to report charges that Douglas Ginsburg, nominated
by President Reagan for the Supreme Court, had smoked marijuana
while on the faculty at Harvard. Three years later she reported an alle-
gation of sexual improprieties by Clarence Thomas, the Bush administration nominee for the Supreme Court. Her report generated another
round of hearings on Thomas' nomination. She valued her reputation
as an aggressive reporter, as a genuine player on the Washington scene.[4]

Some did not like Zelnick's and Totenberg's aggressive—perceived
as liberal—reporting. The pair came to symbolize a retreat from Siemering's more humanistic "alternative" programming philosophy. Siemering
had drawn the analogy of interviewers as therapists, listening with empathy, trying to elicit both the ideas and the emotions of their subjects.
Zelnick and Totenberg were more like prosecuting attorneys seeking to
nail their subjects. In time, Totenberg became the strongest voice within
NPR for values antithetical to those of Siemering, a man she had never
known. She complained loudly, for example, that NPR overcovered
"gay" issues. She sought to purge the staff of anyone she thought was
"a crusader for a point of view, rather than a reporter." She explained,
"There are those extremists who want coverage to be on the outer edge,
not just the cutting edge . . . and I, for one, am not willing to have those
kinds of people on the air, and I will fight tooth and nail to keep them
off."[5] Thus, Zelnick and Totenberg presented another conflict over purpose Quayle would have ignored but Frischknecht needed to resolve.

I understood the distinction between Zelnick's aggressive reporting
and Siemering's celebration of the human experience, but I saw no reason we could not do both. Susan Stamberg, after all, continued to enjoy
more airtime than the prosecutors and personified *All Things Considered* to the public. She and I understood the value of what Zelnick,
Totenberg, and Richard Holwill,[6] a second reporter hired by Zelnick,
added to our organization. Neither of us would have wanted their reporting to dominate NPR, but we saw it playing a legitimate role. For

some of our member stations, however, their reporting symbolized a conventional (liberal-dominated) approach to the news. They complained to Frischknecht, who felt obligated to respond. He saw an either/or choice between Zelnick and Siemering.

"Diversity" added a strong subtheme to this perceived conflict. Before diversity became fashionable, Siemering had proclaimed it as central to his concept of public radio. By the mid-1970s, women, gays, and racial and ethnic minorities adopted identity politics and demanded a piece of the action in many realms, but particularly in the media. Such groups were primarily concerned with getting programming "by, for, and about" themselves on public television. At NPR they found an organization with a hospitable philosophy and better-than-average practice, but a critical difference did exist between their "by, for, and about" demands and public radio's philosophy. Siemering had envisioned diverse voices heard by all rather than the divisiveness of "by, for, and about." Advocates for identity groups looked at the NPR purposes and demanded that the organization implement them as they interpreted them. As president of NPR, Frischknecht felt the need to respond to these demands and attempt to align practice with purpose. Skeptical about affirmative action, Zelnick placed professional excellence above racial diversity. The critics singled him out for attack, and, therefore, Frischknecht singled him out for scrutiny.

Frischknecht also felt the need to clarify the role stations played in producing national programs. In contrast to PBS, which may not produce programs but must acquire them from its member stations, National Public Radio had a mandate to produce programming but could also acquire it. Most educational radio stations possessed barely enough resources to survive. Only by pooling resources in a single entity, NPR, could they develop programs that would demand attention from a national audience. The stations' weakness in those early days would prove the salvation of public radio in the long run, because it allowed—indeed, necessitated—a separate organization to create a strong coherent national program service with a consistent style and appeal. Nonetheless, many stations would have liked to have a piece of the national action, and after five years of development, some felt ready to seize one.

In the spirit of the Carnegie Report, the original NPR board of directors declared decentralization the key to public radio's national programming at the same time as it created NPR, a centralized national production organization. Some probably thought of decentralization as it was at PBS, which had individual stations producing complete national programs or program series. Quayle, however, advocated for a narrower definition of decentralization that most stations accepted. He called on stations to contribute elements to the national magazine program that NPR assembled in Washington. His definition fit the limited capabilities of most stations and allowed public radio to build a consistent sound.

As stations grew larger and stronger, their ability and desire to produce pieces for *All Things Considered* increased, although the ninety-minute length of the program did not. At the same time, NPR's capabilities grew so that it could fill those ninety minutes with quality material without much help from member stations. The quality of station contributions improved, but the number of them that NPR rejected increased. As producer of *All Things Considered*, I thought we had a better program if Susan Stamberg talked on the phone with the man in Montana who grew the world's largest pumpkin than if our Montana station talked to him and sent us a tape. We used both techniques, but as producers we did not set decentralization as our highest priority. I reasoned, naively, that our stations would want a quality program rather than a substandard one that contained a lot of station-produced material. Again, Lee Frischknecht felt the need to resolve the conflict between official network policy and the reality that decentralization might not produce the best programming.

In 1976, making a futile attempt to respond to the diverse criticisms and to resolve the seeming disparity between mission and reality or between competing visions of the mission, Frischknecht wrote a thirty-page compendium of the sins of the NPR staff.[7] It accused the organization, of which he had been president for three years and vice president for three years before that, of thwarting cultural programming, rejecting station contributions in favor of Washington-produced material, and abandoning Siemering's program philosophy to a point that made *ATC* barely discernable from commercial news programs. He went on to accuse NPR's staff of not airing sufficiently diverse voices and of ignoring the concerns of women and minorities. As president of NPR, he would henceforth demand repentance of all these sins and exact a penance of recommitting the organization to its mission.

His indictment was valid only if one compared NPR's reality with an impossible ideal. Ironically, Frischknecht had stood with Siemering's worst detractors and had never taken the program director very seriously while he was still around. Frischknecht's personal values reflected his Mormon heritage more than the emerging Siemering-like attitudes of the 1970s, but his need for clarity and his lack of a personal vision for public radio were the real provocation for his indictment. Without his own vision, Frischknecht sought direction and certainty. He turned to the NPR statement of purposes that Siemering had written, in part to mask the divergent visions for public radio, and found that it contained more contradictions than certainty. He despaired that it did not reflect reality. He was a man besieged by criticisms from all sides and far too conscientious to slough off those criticisms, as his friend Quayle could have. He had to make NPR's performance match its promises.

In a sense one had to admire his resolve, but its impact was destructive to himself and the organization. Feeling attacked, unappreciated, and misunderstood, the programming staff voted to unionize, setting in place a polarization between the NPR programming staff and the rest of public radio that lingered for decades. Totenberg, Zelnick, and others with friends in the press corps managed to spin Frischknecht's actions as an ill-conceived attack on the quality of NPR news. That story appeared in the *New York Times*, the *Washington Post*, and the *Washington Star*. In the end, not much changed in NPR programming, except for the disappearance of Zelnick from the air and from the organization.[8] Frischknecht's indictment served primarily to spotlight irreconcilable issues that had plagued NPR from the beginning and that would plague it in the future. Ultimately it marked the end of the Quayle/Siemering era at NPR.

At the same time that Frischknecht indicted the NPR staff for rejecting station contributions to *All Things Considered*, he faced the same issue on a larger scale with the few stations that felt capable of producing complete national programs totally on their own. Two state networks in particular harbored such ambitions. Wisconsin was the oldest and largest educational broadcaster in the country with a particular heritage in radio drama. Wisconsin's director of broadcasting, Ronald Bornstein, was essentially a television man but saw national opportunities for his radio operation, which was relatively strong in an overall public radio system that was relatively weak. He went to the Corporation for Public Broadcasting and finagled funds for a national radio drama project called *Earplay*, to function totally apart from NPR. Radio drama did not prove the wave of the future for public radio, but Wisconsin's *chutzpah* and success at snaring money that would otherwise have gone to NPR set an example for its neighbor to the west, Minnesota. The president of Minnesota Public Radio, Bill Kling, had bigger and more contemporary dreams of national programming. The heads of the two largest radio operations in the country outside of NPR, who were also the two most dynamic and effective individuals in public radio, saw their own interests as separate from, and in conflict with, those of NPR.

Even more problematic for Frischknecht, Minnesota's Kling and Wisconsin's Bornstein were chairman and vice chairman, respectively, of a much smaller organization, the Association of Public Radio Stations (APRS), the mission of which was to lobby for public radio in Washington. APRS's creation resulted from Don Quayle's belief that NPR could not ethically practice journalism in Washington and simultaneously lobby Congress, the White House, and the Federal Communications Commission. Some entity needed to do the lobbying, of course, but Quayle insisted that that entity stay separate from NPR. With that principled decision, Quayle left no choice but for public radio stations to create a rival national organization to represent them, and by the mid-1970s, two very strong leaders not particularly loyal to NPR led that organization.

To make matters worse, public radio's lobbying efforts were not going well in the mid-1970s. Its most notable defeat was the Corporation for Public Broadcasting's decision to change the way it divided its money between public radio and public television. Public radio had received about 17 percent of the total though the early 1970s. In 1976, CPB would guarantee radio only 10 percent, with the mere possibility of going higher. NPR blamed APRS for the defeat. APRS fired back that NPR had undercut its efforts when Frischknecht seemed to accept CPB's position in a meeting he attended. Frischknecht said his words were misconstrued, but the more important point was that the president of National Public Radio had attended a meeting in which APRS should have represented radio. Given NPR's size and prominence and APRS's obscurity, it was not surprising that many assumed NPR spoke for public radio. Both sides agreed, therefore, that public radio needed to speak with one voice in the future and that the two organizations should merge.

In an amazing display of political gamesmanship on the part of Kling and Bornstein and an equally amazing display of political ineptitude by Frischknecht, NPR with its 100 or so employees and budget in the millions merged *as an equal* with APRS, an organization with but two employees and heaps of debt. Not only did the two organizations merge as equals, but the two most powerful personalities on the merged board were Bill Kling and Ron Bornstein. The newly merged organization took the name National Public Radio, but it was a "new" NPR which would usher in new management and a whole new era for public radio.

Rather than seek the NPR presidency for himself, as cynical observers assumed he would after orchestrating the coups against Frischknecht, Wisconsin's Ron Bornstein asked to chair the presidential search committee. He wanted a president who was "somebody," whose credentials went beyond the small world of public radio and the somewhat larger world of public television. A member of the search committee with Georgia connections asked for suggestions from the Jimmy Carter White House. The White House suggested Frank Mankiewicz, presidential candidate Bobby Kennedy's press secretary in 1968 and presidential candidate George McGovern's campaign manager in 1972, a loyal and talented Democrat, but definitely a Hollywood/Hyannisport Democrat who did not fit comfortably in a Georgia-accented Carter White House. So the White House suggested he might fit better at NPR.

In 1977, Mankiewicz was a skilled, connected political operative. He would give public radio an effective voice in Washington. He regarded himself as a journalist. He had reported, published books, written a syndicated column, and anchored local television news. Once an entertainment industry attorney and the scion of the Hollywood Mankiewicz family—his father Herman wrote *Citizen Kane*, his uncle Joseph was a major film producer and director—Frank knew show business. But most of all, he was a witty, confident public personality, someone whose phone calls were always returned, someone with ready access to power and to the media. Simply the act of hiring Mankiewicz would give NPR more publicity than it had had in its entire seven-year history.

Bornstein and his search committee rammed their selection down the throats of a reluctant NPR board, most of whose members supported one of several "inside" candidates.[9] Afraid the full board might not chose Mankiewicz if offered a slate of candidates, the committee decided to give the board only one option: Frank Mankiewicz.

"Who else did you consider?" board members asked.

Bornstein responded that revealing the rejected candidates' identities would embarrass these very fine individuals and violate confidentiality. The committee had one recommendation: Frank Mankiewicz. Frustrated as some board members were, they had the choice of appointing Mankiewicz or repudiating their search committee and starting over. The minutes of that meeting state: "Following extensive discussion of the Search Committee Report and recommendation, the motion made by Mr. Bornstein was approved by the Board."[10] Like it or not, a "somebody" would lead public radio. That Mankiewicz himself had never heard of public radio before the search committee approached him provided sufficient evidence to him and to the search committee that the organization needed someone like Frank Mankiewicz to put it on the map. He did not disappoint.

The appointment of this "journalist" to head NPR dampened, but did not end, the debate about NPR's programming philosophy and its role in news. Mankiewicz saw NPR as first and foremost a news organization. He knew what a news organization should be and had no doubt that NPR should be the country's leading broadcast news organization— the *best*, but not essentially different from other news organizations. You can provide an alternative by doing what the other guy does but doing it better, he often proclaimed, dismissing the debates that had plagued public radio for its first seven years. Frank Mankiewicz had little patience for the academic navel gazing that came so naturally to a group of radio stations conceived in academia and to the radio network created to serve them. Mankiewicz was a man of action, accustomed to moving quickly to accomplish goals that seemed inarguable to him. Right or wrong, he knew where he wanted the organization to go, and he convinced the organization it could get there.

The first pressing matter Mankiewicz faced was getting money out of Congress. As the first Democratic administration since Lyndon Johnson launched public broadcasting, the Carter administration sought to undo some of the damage inflicted on public broadcasting during the Nixon years. The administration's most significant goal involved strengthening public television's national programming, and that goal captured public attention when Carter sent new public broadcasting legislation to Congress in 1978. The legislation would provide more money to public broadcasting overall, but it allocated a significant amount to national programming for public television. This allocation would come at the expense of other parts of CPB's budget, including its allocation for NPR and public radio. Taking the offense instead of playing defense, Mankiewicz asked the White House and Congress to set aside 25 percent of the Corporation for Public Broadcasting's total appropriation for radio. While he failed to get that allocation written into the law in 1978, a "report" that accompanied the legislation expressed the "intent of the Congress" that CPB allocate 25 percent of its funding to public radio. Three years later, that language was incorporated into the body of the legislation.

It was an amazing victory, far beyond anything public radio had any right to expect and possible only because Mankiewicz was "somebody" willing snub the rest of the public broadcasting family and able to wield personal influence in the halls of power in Washington. Through the efforts of Jerry Sandler, public radio had snuck into the Public Television Act of 1967, where it was not wanted and had little right to be. Eleven years later, Mankiewicz had the audacity claim 25 percent of a much larger appropriation. Public television proponents were angry, of course, but Mankiewicz did not much care. In politics you play to win. He had the votes. He won.

That 1978 legislation contained another critical provision. It provided funding for public radio and public television to acquire satellite capacity and build ground equipment to distribute their programming by satellite rather than by telephone company land lines. NPR would operate its satellite on public radio's behalf. Bill Kling of Minnesota made sure that public radio's satellite system was unique. His seat on the NPR board and his domineering chairmanship of the board committee responsible for the system allowed him to become its principle architect. Radio's satellite system could carry twelve different channels of programming simultaneously, six if in stereo, providing options and flexibility in the system. No longer would NPR need to choose between continuing the live broadcast of a Congressional hearing and starting *All Things Considered* as scheduled at 5:00. The satellite's capacity allowed it to offer both, allowing each station to make its own editorial decision.

The new system's most distinctive characteristic, however, was its ability to send programming to the satellite from multiple locations. Ultimately, CPB would equip sixteen public radio stations to feed programming to the satellite, vastly increasing the system's expense and complicating its operation, but making a strong statement about the importance of "decentralization." The headquarters of Minnesota Public Radio in St. Paul would, not surprisingly, get one of those uplinks. Its president, after all, was Bill Kling, architect and principal advocate of the complex system. Kling's insistence on decentralization and an uplink system that encouraged it reflected his desire to break NPR's stranglehold on national programming. He wanted something more like the public television system in which several large stations produce most of the system's programming, coordinated, but not really controlled, by NPR in Washington. That public radio's remarkable progress grew largely from the ability of NPR to produce programming and impose a standard and a style on national offerings did not deter Kling's desire to grab a piece of the action for himself and others like him. An uplink in St. Paul allowed Kling to feed Garrison Keillor's *A Prairie Home Companion* live to stations across the country every Saturday evening. Keillor's show was the first highly touted national offering from outside Washington and independent of NPR. It also proved extremely popular among public radio listeners, second only to *All Things Considered* and, eventually, to *Morning Edition*.

Kling claimed, and NPR did not deny, that he had offered *A Prairie Home Companion* to National Public Radio and decided to distribute it independently only after the network rejected it. Reportedly, NPR refused it because the programming vice president feared *A Prairie Home Companion* might seem "too regional," and Mankiewicz simply did not like it. But the reasons go deeper than Mankiewicz's distaste for a program that, in his view, packaged downscale music and entertainment for an upscale audience. *A Prairie Home Companion* required far more money to produce than NPR was accustomed to paying, and NPR was unlikely to cover those costs even if Mankiewicz had personally identified with Lake Wobegon. While large, NPR's budget was fixed. It consisted almost totally of the $12 million the Corporation for Public Broadcasting sent to NPR each year. NPR had already allocated that money to its own programming, primarily its news programming. It had budgeted little for "program acquisition."

A little quick arithmetic would demonstrate that Kling could do far better financially marketing a program independently of NPR. If the program were worth an average of $25 a week to each of 200 stations, Kling could collect $260 thousand a year from station fees alone, far more than NPR would ever pay to acquire a program from an outside producer. For the right program, many stations would spend more than $25 a week, and carriage could easily go well beyond 200 stations if the program became a "hit." If the program were sufficiently popular, an "underwriter" might sign on and provide another source of income. More money might come from the National Endowment for the Arts and maybe from CPB, especially if its management were sufficiently angry at Mankiewicz to seek alternatives to NPR for spending national programming money. While the magnitude of the opportunity was not recognized at the time, an entrepreneurial producer could rake in even more money by marketing tee shirts and other merchandise to listeners. In short, Kling could generate income to support the program from a variety of sources beyond the annual single source subsidy from the Corporation for Public Broadcasting, on which NPR relied totally.

For public consumption, however, Kling's accusation that Mankiewicz rejected Garrison Keillor because he did not like the program made good press. More importantly, he planned to establish his own network to compete with NPR from St. Paul. The public radio satellite system made possible American Public Radio (later to change its name to Public Radio International) as an alternative to National Public Radio.[11] Had Mankiewicz known Kling's plan, he might not have worked so hard to secure funding for the satellite project.

American Public Radio would differ from NPR. It would resemble The National Public Radio System Hartford Gunn proposed before the creation of NPR. Member public radio stations would not elect its board as they did for NPR. Rather, a handful of major public radio stations would operate American Public Radio as an independent not-for-profit corporation. The board of directors would include members who had access to corporate and foundation money and who were expected to use that access to help fund the service. Unlike NPR, the new network would not produce its own programming. Instead, it would acquire, schedule, and distribute programs produced by its governing major market stations, most notably Minnesota Public Radio. It returned to the old-fashioned program-by-program concept of radio scheduling rather than the integrated format concept that was quickly gaining acceptance among public stations. Kling envisioned National Public Radio and American Public Radio offering competing menus from which stations could purchase individual programs they found appetizing. Besides his outdated program philosophy, a principle flaw in Kling's grand scheme was that all of CPB's national program money continued to flow directly to NPR. If stations were to buy programs from APR, they would have to find the money to do it or find local underwriters to pay the bills. In 1979, that was radical thinking in a system of stations accustomed to cashing checks only from their universities or the government.

The popularity of *A Prairie Home Companion* and the development of an entrepreneurial rival in St. Paul, however, did not diminish the reality that National Public Radio dominated the public radio system in the public mind and that the personality of Frank Mankiewicz dominated National Public Radio. Mankiewicz's most spectacular coups was corralling the president of the United States. In 1976, an obscure dark horse presidential candidate, Jimmy Carter, hardly thought NPR worth an hour of his time for a national call-in program in which NPR had invited him to participate. Two years later, President Jimmy Carter sat down with Susan Stamberg in the White House for a live conversation and national call-in.[12] Television cameras, still cameras, and print reporters captured the historic event, but NPR took center stage. The show's impresario was Frank Mankiewicz.

The presidential call-in topped Mankiewicz's first publicity coups, which had seemed pretty spectacular at the time. When the U.S. Senate opened debate on President Carter's proposed Panama Canal treaty in 1978, Mankiewicz proposed that NPR broadcast the debate live. While radio and television had broadcast Senate committee hearings, broadcast media had never had access to the Senate floor. (C-SPAN television coverage came much later.) To receive permission to broadcast from the Senate floor, NPR would have to break tradition and tackle the clubby, ritualistic U.S. Senate. Mankiewicz worked the system and his connections.[13] He personally contacted the Senate leadership and negotiated most of the details. Tradition fell; Mankiewicz scored. Permission for NPR to broadcast from the world's greatest deliberative body was Mankiewicz's personal achievement. Public radio was on the map.[14]

Mankiewicz generated even more publicity with his campaign to reinvigorate radio drama with a radio adaptation of the *Star Wars* film. As in news, doing what the other guy does but doing it better was good enough for Mankiewicz. Maybe *Star Wars* did not qualify as an alternative in the broader world of pop culture, but it was an alternative to other things on the radio. Besides, he reasoned, it might bring new listeners, particularly younger listeners, to public radio. An interest in radio drama came naturally to Mankiewicz. While most famous for writing *Citizen Kane*, Mankiewicz's father Herman began his collaboration with Orson Welles earlier with the *Mercury Radio Theater*; this included its historic broadcast of "War of the Worlds." Mankiewicz recalled Welles and other actors coming to his family home to rehearse those radio dramas. He saw no reason why he could not revive that tradition. His selection of *Star Wars* as the vehicle for that revival signaled a Hollywood pop-culture approach rather than the New York theatrical approach taken by the existing public radio drama series, *Earplay*, based at Bornstein's Wisconsin Public Radio.

Earplay proved frustrating for Mankiewicz. First, it remained the only national program supported by the Corporation for Public Broadcasting outside the control of NPR. That alone was enough to stick in the Mankiewicz craw, but what gagged him was the series' focus. *Earplay* commissioned plays from leading contemporary playwrights. Sometimes the works were intended for the stage but adapted for radio's less-expensive production costs. Others were radio adaptations of already-produced works. Archibald MacLeish, Edward Albee, David Mamet, and Arthur Kopit wrote for *Earplay*. Kopit's *Wings* debuted on *Earplay* before its successful run in New York. *Earplay* was committed to serious drama by theatrical writers who often fostered heavy, dialogue-laden scripts that were much too long for radio listening patterns. Although critically successful, *Earplay* did not attract audiences and had not revived radio drama. In the tradition of educational radio, *Earplay* approached radio drama as an art form. With little patience for tradition or the remnants of educational radio, Mankiewicz approached radio drama as pop culture.

In a move that separated him from his collaborator Kling, who always sought to limit NPR's funding and control, Bornstein agreed to cede *Earplay*'s radio drama money to NPR with the understanding that a portion of it—but not all of it—would come back to Madison to support a limited number of *Earplay* productions.[15] Clearly he trusted Mankiewicz's leadership and felt all of public radio needed to unite behind this "somebody." He may even have begun to come around to the view that radio programming differed from television and required a central authority to establish and maintain a coherent sound or personality to make public radio stand out on the crowded radio dial.

Mankiewicz's promotion crew unleashed its full talents on *Star Wars*. His team was wildly successful in generating press. *Time* headlined its story, "Radio drama is making a resounding comeback."[16] The *New York Times* was more skeptical: "Will *Star Wars* Lure Younger Listeners to Radio?"[17] *Star Wars* even rated a one-page story in *Playboy*.[18] Media far and wide touted *Star Wars*. Unfortunately, the series was unlike the programming normally found on public radio. The intended audience was different from public radio's audience. All the publicity for *Star Wars* might bring new listeners to public radio for the program, but the more important question was whether those new listeners would stay with public radio after the series ended. *Star Wars* was a publicity coup. It probably introduced some new listeners to NPR, but its long-term impact was minimal. Public radio, like all radio, builds audience through loyalty, which means giving listeners relatively consistent service 365 days a year, rather than half-hour events heard once a week for thirteen weeks and then disappearing.

As intriguing and attention-grabbing as *A Prairie Home Companion* and *Star Wars* might have been, the core identity of public radio on a national level remained *All Things Considered* and its related news coverage. And the central concern of Frank Mankiewicz remained *All Things Considered* and its related news coverage. He and his program vice president emphasized "professionalism" over the "charm" of the early *All Things Considered*. They expected the news department—and that is what they called it—to follow journalistic convention. They established a system of "editors" mostly drawn from the world of print journalism to oversee reporters' work. An editor would work with a reporter in a collaborative effort to produce a story. Previously, reporters had worked pretty much on their own, in their own style, pursuing their own interests, and sometimes imposing their own point of view over journalistic "objectivity" or "fairness and balance." To add further assurance of journalistic professionalism, each program would have an "editor," a content-oriented (print) journalist to collaborate with the program producer. The producer would become responsible for the "radio" part of "radio journalism," the editor for the "journalism" part. While few noted the change at the time, the increased level of "professionalism" implied a departure from Siemering's programming philosophy. The high standards this "professionalism" implied were standards universal to the profession of journalism not unique to public radio. Increased professionalism decreased distinctiveness. Gone was the notion, so central to the thinking of the first NPR board, of public radio as the people's instrument. The *vox populi* became the voice of the best professionals.

If Susan Stamberg symbolizes that earliest "alternative" phase of National Public Radio and Nina Totenberg the aggressive Zelnick influence, Cokie Roberts, and to a lesser extent Linda Wertheimer, represent the Mankiewicz era. He hired Roberts and promoted Wertheimer and helped them become essential listening to anyone who cared about what was happening in Congress. Wertheimer and Roberts came to represent the highly competent, lucid, yet essentially mainstream, reporting that flourished under Mankiewicz. Staffers, particularly those from the old school, resented their exalted position in the organization, the united front they (along with Totenberg) always presented, and their heavy-handed influence within the organization. They were known, not lovingly, as the fallopian troika. Each was tied to the Washington political establishment. Wertheimer was the wife of Common Cause President Fred Wertheimer. Roberts was the daughter of the late House of Representatives Majority Leader Hale Boggs and his successor Congress-woman Lindy Boggs, and sister of a Washington power broker, Tom Boggs. Totenberg married former Senator Floyd Haskell of Colorado.

More important, each was a member of the journalism establish-ment in Washington, and each was honing her own reputation, as well as NPR's, among professional colleagues in the capital press corps. They proved that NPR was no longer on the fringe, no longer an "alterna-tive" medium. While conservatives might be skeptical, they also proved that NPR was not a "liberal" mouthpiece, unless, of course, one as-sumes that all Washington media are "liberal." Wertheimer never left NPR for the glamour of commercial television, but at one time she as-pired to, which required her to assume the attitudes of commercial tel-evision. At minimum, she sought the acceptance and respect of her television news colleagues in a way that implied sharing their values. Roberts did move gradually and gracefully into commercial television. She could not have made this transition so smoothly had her approach to journalism or her views been insufficiently mainstream for commer-cial television.[19] As a Washington insider, Cokie Roberts was second to none, with the possible exception of Frank Mankiewicz himself. An NPR of insiders had its virtues, of course, but they were very different virtues that NPR pursued under Siemering, Quayle, and Frischknecht.

CHAPTER 7

Morning Edition

M ankiewicz fostered an NPR sound that was more professional, more reliable, and more like a mainstream news operation, but even under Mankiewicz, inside-Washington reporting did not replace all other values. Susan Stamberg continued to host *All Things Considered* and hence remained the primary public voice of the network. Robert Krulwich also carried over from pre-Mankiewicz days. He was the most quirky and creative of NPR reporters. In contrast to the ultimate establishmentarian, Cokie Roberts, Krulwich came to NPR from Lewis Hill's Pacifica Foundation, still known for its free-speech, alternative, and decidedly leftish mind set. Krulwich's idiosyncratic creativity contrasted sharply with conventional journalism. Krulwich always seemed to have a good time. He was both amused and bemused by the world. Longtime listeners to public radio can still recall the comic opera and the cast of mice he used to demonstrate important lessons about the economy. Ultimately, he took his unique talent to commercial network television, where the necessity of pictures limited his magical adventures in sound. There was also Ira Flatow, who followed Siemering from Buffalo to Washington and could explain science with ingenuity and charm. Scott Simon was yet another idiosyncratic contributor. As NPR's Chicago-based reporter, he produced real "stories." He saw and heard

Author's Note: I participated in the events described in this chapter in a minimal way as an advisory panel member during the development of *Morning Edition*. I participated more directly when I was elected to the National Public Radio board of directors in 1982, just as the organization plunged into bankruptcy.

details others overlooked and wove them into human sagas that touched the heart as well as the mind.

Excellent reporters, mainstream and idiosyncratic, helped make NPR a competitor in national, particularly Washington, journalism; *Morning Edition* helped make NPR a competitor in the world of radio. If it had not been for Quayle's prejudices and staff convenience, *All Things Considered* would have debuted in the morning. Eight and a half years later, a *Morning Edition* of *All Things Considered* finally acknowledged the importance of radio listening patterns. Mankiewicz's programming vice president, Sam Holt,[1] fathered *Morning Edition*, as Bill Siemering had fathered *All Things Considered*. The differences between these father figures explains in part the differences in the two programs' development. The analytical Holt attacked problems differently than the poetic Siemering. Holt enjoyed both the advantage and the disadvantage of working in an organization that had experienced some success. *ATC's* creators had worked in a vacuum and expected only to concoct an original program, an "alternative" to both commercial radio and traditional educational radio. *Morning Edition's* creators needed to meet high expectations of stations and listeners, who now had a model, *All Things Considered*. A totally original program would disappoint them. The new program had to adapt *ATC* to the morning.

In subsequent years, some would argue that *Morning Edition* grew out of research whereas *ATC* had not. In fact, neither program employed focus groups or other original testing of potential program elements known as "formative" research. Siemering and the crew who created *All Things Considered* just followed their instincts, pursuing topics that interested them personally or that reflected their interpretation of NPR's mission. By contrast, Holt and the crew who developed *Morning Edition* gathered statistical information on radio listening that Siemering would not have bothered to read. Dr. Larry Lichty, NPR's research director, was almost as influential in shaping the program as Holt was. A former professor of radio and television, Lichty developed a close rapport with Sam Holt. His forceful personality and high energy level gave him more influence over *Morning Edition* than a research director should have. Holt and Lichty used statistical information to help decide *Morning Edition's* structure, but they did not use research to determine its content; the content of *All Things Considered* plus the gut instincts of its staff determined the daily content of *Morning Edition*.

Holt was a master at consulting with member stations, simultaneously soliciting their views while selling them a concept. He argued consistently that radio, even public radio, should offer a format, a consistent sound, rather than a series of programs. Consequently, he proposed scrapping a number of NPR's individual programs and using their resources—and the additional resources now available to NPR thanks to the Mankiewicz's political maneuvers—for a morning-long program service without a clear beginning, middle, or end. Listeners could opt in and out of the service as they went about their morning routines. Holt's service would provide what listeners wanted to hear in the morning: frequent national news summaries and short updates on local news and weather. It would provide segments even shorter than those on *ATC*, and the segments would include topics formerly covered by the programs Holt proposed to sacrifice. The most notable of those sacrificial programs was a weekly arts magazine and a daily omnibus hour that covered topics like education, science, history, literature, and others that came out of an educational-radio heritage. The new format would trade extended treatment of these topics for short reports that potentially reach more listeners. Holt's vision reflected his deep understanding of contemporary radio and his personal values as a closet academic.

Holt designed the superstructure. Lichty added details. Colleagues wanted to start *Morning Edition* at 7:00, the same as television's *Today Show*, but Lichty cited statistics to convince them that a morning radio program should start no later than 6:00. Noting that weather was the first reason listeners gave for turning on the radio in the morning, Lichty insisted on providing frequent opportunities for stations to broadcast local weather and announcements. He argued that radio, even public radio, had to provide the information listeners sought and had to provide it frequently. The commitment to provide local breaks every ten minutes forced the national program to confine its segments to a fixed length of nine minutes, a prospect that *ATC* host Susan Stamberg decried as too confining and too choppy for continuity. Her criticism would have hit the target if Holt and Lichty were designing *Morning Edition* as a "program" to listen to from beginning to end, but she missed the point that *Morning Edition* was not a program. It was a format. Holt and Lichty were designing a programming format that no one expected listeners to hear in full, a service into and out of which listeners were continuously tuning. Any moment in the format could become the start or stop for a listener whose morning schedule—not program content—dictated when he or she would flip on or off the radio.

The third architect of *Morning Edition* turned up after Holt and

Lichty had designed its structure. Since I had left NPR in 1976, the news operation had no single department head. Mankiewicz, of course, wanted his own man in such a key position, or, as it turned out, his own woman. He invited Barbara Cohen to lunch at a fancy restaurant. Cohen was a young editor at the recently defunct newspaper, the *Washington Star*. NPR legend holds that at the end of the meal, he found, not untypically, that he had no money to pay the bill. Cohen picked up the tab and a job as NPR's news director. Barbara was married to *Washington Post* columnist Richard Cohen, and the two moved in the smartest of Washington social circles.[2] If Mankiewicz wanted a Washington insider, he could hardly have done better. If he wanted someone to bring mainstream news values to an organization with an "alternative" self image, Barbara Cohen was, again, the perfect choice.

A conversation with Cohen not long after she arrived dramatized for me the changed values of NPR under Mankiewicz. We discussed possible funding for NPR coverage of developments in academic research, such as covering the annual convention of the American Psychological Association. Cohen expressed interest and explained that NPR had sent a reporter to the APA convention that year but had to pull the reporter from that meeting to cover a Sacramento press conference by Governor Jerry Brown. Her explanation surprised me. In the days before Mankiewicz and Cohen, NPR would almost certainly have kept the reporter at the psychology convention. I would have counted on that meeting to generate important stories about new insights into human behavior that would interest public radio listeners but not attract much coverage by other broadcast media. Cohen's decision to send the reporter to Sacramento traded unique coverage of meaty and interesting "public radio" issues for coverage of a press conference that other media blanketed. Under Cohen, NPR no longer avoided putting "just another microphone at a press conference." Instead, Cohen worried that other media would scoop NPR and believed that if other media covered an event, NPR must. By conventional news standards, Cohen's journalistic judgment was sound, but Siemering had promised that NPR would operate by unconventional standards.

In most respects, Holt, Lichty, and Cohen did things right and with more care and professionalism than had the crew that created *ATC*. In one respect, however, they could have learned an important lesson from our earlier experience. Siemering focused first and foremost on the humanity of the people he hired. He always selected people he felt good about, people who seemed to express the appropriate values and atti-

tudes. Professional background, experience, or skills were less important to him than a shared vision, a shared sensibility. He trusted that
the right people could learn the necessary skills and that the right
people would eventually create the right product.

In 1979, NPR's leadership took the opposite approach. Holt and
Lichty developed the *Morning Edition* format, and then Cohen hired
staff to implement it with their skills rather than their sensibilities. As
executive producer she hired a commercial-broadcast newsman with impeccable credentials. He was news director of the top AM commercial
station in Washington, the highly respected WMAL, which, in those
days, was about as serious a commercial radio news operation as one
was likely to find. He brought with him the station's top female anchor
reporter, a very familiar voice to Washington radio listeners, to co-host
the new morning effort. Her style was professional, not warm and
human, and her voice powerful, not intimate and conversational. She
was excellent for commercial radio, but, as Cohen would soon discover,
NPR was not commercial radio. Her co-host, Pete Williams, was un-
known to Washington radio listeners but would become prominent a
decade later when he emerged as the chief Pentagon spokesman during the Gulf War and then as a correspondent for NBC Television.
Williams came across as a little more human than his co-host, but overall, *Morning Edition* sounded an awful lot like a good commercial news
program. Dry runs the week before its debut generated negative reactions among NPR member stations and among the troops at NPR.

I happened to visit NPR on other business the Thursday before the
scheduled Monday launch of *Morning Edition* in November of 1979.
As I headed to my meeting room, I ran into a very distraught Cohen.
She had just fired the executive producer and the two *Morning Edition*
hosts. As he had each morning of the dry runs, Lichty gathered a small
coterie of staff at a nearby coffee shop to critique that day's practice
broadcast. That Thursday morning, they reached consensus that the
program would not work with the current cast, and Cohen took the necessary action. She and Holt were regrouping.

That afternoon, a young producer named Jay Kernis appeared in the
office where I was holding my meeting. Kernis had started at NPR as
a promotion assistant not long after the organization began. He later
served as associate producer and then producer of the arts magazine
that Holt killed to free resources for *Morning Edition*. Kernis, acknowledged as one of the most creative and sensitive producers in the
organization, had done a splendid job with the arts magazine and now

had the task of assuring that the nine-minute arts segment at the end of each *Morning Edition* hour attained the quality established by his now-cancelled program. He had already contributed significantly to the sound of the evolving program by working with composer B. J. Lieder-man on the strangely melancholy *Morning Edition* theme.

Kernis entered the office trembling and asked my meeting mate, "Have you heard what they want me to do?" What they wanted was for him to take over as producer of *Morning Edition*. He would have three days to get the program ready for its Monday debut. Kernis doubted that he could do the job. "This is supposed to be a news program," Kernis lamented, "I don't know anything about news." My meeting mate reassured him and reminded him that NPR was full of people who knew about news. All Kernis had to do was "to make pretty radio" out of what the news people gave him. It seems significant that Kernis, who ultimately forged *Morning Edition*, was an arts producer, a pre-Mankiewicz veteran, whose sensibilities would soften the news-driven values of Mankiewicz, Cohen, Roberts, Wertheimer, and Totenberg.

More than any other individual, Jay Kernis helped develop NPR's carefully crafted sound, first as producer of *Morning Edition* and later as producer of *Weekend Edition*. Kernis left nothing to chance. He would slave over a piece of tape until he had it just right, and those who worked for him copied his perfectionist habits. The print-oriented journalists hired as editors checked over every word in every sentence for accuracy and nuance. The producers who worked for Kernis applied equal care to the sound and the pacing and the music that carried the content. They also ensured that Washington-centered public affairs journalism did not squeeze out attention to the arts, pop culture, science, and offbeat features.

Lost in this quest for perfection was spontaneity. Kernis' emphasis on scripting eliminated most errors and most serendipity. Placing the emphasis on heavily edited, pretaped material meant that even the seemingly spontaneous interview was carefully shaped and pruned. Undesirable negative spontaneity disappeared, but, ideally, the wonderful spontaneous moment remained. This scripting was far different from the relatively unscripted way *All Things Considered* began under Robert Conley and the semiscripted approach under Mike Waters that followed. This care and attention to detail was a logical result of the growth in budgets and personnel that made it possible. This change was most pronounced under *ATC* executive producer Jim Russell, the de facto leader of the news department in the transition years between Frischknecht and Mankiewicz. While some might regret this increasing bureaucratization of quality, it was not a rejection of NPR's original purposes. Rather, it emphasized two goals in Siemering's laundry list of laudable purposes that reflected the diverse dreams public radio had at its founding in 1970. Those two purposes were to reach the highest standards of broadcast journalism and to perfect the art of audio production.

In desperate need of a credible host or hosts for what was expected to become public radio's most important program, NPR's management tried to draft the most "public radio" of public-radio hosts, Susan Stamberg. She declined. She still valued maintaining some approximation of a normal family life and saw the morning shift as incompatible. Management's fallback was Stamberg's *ATC* co-host, Bob Edwards. Few people perceived Edwards as a strong enough personality to carry a program, especially in the morning when personalities traditionally ruled radio. As a stopgap, however, he would provide the new program with instant credibility among public radio listeners and a public radio "sound." Management reasoned that after two months he could return to *ATC*, having provided them time to find a host more appropriate for morning drive time. That two-month assignment lasted a quarter of a century. Kernis accepted the limitations Edwards brought to the program—his lack of curiosity, which limited his ability to conduct an interview, and his total lack of enthusiasm for any task assigned to him. With a different host, Kernis would have created a different program, but Edwards was his star, and Kernis designed the program around him. His job, he said, was to make Edwards sound good. Kernis later left NPR for CBS Television, only to return as vice president for programming. In 2004, the man who had worked to make Edwards sound good removed him from his "temporary" assignment. That decision caused an angry outpouring from listeners who had grown comfortable with Edwards, but only relief from the people who had inherited the assignment of making him sound good.

The 1979 decision to change the *Morning Edition* team at the last minute had a deeper significance for NPR veterans, who lamented that the outsiders just did not understand public radio and its special sensibility. Privately, some were pleased that the outsiders had failed, and that, in the end, NPR had to turn to people like Kernis and Edwards to deliver a public radio program. NPR might move in the direction of conventional news values, but it was still different, so profoundly different, that even the best professionals from commercial broadcasting could not do a program that felt like public radio.

Morning Edition transformed public radio like no other single program. Within two years of its introduction, the weekly audience of NPR member stations increased from 5 to 8 million, the biggest single percentage jump before or since.[3] As important, those new listeners spent more time with public radio. In the past, they might have listened to *All Things Considered* as they drove home from work but, most likely, to a commercial station as they drove to work in the morning. With *Morning Edition*, they could listen to NPR news magazines as they drove to work and as they drove home. Many more listeners, each spending more time with his or her public radio station, resulted in an incredible doubling of the average number of people listening at any given time to NPR member stations in the two years after *Morning Edition*'s debut.[4]

Lichty's student and successor as head of research for NPR, David Giovannoni, has explained how *Morning Edition* transformed public radio.[5] According to Giovannoni, the new service was on at the right time: in the morning, when the largest number of people turn on the radio. It was on not just for an hour or ninety minutes but for two full hours. Moreover, most stations "rolled over" the two hours, filling their morning drive time, 6:00 to 10:00 in many major East Coast markets and 5:00 to 9:00 in many Central and Pacific Time Zone markets. He pointed out that, with the addition of *Morning Edition*, listeners could tune to their public radio station as they awoke, brushed their teeth, ate breakfast, or drove to work and then catch *All Things Considered* while they drove home or prepared dinner. The two programs complemented one another, providing information at the two times of the day when public radio listeners most wanted it.

Morning Edition also forced stations to reconsider their entire schedule. The modularized nature of *Morning Edition* encouraged stations to adopt the same approach. Some replaced hour-long local discussion programs with short, polished "features" incorporated into the local *Morning Edition* broadcast. Giovannoni observed,

Before *Morning Edition*, most hours devoted to information were filled with, usually erudite, talking mouths. Professional radio journalists have known for years that very few people remember, desire, or listen to more than a few minutes of investigation into all but the most important issues. *Morning Edition* allows public broadcasters to retain their commitment to local issues while ridding themselves of ineffective "long form" programming.[6]

Whether or not he was correct about the relative effectiveness of long-form and short-form program styles, Giovannoni's interpretation gradually became dogma in public radio. Replacing long talks with short reports on local issues in *Morning Edition* and *ATC* cleared the middle of the day for extended runs of classical music, still the program category that the largest number of public radio listeners preferred. *Morning Edition* followed by classical music followed by *All Things Considered* became public radio's "standard format," pleasing its two largest listener constituencies.

By 1979, the message of "formats" had reached most public radio managers. Sam Holt had delivered the message again and again in planning meetings with stations, wedding this commercial concept to an obvious commitment to mission that resonated with the values of public radio managers and programmers of the time. He, like they, in the spirit of Lord Reith, wanted to reach as many listeners as possible with the quality material they produced and valued. Lichty, Giovannoni, George Bailey (another former Lichty student), and Tom Church, director of radio research at CPB, bludgeoned managers and programmers with the same message but without the idealism and sense of mission. They brutally told public radio meetings that nobody was listening (which was not quite true) and that public radio would need to emulate the practices of commercial radio if that situation were to improve (which probably was true). While they offended many in the process, the disciples of audience growth through formatting were impossible to ignore. Public radio learned that it had to package public-radio content to follow the rules of radio, even if those rules had been set by commercial broadcasters. When *Morning Edition* arrived, many stations were primed to change.

By 1983, public radio was reaching 8.5 million people each week, and at any given time about half a million people were listening. Public radio had come a long way in the twelve years since *ATC*'s debut when educational/public radio served just over 2 million people each week and the number listening at any given time seemed too inconsequential to measure.[7] Unfortunately, 1983 was also the year that the house that Mankiewicz rebuilt came dangerously close to blowing up. Frank Mankiewicz's personality and policies, mixed with the internal politics of public radio, planted the bomb. The new Reagan administration's distaste for public broadcasting lit the fuse. The resulting explosion almost reduced NPR to rubble.

The Reagan administration cut the funding for the Corporation for Public Broadcasting by 20 percent at the start of the 1983 federal fiscal year, October 1982. The impact on public broadcasting as a whole was less serious than one might think. Federal support through CPB had never grown to the levels Lyndon Johnson and the Carnegie Commission envisioned. In 1982, CPB provided only about 20 percent of all the revenue for public radio and television. A 20 percent reduction in 20 percent of their budgets translated into a real cut for most public broadcasters of less than 4 percent of total revenue. Individual stations could cover the loss through increased revenues from nonfederal sources or reduced expenses, and all of the publicity over the Reagan "attack" on public broadcasting generated increased private donations to stations that in most cases more than made up for the federal cuts.

Not so for National Public Radio. CPB had created National Public Radio and totally funded it. Having a single source of relatively assured funding had helped give NPR the ability to create a distinctive program service over a period of a dozen years, in contrast to television which faced constantly shifting fortunes. NPR's advantage turned to a significant disadvantage when its single source of funding was no longer assured. For NPR, a 20 percent cut in funding from CPB translated into a full 20 percent cut in its budget. The independence NPR enjoyed from its member stations—its freedom to lead, its freedom to innovate—turned into a serious liability. The logical course for NPR would have been to ask its member stations to come up with money to pay for part of the NPR operation, just as public television stations directly funded, and controlled, PBS. The stations, after all, were barely hurt by the Reagan cuts and some were doing better because of the listener support the cuts generated. Stations had a critical interest in maintaining the quality—or even the existence—of *All Things Considered* and *Morning Edition* since those programs now attracted most of their listeners, surpassing the attraction of classical music. They would have grumbled, of course, but if they had no choice, they would have paid, and most could afford to.

In spite of his success on their behalf, Mankiewicz was far from loved by those in the public radio system. They thought he was too high-handed, too egotistical, too contemptuous of the academic attitudes and provincialism of many public radio stations, and, ironically, perhaps too successful. Stations felt they had lost control of their organization to a man who operated in a world alien from their own.[8] Stations would not react positively to a plea for help from this man. The thought of asking stations for money did not appeal to Mankiewicz either. To the extent that he relied on stations for income, he became subjugated to them. If stations paid the piper, the stations would call the tune, and Mankiewicz was not about to dance to that tune. Success in the future, as in the past, depended on freedom to act independently from the stations, to lead rather than follow.

Boldly, if not wisely, Mankiewicz moved in the opposite direction from what was logical and expected. He proposed that CPB money going to NPR go instead to the member stations to use for their own purposes. NPR, in turn, would raise its own money from private sources, thus obtaining freedom from both its member stations and the equally irksome Corporation for Public Broadcasting. Mankiewicz vowed to have NPR "off the federal fix by '86." He left unanswered the question of how NPR would get by between 1983, when it would lose 20 percent of its revenue, and 1986, when it would have developed totally new sources of revenue.

Compounding this problem was the old axiom that it takes money to make money. NPR might seek "underwriting" support—soft-core advertising—from businesses and foundations, but that would require investment in a staff to sell and track it. In the long run, such an investment would almost certainly pay off. In the short run, it was an additional cost for an organization already losing 20 percent of its budget. Mankiewicz saw income potential in for-profit uses of the NPR satellite channels by partners or customers interested in high-tech communication. NPR would need to invest in staff with experience in this area to seek out and negotiate with vendors and partners, even though no one foresaw any actual income from such ventures for at least another year. Most of these income-producing schemes would require the use of the FM subcarriers of NPR member stations. Someone had to negotiate agreements with stations, most of which were housed in universities unaccustomed to such entrepreneurship. Someone had to convince the Federal Communication Commission to permit use of these noncommercial stations and the noncommercial satellite to generate revenue from commercial sources. None of this could happen quickly. To compound matters, the potential partner with whom NPR seemed closest to a "deal" for data transmission turned out to have a $2 million debt itself and was headed by a president accused in the past of questionable business practices.

A journalist, a politician, a showman, a publicist, a lobbyist, Mankiewicz never claimed to be a businessman. A son of Hollywood, Mankiewicz came from a go-go world in which prudence played but a tiny role. Mankiewicz had never had to think much about money. A political operative, Mankiewicz also came from the go-go world of political campaigns, in which the candidate spent whatever it took to win. If the candidate won the election, those currying his or her favor would happily pay off the debts. If the candidate lost the election, creditors had little choice but to negotiate payments of pennies on the dollar. The thought probably never crossed Mankiewicz's mind that an organization should curb its spending simply because it did not have the cash on hand to pay the bills. Indeed, he seemed to believe that tough times demanded spending more money. If NPR would depend in the future on underwriting instead of the largess of CPB, it would need to expand its program offerings to produce more inventory for the sales staff to sell. To attract underwriters interested in associating themselves with a quality service, NPR would need to increase its spending on news and entertainment programming to maintain or increase the quality potential underwriters sought. It was all somewhat logical. It was all somewhat mad.

Bill Kling's American Public Radio added the straw that ultimately broke NPR's back. Kling proposed that public radio stations deal with the Reagan budget cuts by reducing the costs each station paid to supply their listeners with classical music. Kling's Minnesota Public Radio could produce twenty-four hours a day of high-quality classical music hosted by impeccable announcers and sell that service through Kling's American Public Radio network to stations at a small fraction of the amount stations paid to maintain their own music libraries and own classical music announcers. Stations would save money. The quality of music presentation on public radio would improve. And Kling would make MPR and APR as important to public radio in music as NPR was in news.[9] Stations could reduce costs and "cope effectively with the reality of reduced staffs during these turbulent times," wrote Kling, by buying high-quality, inexpensive classical music from APR.[10]

The highly competitive Mankiewicz could not let this happen, even if it seemed to make sense for all concerned and hurt only NPR's ego. If stations needed such a low-cost, high-quality classical music service, Mankiewicz wanted them to buy it from NPR, not from the upstarts in

St. Paul. He countered with a package more extensive and less expensive than Bill Kling's. He would offer the classical music at a lower price than Kling proposed and would throw in a stream of jazz programming and augmented news programming. Faced with competition from NPR, and recognizing the precarious economics of such an enterprise, Minnesota and APR dropped their project. NPR did not. Instead, it rationalized the new twenty-four-hour music service as a spectacular opportunity to sell underwriting. The network could squeeze a lot more underwriting announcements into a twenty-four-hour service than into the ninety minutes of *All Things Considered* and the 120 minutes of *Morning Edition*. *NPR Plus*, as they dubbed it, was no longer a competitive response to Bill Kling; *NPR Plus* was essential to the future economic viability of NPR. In the meantime, of course, it would generate immediate costs and only the possibility of future income to the already financially desperate NPR. In January 1983, three months into the fiscal year, NPR's outside auditors predicted a "cash-flow" problem later that year.

As a recently elected member of the NPR board, I joined my board colleagues in March for an emotional special meeting. At the end of the day we had agreed to cut most of NPR's cultural programming and fifty-six jobs, or 10 percent of the workforce. Mankiewicz neither endorsed nor opposed the cuts that his executive vice president had recommended. In April, now very angry board members met again to make another round of cuts of similar magnitude to the first. When I looked at the numbers, I had to agree with the executive vice president that no amount of cutting could bring the budget into balance. NPR was insolvent, even though Mankiewicz continued to characterize the situation as a cash-flow problem that would ultimately resolve itself as investments began to generate revenue. Board members now realized that we had to go to our stations to rescue the organization from its financial woes. They then turned their anger on Mankiewicz, whom several had always disliked.

To stave off an effort by station-manager board members to fire him on the spot at that April 1983 special board meeting, Mankiewicz promised to resign the next week at the annual meeting of public radio managers. He hoped that at that meeting the member stations would vote to bail NPR out of the mess he had created.

The next day I went to Mankiewicz's office and found him in an intense telephone conversation with one of NPR's potential Venture partners, acting as if he were back in charge of the McGovern campaign and hitting up a major contributor. I heard him say, "If I can't come up with $1.5 million by Monday, I will be in big trouble," except that he said it more colorfully. He did not sound like a man preparing his resignation speech.

I said to him, "You know, you are going to have to resign. I voted with you yesterday, but that does not mean I think you can stay."[11]

He acknowledged that he had promised to resign, but the time and place now seemed fluid. He certainly did not plan to do it soon. Not only was the organization insolvent, its president would not leave gracefully.

Five days later, at the annual awards banquet of the public radio managers' meeting, Sharon Rockefeller, wife of the senator from West Virginia and chairperson of the Corporation for Public Broadcasting (NPR's sole source of income), blasted NPR's management for its irresponsibility and its board and stations for allowing the behavior to continue. Early the next morning, Mankiewicz, furious at Rockefeller for her remarks and vowing that "her husband will never be president of the United States, and she will never live in the White House,"[12] bowed to the inevitable and gave the board his resignation letter.

Even Mankiewicz's resignation was not enough to convince stations to offer up the money to make up the deficit. Perhaps not comprehending the seriousness of NPR's financial situation, stations chose to vent their resentment of Mankiewicz's high-handed style, even if it meant jeopardizing public radio's most important asset.[13] Wisconsin's Ron Bornstein volunteered to take over as acting CEO of NPR and try to clean up the mess that he indirectly caused when he insisted that NPR hire Mankiewicz six years earlier. He asked me to go with him to Washington to temporarily head its programming operation.

The first five years of the Mankiewicz presidency were successful beyond anyone's hopes. The sixth year was worse than anyone's fears. Looking back, the accomplishments of his first five years outweigh the explosion of his last, but it is tragic, in the classical sense of the term, that his flaws nearly wiped out his heroic contributions to NPR and public radio.

CHAPTER 8

Weekend Edition

Ron Bornstein had a simple plan to clean up the 1983 financial explosion, but his simple plan was difficult to execute. Insolvent, NPR would first need to borrow enough money—about half of its annual budget—to get through the final months of its fiscal year. To borrow money, NPR needed to assure a lender that it could repay the loan. Then, NPR would need to trim its size by about 25 percent to fit its likely income in the following fiscal year. Bornstein would do exactly what Mankiewicz would not.

The Corporation for Public Broadcasting, NPR's sole source of significant funding, forbade Bornstein from seeking money from a bank, as if any bank would willingly grant a loan to a bankrupt organization with few tangible assets. CPB set itself as the only source for an NPR loan, and any loan it would grant would come with unpleasant strings attached. Mankiewicz had sought to escape CPB's clutches when he promised to get off the federal fix by '86, and Bornstein was equally reluctant to turn to CPB as his rescuer. CPB was political; its board members were presidential appointees whom Congress confirmed. Legally responsible for the proper use of the tax money it provided to NPR and other recipients, CPB legitimately required accountability, which sometimes translated into illegitimate control. CPB insisted that NPR member stations guarantee repayment of any loan it made to NPR. Getting

---

Author's Note: I participated in these events as the interim head of NPR's program department through part of 1983, as an NPR board member beginning in 1984, and as board chairman beginning in 1985.

that guarantee from the stations presented quite a hurdle, given the anger stations still felt toward NPR and the reality that most belonged to universities not inclined, and in many cases not allowed, to guarantee anybody's loan. Mankiewicz would have refused such a string on a loan from CPB, since he feared station control over NPR as much as he abhorred CPB's. As a veteran public broadcaster, Bornstein understood the centrality of stations to the public broadcasting culture and was prepared to live with it.

The second part of Bornstein's plan, cutting expenses to match anticipated income, pretty much eliminated the possibility of achieving financial independence, because the investments necessary to launch NPR's entrepreneurial ventures were the first in line for the chopping block. Programming faced the axe as well, and I had the task of wielding it. I had to eliminate nearly the entire cultural programming department. I would retain a tiny staff on which to rebuild if times got better. I would cut the news department budget by less than 10 percent, but, because the department was spending far beyond its budget, it needed to cut more than 10 percent from its actual level of spending. Although her department was taking the smallest cut of any unit in the organization, news Vice President Barbara Cohen declared the cuts impossible. She would quit rather than live with them. Coached by Mankiewicz, news staff members launched a public campaign to preserve their budget, suggesting that the crisis was no more than a cash-flow problem, and that the proposed cuts in news were unnecessary, part of a political vendetta by Mankiewicz's enemies in the Reagan administration and in public broadcasting.[1]

My meeting with the news staff to discuss the reductions was a more bitter than sweet reunion with my former colleagues. They and the many new staffers Mankiewicz had added were not interested in why the cuts were needed nor in my suggestions on how to make them. They directed their anger at me and Bornstein rather than at Mankiewicz, whom they argued was a victim of a Bornstein/Kling intrigue, probably in concert with the Reagan administration. They believed these enemies of NPR wanted to destroy the organization, not save it. Had not Bornstein once worked for the CPB, which had an antagonistic relationship with Mankiewicz and whose board Ronald Reagan had appointed? Had not Bornstein joined Kling in advocating a PBS-like program marketplace that would allow "NPR's" money to go to other producers?

They thought my budget levels would destroy NPR news, and they believed we intended that outcome. They said NPR's enemies feared

NPR news's increasing quality and influence. They accused me of wanting fewer reporters and more host telephone interviews. I reminded them that NPR had done very good radio when it had fewer reporters and more host interviews. They insisted NPR had advanced beyond the standards I left behind in 1976 and could not slip back. They said the excellence of NPR news as it developed under Mankiewicz was responsible for the success of public radio nationally and any cuts from the status quo would jeopardize all of public radio.

I pointed out that the cut to news was relatively modest compared with the devastating cuts elsewhere in the organization. News, I said, was our first priority, and we were protecting it within the limits of a finite amount of money. They responded that the money could not be finite, and that it was Bornstein's obligation to go out and raise the money rather than cut the budget. If necessary, they would take the matter in their own hands.

They did. A "Friends of NPR" organization, prominent acquaintances of news staff members, sprang up to raise money by advertising for donations in newspapers. If Bornstein would not go out to find the money to save NPR news, these prominent citizens would do it for him.

One hundred influential members of Congress signed a letter to us demanding that we preserve NPR news. Were it not for rules prohibiting reporters from lobbying, I might have suspected that NPR's potent congressional reporting team of Wertheimer and Roberts might have had something to do with that letter.

The news staff did not understand, or would not accept, that a few hundred thousand dollars one way or another in the news budget was not the issue. The very survival of the organization was at stake, and survival required a realistic demonstration that NPR would live within its means. We were going to have to borrow money to survive, and creditors like budgets that balance.

Ultimately, I presided over a compromise by which the news department could restore the 10 percent cut in its budget—but not its spending over the budget—by conducting an emergency on-air fundraising drive, a delicate matter because stations jealously guarded their exclusive right to ask their listeners for money. Under the plan, the proceeds would go to the individual stations, which would use them first toward any responsibilities they took on to pay the NPR debt. They would donate half of any money left to NPR to restore the news budget. Most stations did not participate in this three-day "Drive to Survive." Many on the NPR board were unhappy with even this small infringement on the stations' exclusive right to raise money from their listeners. Nonetheless, the special drive proved a pragmatic solution for both the participating stations and the news budget, and achieved a measure of peace in the public radio family.

Meanwhile, the loan negotiations were not going well.[2] They dragged on for two months up to the day before the August 1 deadline set by NPR's landlord to pay the back rent or see the doors padlocked, the deadline set by the phone company to cut off service, and the day before paychecks would go out with insufficient funds to cover them. It was time to get serious, but several issues blocked agreement. Many stations had not or could not promise to guarantee the loan, one of CPB's prime conditions. Another was that, until NPR repaid the loan, CPB wanted to exercise stringent financial controls, essentially approving all NPR's expenditures. Bornstein found that unacceptable, arguing that expenditure-by-expenditure, financial control would result in editorial control by a political body. Finally, CPB wanted to take the operation of the public radio satellite away from NPR and hand it to a consortium of stations led by Bill Kling's Minnesota Public Radio. Such a transfer would reduce NPR from "the" public radio network to a status essentially no different from American Public Radio and any other potential producer or distributor of public radio programming. This transfer had more symbolic than practical importance, but those on both sides of the argument perceived the symbolism as critical.

They played chicken until the last possible moment. Thursday evening, July 28, 1983, with just one working day left before NPR would have to close, I encountered NPR Board Chairman Don Mullally, a professor in charge of broadcasting at the University of Illinois, sitting outside Bornstein's empty office. Mullally was in an expansive mood, anticipating phone reports from the CPB conference room a few blocks away. The final negotiations had begun and would continue as long as it took to reach an agreement. Mullally told me the CPB had a group of station managers standing by to take ownership of NPR's satellite equipment once the NPR negotiators caved on this issue.

NPR had someone standing by as well, Mullally said. Congressman Timothy Wirth of Colorado, chair of the House subcommittee responsible for public broadcasting legislation, was parked with a car phone just outside the CPB Building. Inside the CPB conference room, Bornstein sat so that he could watch the lights on the conference room phone. At key points in the negotiation he would send a staff member out to Congressman Wirth's car. A few minutes later, he would watch to see the phone line blink. He knew that the call was for the CPB president, that Congressman Wirth was on the other end, and that CPB would back down on whatever point was blocking accord.[3] At 4:30 Friday morning, they reached an agreement:

Many stations had not signed on to guarantee the NPR loan, but enough had for CPB to save face on its first condition. NPR would accept the CPB's financial oversight, but with the explicit understanding that the oversight would not extend to editorial decisions. And the two sides agreed that NPR would continue to operate the satellite distribution system, but with ownership of some key equipment transferred from NPR to three trustees, one of whom was Elliot Richardson, the Nixon administration's attorney general who resigned rather than fire the Watergate special prosecutor.[4] Based on those compromises, CPB approved the loan of $9.1 million. Bornstein left the building at dawn that Friday morning with check for $500 thousand. Later that morning he walked to the bank to deposit it.[5] The salary checks issued that day did not bounce, the landlord and the phone company were paid, and listeners would hear NPR on Monday morning.

Six months after he took over as interim CEO, Bornstein was able to turn over to his successor a smaller, but solvent NPR, the main products of which, *All Things Considered* and *Morning Edition*, were virtually unscathed. Radio drama—both of the *Earplay* artistic variety and the *Star Wars* pop variety—was gone, along with most of NPR's other cultural offerings and most of the Mankiewicz publicity machine.

Doug Bennet, who took over from Bornstein, had a political background similar to Mankiewicz, and yet the two could not have been more different. Mankiewicz was a brash Hollywood wheeler-dealer. Bennet was a reserved Connecticut academic, a Harvard PhD in international economics. Yet each had been active in Democratic politics, each had run unsuccessfully for Congress, and each had helped manage presidential campaigns. Indeed, they had served in opposing camps in 1972 when Mankiewicz's candidate, George McGovern, beat Bennet's candidate, Senator Edmund Muskie of Maine, for the Democratic nomination for president. Four years earlier, in 1968, Mankiewicz served Bobby Kennedy and the antiwar movement, while Bennet wrote speeches for Hubert Humphrey, Lyndon Johnson's vice president and an eventual presidential candidate. At that year's infamous Chicago convention, Bennet was inside the Humphrey headquarters hotel while Mankiewicz's antiwar demonstrators marched and chanted outside.

Doug Bennet stayed with Senator Muskie after the unsuccessful

1972 campaign. When Muskie became chairman of a newly formed congressional budget committee charged with gaining control of all government spending, he selected Doug Bennet to run the committee staff. When Muskie became President Carter's secretary of state, he took Doug Bennet with him to the State Department, first as head of congressional relations and then as head of the Agency for International Development. Ronald Reagan's 1980 election victory cost Doug Bennet his job at AID. He served briefly as president of a foundation, but when NPR needed a president in 1983, Bennet was unemployed. While not a public figure as Mankiewicz was, he knew the congressional players and process as well as his predecessor. He would not claim he was a showman or a newsman, but he had one skill that, in 1983, NPR needed more than showmanship or journalistic prowess: He was a trained economist. He had overseen the federal budget for Congress. That the federal budget balanced no better than that of NPR under Mankiewicz did not deter the selection committee. It assumed that Bennet could put NPR's financial house in order. Like Mankiewicz, Bennet had barely heard of National Public Radio when he accepted the job. He did say, however, that he enjoyed classical music.

Doug Bennet's voice rumbled in the same low registers as that of Don Mullally, the University of Illinois professor who chaired the NPR board that hired him. The two resonated in so many ways that it was difficult to know for certain where one ended and the other began. The quintessential staff man, Bennet was far more comfortable than Mankiewicz in allowing his board chairman a public role equal to, or greater than, his own. Bennet and Mullally formed a true partnership creating a distinctly different NPR from Mankiewicz's organization. They focused on repairing NPR's relationship with its member stations, who carried the responsibility for paying off what ultimately was a $6.5 million debt to CPB.[6]

About a year after Bennet took on the job, he and Mullally took a step that cemented the interdependence of NPR and its member stations and severed its taut ties to CPB. They proposed that the CPB end direct support of NPR programming, but they did not suggest, as Mankiewicz had, that NPR could somehow raise its own revenue independent of CPB and the stations. Radio, they proposed, should adopt television's pattern of sending money to stations, who would then "buy back" programming from the network.[7, 8] CPB liked the idea because it wanted to shed the embarrassment NPR's financial collapse had caused it in Congress. It was also relieved to end the years of discord that began with the feisty and independent Mankiewicz. CPB leadership had found Bornstein as difficult to deal with as Mankiewicz, and Bennet was not proving much more cooperative than his predecessors. Direct funding of NPR was a headache CPB wanted to cure. Since the crisis, CPB had tried to exercise more control over NPR than had been possible under Mankiewicz. Not surprisingly, Bennet did not like the arrangement. In fact, he quickly developed an antipathy for CPB's top management that equaled Mankiewicz's and Bornstein's.

Minnesota's Kling and Wisconsin's Bornstein had long advocated the television scheme of putting all CPB money in the hands of the member stations, which could use the money to buy the national programming they wanted. In television, PBS served as broker between program producers and station program purchasers. Kling in particular wanted a program marketplace in which many producers competed to sell their wares to stations. He was disappointed, therefore, in the details of the NPR "business plan." NPR's leadership wanted to get rid of direct funding from CPB, but they had no desire to create a genuine program marketplace. For all of the reasons enunciated by the founding NPR board and generally accepted by the public radio system, Bennet and Mullally thought NPR should remain free to create an integrated program service rather than provide individual programs that stations could buy *à la carte* from NPR or other producers. Bennet and Mullally would allow the CPB money to go to stations but would then "tax" each station a fixed percentage of its total income to buy access to everything NPR produced. They offered no choices. It was all or nothing, and since few stations could get by with nothing, nearly all stations had to buy all, in effect, leaving the total NPR program package intact and freeing little if any money to buy programming from other producers.[9]

NPR would use the tax-generated funds to produce an array of programs to meet system needs. For example, NPR might produce a Spanish-language program even though it would air on a small number of stations and not be viable in strictly market terms. NPR would use the tax to pay for the program on the assumption that it served an overall good in the public radio system. All stations would help pay for such a program even if only a few used it, just as all taxpayers support the fire department, police, schools, parks, and libraries, whether or not they used them. Bennet was thinking like the civil servant that he was rather than like the entrepreneur that Bill Kling would have preferred.

While Kling and those who thought like him[10] resented Bennet's unwillingness to embrace market mechanisms, most NPR members probably saw that lack as the plan's strength. They wanted NPR freed from CPB; they did not want a program marketplace. Many also liked the "all ships rising (or falling) together" characteristic of the fixed percentage tax. As stations prospered financially, so would NPR. NPR would have an incentive to work toward the financial success of stations. While the scheme allowed NPR to produce programs not viable in strictly market terms, it forced the network to provide an overall program service that would contribute to the stations' financial success. It made NPR subject to market incentives for its overall service, but not for each program.

In a daylong meeting of public radio stations, those who thought like Kling managed to amend the plan, replacing the fixed percentage tax of station income with a tax rate established each year by the NPR board, much like a school board adopting a budget and assessing a property tax rate for the year. Like the school tax, each year involved a difficult battle between those who wanted more service and those who wanted to hold the line on taxes. Not surprisingly, the man who had presided over the budget process for the entire United States government won every skirmish. Doug Bennet could play the budget game far better than the brigade of station managers who marched in front of the board each year to protest his proposed spending levels. Bennet charmed, reasoned, and threatened as necessary to gain significant budget increases every year of his presidency.

The new way of doing business that Bennet adopted in 1985 signaled the end of the crisis mentality and a third beginning for NPR. It paved the way for *Weekend Edition*, the first new program added under Bennet, and launched twenty years of growth that continues to this day. It also signaled some subtle changes in the organization. Jay Kernis, the arts producer who did not "know anything about news," had overcome his terror at the prospect of producing *Morning Edition*. His reward was the opportunity to create a Saturday *Weekend Edition* that NPR's most gifted story teller, Scott Simon, would host. Working with a constricted budget more reminiscent of the birth of *All Things Considered* than that of *Morning Edition*, Kernis and Simon had to create a program without the reporting support that Mankiewicz had mustered for *Morning Edition*. NPR would not stretch the workweek of its star reporters to include the weekend. The news staff would continue to focus on *Morning Edition* and *All Things Considered*. Kernis and Simon needed to come up with inexpensive, creative ways to generate two hours of magic each Saturday morning.

The once-a-week schedule gave the pair a full week to develop long sound-based, often emotion-laden, features built on Simon's reporting and narrative ability and on Kernis' audio craftsmanship. In place of the five-day-a-week reporting staff, Kernis created a major role for Daniel Schorr, the curmudgeonly refugee from CBS. Schorr they reasoned, could "talk about" the hard news of the week, tap his decades of experience in reporting and analyzing news, and exercise the privilege of age to "interpret" the news in a manner denied his younger colleagues. They also used recurring segments with distinctive commentators on "frivolous" topics such as sports and entertainment. Kernis and Simon assembled a cast of "regulars" who turned *Weekend Edition Saturday* into a comfortable radio community. That community talked about the news and anything else Kernis and Simon found interesting.

A year later, a Sunday version of *Weekend Edition* joined the NPR lineup with Susan Stamberg as host. Having anchored NPR's signature program five days a week for fifteen years, Stamberg had earned the right to a less demanding and more liberating assignment. The discovery that she had breast cancer made a lighter schedule imperative. Like Scott Simon on Saturday, Stamberg would have relatively few resources and virtually no support from the news staff on Sunday. Out of necessity, she took a softer approach to the program, an approach reminiscent of *ATC*'s early years, when personality and ingenuity, rather than journalistic prowess, had to carry the program. Stamberg's personality and interests could emerge without apology or compromise on the Sunday program. Reflecting her interests, *Weekend Edition Sunday* strayed even farther from hard news than did the Scott Simon version on Saturday.[11] Stamberg focused on literature and the arts. She chatted with authors and critics. She presided over the creation of a serial novel in which a different author added a chapter each week, taking the story off into some very unexpected directions. Not great literature, perhaps, but an intriguing tale and, above all, an innovative process that took creative risks. She added a "puzzle master" to the Sunday show, reviving the lost *ATC* tradition of contests to generate creative responses from listeners. Most controversial among the more mainstream news people who increasingly dominated the staff at NPR and at NPR member stations, Stamberg used a pianist to play live musical interludes and add musical punctuation to the Sunday morning program.

While *Weekend Edition Sunday* provided an ideal vehicle for her, Stamberg's departure from *All Things Considered* would solidify the changes that had crept into the nature of the program over the years.

Stamberg had been the program's "personality," a buffer against an increasing emphasis on professional news coverage. *All Things Considered*'s producer, Art Silverman, shared the views of many veterans when he observed that Stamberg was "the only one who really fulfilled the mission of the show, which was to be smart and sassy. She would always ask the good dumb questions that got the best answers."[12] Professional reporters asked questions in developing their reports, but their finished pieces sought to provide well-informed intelligent answers rather than ask good dumb questions.

Stamberg's departure from weekday hosting came in roughly the same period as Garrison Keillor's "retirement" from *A Prairie Home Companion* to move to Denmark with his new wife. Bill Kling hired Stamberg's *ATC* co-host, Noah Adams, to attempt filling Keillor's shoes in Minnesota. The same era saw Robert Krulwich take his quirky reporting style to CBS (and later ABC) Television; Ira Flatow took his human approach to science reporting to PBS, and Cokie Roberts moved her insider knowledge to ABC Television, which became her primary home, although she never fully cut her ties to NPR.

Bennet looked at all these defections and concluded that personalities were fickle. NPR might develop them, but either it could never pay enough to hold them if they became desirable to other media outlets, or else, they became difficult-to-handle prima donnas. In the future, he told me, NPR would de-emphasize distinctive personalities. NPR would attract listeners not with personalities but with its institutional integrity. NPR would have interchangeable and replaceable hosts and reporters. None would really stand out much from the others. All would embody the NPR style. All would reflect NPR's commitment to quality reporting. In the future, listeners would tune in to hear a solid and dependable NPR news product, not a Susan Stamberg, Noah Adams, Robert Krulwich, Ira Flatow, Cokie Roberts, Daniel Schorr, Scott Simon, or Nina Totenberg. When it came time to pick a replacement for Stamberg on *All Things Considered*, the assignment went initially to the solid Renée Montagne and then to the frosty competence of Linda Wertheimer rather than to the early favorite, the more memorable and controversial Margot Adler. Adler was a New York–based reporter, whose distinctiveness included her public commitment to and published works about Wicca, the religion of witchcraft. NPR might have a commitment to diversity, but having "a witch" as *ATC* co-host seemed a little too diverse.[13] Besides, personalities were passé. Ruth Hirschman, manager of KCRW in Santa Monica, observed "I'm sure people are not knitting sweaters for Robert Siegel or sending chicken soup . . . like they did to Susan Stamberg."[14] Montagne and Wertheimer fit Bennet's expectation for a next generation of competent but colorless NPR "personalities."

Ironically, the creation of two personality-based programs—*Weekend Edition Saturday* and *Weekend Edition Sunday*—signaled not the triumph of personalities but their marginalization. Putting personalities and "soft" features on the weekend allowed NPR to emphasize neutral professionalism and hard news on weekdays. *Weekend Edition* and its Saturday and Sunday morning hosts were the exception that proved the rule. NPR was primarily a news organization seeking to maintain the highest professional standards—professional standards that NPR upheld better than nearly any other news organization but professional standards that, by definition, were not essentially different than the professional standards other journalistic organizations espoused but often ignored.

Not even the weekend ghettos, however, were immune from NPR's commitment—and increasingly, its member stations' commitment—to covering breaking news. Just as it had with *ATC* in 1972, family life in the Stamberg household placed a limitation on *Weekend Edition Sunday*. The host of the Sunday-morning news magazine did not want to work Sunday morning. Therefore, Stamberg and her staff taped *Weekend Edition Sunday* on Friday afternoon. They left space to insert news developments and understood that from time to time the program might need an update after the Friday taping. Given the program's non-news focus and the Monday through Friday nature of most news, this approach seemed reasonable, until the Chinese government chose Sunday morning to open fire on the students occupying Tiananmen Square, and *Weekend Edition* was not able to react with the speed of a first-rate hard news organization.[15]

I did not regard this failure as fatal. Most news junkies, I assumed, would turn to CNN to see what happened. Like me, they would tune to NPR later to find out what it meant. Mine was a minority view, however. Most in public radio were embarrassed, others outraged. Henceforth, *Weekend Edition* would broadcast live. If Stamberg would not give up her Sunday mornings to do it, someone else would. That someone was Lianne Hanson, a Stamberg admirer, who continued much of her mentor's style but broadcast live on Sunday morning, ready to fulfill NPR's emerging role as radio's most through and reliable source of news.

CHAPTER 9

Performance Today

M ost who scan this book's chapter titles will undoubtedly recognize *All Things Considered, Morning Edition*, and *Weekend Edition*. Many will recognize *Talk of the Nation* and *Marketplace*. Only a few will recognize *Performance Today*. It was not supposed to be that way. NPR wanted *Performance Today* to become public radio's showcase arts and performance program, the cultural department's equivalent of the news department's *Morning Edition*. That it failed exemplifies both public radio's problems in doing cultural programming and the environment into which NPR introduced it, during the presidency of Doug Bennet in the late 1980s when the two versions of *Weekend Edition* went on the air.

The watchword of that era was "audience building." Public radio learned that the rapid audience growth it had experienced under Mankiewicz had screeched to a halt during and after the 1983 NPR financial crisis. NPR staff attributed the stagnation to the 25 percent spending cuts that Bornstein imposed on the organization. They might have been right that listeners noticed some diminution of quality and stopped listening, or stopped listening as often, but that argument seems improbable given the vast gap in quality between public radio—even with reduced budgets—and commercial broadcasting.

It seemed more probable to me that the Corporation for Public Broadcasting's reaction to the Reagan cuts contributed to the stagna-

Author's Note: I participated in these events as chairman of the National Public Radio board of directors.

119

tion of audience growth. Facing a 20 percent budget reduction, CPB acted to preserve what it had built by halting its aggressive station expansion program. That expansion program had helped institutions and organizations all across the country to build new public radio stations or to upgrade inadequate facilities to serve a broader public. Moreover, each new station had filled another spot on the finite FM spectrum, leaving far fewer possibilities for new stations in 1983 than there had been in 1973. While Mankiewicz had been quick to attribute the audience growth during his regime to his programming and promotional innovations, he neglected to mention how much of that growth was due to the rapid increase in the number of public radio stations and the increase in the number of people able to hear public radio. NPR also got a big boost from the decision of automobile manufacturers to make FM radio virtually standard in new cars during the late '70s and early '80s. It seemed to me that Mankiewicz had had a lot of help generating record audience growth and Bennet lacked that help as he tried to continue it. Whatever the reason or whoever was to blame, public radio listening was flat in the middle of the Reagan years at the same time stations were becoming more dependent on listeners for support, a combination that did not bode well for the future.

When Doug Bennet arrived as NPR's new president late in 1983, he found a lengthy memo from research consultant David Giovannoni proposing that public radio make audience growth a priority. Giovannoni wrote, "Public radio has a very long history of being genuinely well-intentioned but generally ineffective." He attributed those good intentions to the system's educational roots, the subsidies and expectations of Congress, and the example of the BBC. The overall result, he said, were public broadcasters "so absorbed in airing what they believed people should listen to that they were not really paying much attention to what people would listen to."[1] Giovannoni overstated the case but identified an essential truth. Public radio had descended directly from educational radio, which had descended from the Reithian BBC and the progressive movement, all of which sought to educate and uplift rather than give the public what it wants.

Even though Siemering began his NPR purposes with a commitment to "serve the individual," his intent was to provide programs that would contribute to a better, more humane world. In the tradition of educational broadcasting, Siemering never proposed to simply give the public what it wants. He proposed programs that reflected his values. His values, however, were more humanistic than traditional educational broadcasters', and he packaged them in contemporary radio formats to appeal to as many people as possible, but he would never sacrifice his values for appeal. Even Frank Mankiewicz was willing to "pander" to audiences only in the case of *Star Wars*, which had not proven particularly successful. He built an institution that presented quality programming—particularly news—as he understood quality. He assumed his quality programming would attract listeners sharing his understanding of quality, or better yet, expose untutored listeners to his understanding of quality. Mankiewicz was a showman, but a showman in the public service tradition. The cliche that "you can't save souls in an empty church" applied to the secular religion of public radio, but both Siemering and Mankiewicz thought first about the gospel they would preach and only later about filling the pews.

Giovannoni did not really disagree with those priorities. He did not advocate increased listenership for its own sake but to reach more people with programming in the public radio tradition. He argued in his memo to Bennet that better packaging of quality content could explain the audience growth under Mankiewicz:

> Public radio has learned to package its content in order to make it more accessible to listeners, without sacrificing the integrity of the content itself. . . . And through careful attention to the form of presentation, public radio now serves hundreds of thousands of listeners, where it used to serve merely hundreds.[2]

Giovannoni's concern with audience growth was not totally academic. In the Reagan era, public broadcasters continued to pursue government financing aggressively, but they could not fully depend on government largess, federal, state, or local. Since corporate underwriting made some public broadcasters uneasy, they looked to listener support for a more comfortable and more certain alternative to government. From 1970 to 1985, listener support rose from 8 percent to 20 percent of station budgets, but still remained much less than the portion from government, which was about 60 percent in 1985.[3] That listener-support percentage needed to go up substantially to guarantee a future for public radio. Getting more listener money required more listeners. While public radio staff members could not stop the political tide sweeping away their government subsidies, they could make programming decisions that would attract listeners and influence their willingness to contribute.

So public radio set out on a campaign to duplicate its 1977–1982 audience growth and to double its audience again by 1990, five years hence. As the chairman of the NPR board, I appointed a task force, headed by Professor Don Mullally of the University of Illinois and the former NPR board chairman, to tell us how to do it.[4] The task force report[5] reflected the philosophy and sometimes accusatory style of its chairman. It argued that public radio needed to think more about what listeners want to hear and less about what its producers want to produce. It did not propose any basic change in programming; public radio would still center on intelligent news and talk and classical music. Mostly, the task force complained that public radio did not package this material in ways most appealing to listeners. A devoted classical music listener himself, Mullally cautioned, for example, against "excessively arrogant and supercilious stylistic affectations by announcers" who create "the impression of a private club of *cognoscenti*, rather than an open and inviting radio service."[6] Focusing on audience, once considered a fringe concern of people who did not really understand public radio, suddenly became dogma as a task force led by the most traditional and programmatically conservative of public radio leaders endorsed it.

The task force made the critical decision to define doubling the audience as doubling the number of people listening to public radio *at any given time* (average quarter-hour audience) rather than doubling the total number of different people who *ever* listened to public radio during a week (cumulative audience). Focusing on the average number of listeners rather than on the total number of different listeners implied that public radio could double its audience without doubling the number of individuals who tuned in. Public radio could achieve its goal by doubling the amount of time current listeners spent with public radio.

This distinction was crucial. Had it chosen to focus on *cumulative* audiences, the task force might have recommended increasing the variety of programming offered so as to appeal to additional groups. It certainly would have called for expensive advertising and promotion to reach new people. However, doubling the *average quarter-hour* audience required no new types of programming nor additional promotion. Public radio listeners spent less time with their public radio station than commercial radio listeners spent with their favorite commercial station. If public radio listeners showed the same loyalty to public radio as commercial radio listeners did to commercial stations, public radio's average quarter-hour audience would almost double even without attracting any new listeners.

The task force told stations to eliminate anything that might send its current listeners away. Some steps were simple. The task force suggested that program hosts never say "goodbye." Instead, the hosts should engage in "internal promotion" and ask listeners to "stay tuned" for whatever segment or program was next. The task force called on stations to build a consistent sound and easily comprehended schedule. It wanted stations to focus on doing one or two things very well all the time so that they could attract *and hold* listeners who prized whatever their proficiency was. Stations needed to assure listeners that they would always give them what they wanted when they wanted it, the same as all-news stations or classic rock stations always deliver news or classic rock. Assuring listeners of this consistency meant that a station had to dump marginal types of programming that its primary listeners might find distasteful. Such assurance jeopardized specialized programming intended for a select group of listeners, for example, a weekly hour of Spanish language programming or presentations of atonal contemporary music that might drive listeners to other stations. This average quarter-hour strategy upset public radio zealots far more than the goal of doubling the audience. To them, this strategy seemed to endorse a colorless, homogenized service that encouraged habit by discouraging surprises.

Mullally's task force told CPB to demand audience research before funding new program projects. It told NPR to provide programs when listeners wanted to hear them rather than when the staff wanted to present them. This dictum meant starting *Morning Edition* at 5:00 AM rather than 6:00 AM and *All Things Considered* at 4:30 PM rather than 5:00 PM Eastern Time.[7] It also instructed concert syndicators to blend their presentations unobtrusively into radio formats rather than attempt to transport audiences to the concert hall.

The task force report produced hostility but little change at NPR, with the staff of journalists and artists resistant to substituting audience judgements of quality for their own. The report did, however, provide an occasion for the periodic soul-searching on which public radio thrives, and many stations did take action to "minimize tune-outs" and "extend time-spent-listening."

NPR gave birth to *Performance Today* in the wake of the task force report, and that environment explains in part the decisions made about that program. The audience-building task force directed producers to develop programming that blended into a station's overall sound and avoided unhappy surprises that might cause listeners to tune elsewhere.

It prescribed a vanilla approach to programming, and, in a sense, *Performance Today* became a vanilla program. Dean Boal, who presided over the remnants of the cultural program department that survived the 1983 financial crisis, liked vanilla. Prior to taking charge of the department, Boal had developed the low-cost, generic classical music service of the ill-fated *NPR Plus* project that contributed to NPR's financial debacle. Boal understood formatted music programming better than most. *NPR Plus*—cheap to produce, inexpensive to buy, and easy to use—had presented a stream of classical recordings with very little host-talk. It would not win awards, but it would give classical music listeners a solid, reliable, professional presentation of the music they loved. It filled the audience-building task force's prescription. Boal thought *NPR Plus* had traveled the right track and that the remnants of its staff could apply their experience to the new project, the proposed two-hour daily classical music program called *Performance Today*.

Bennet, however, needed to raise money for the project, and few funders care to give money to projects that are not outstanding, both in quality and in the actual ability to "stand out." Bennet demanded a program that would do for cultural programming what *Morning Edition* and *All Things Considered* did for news. Boal had to create an outstanding program that listeners were not supposed to notice. Bennet had to find funders for a program that would blend unobtrusively into a program stream.

Thus, *Performance Today* emerged as a compromise. To satisfy the admonition of the audience-building task force and the expressed need, particularly of smaller stations, for an *NPR Plus*-type classical music "service," the program would provide mostly "background" music for busy listeners. To satisfy the need for a performance "showcase" worthy of National Endowment for the Arts and philanthropic underwriting support, most of the music presented would come from performances that NPR member stations recorded recently around the country, a much more costly approach than spinning discs. To add further distinctiveness to the service and to expand the range of "performance" beyond classical music, the program would incorporate reviews, interviews, and produced features about all of the arts. These additions rammed *Performance Today* smack up against its contradictory mission: All the "talk" definitely would detract from its usefulness as a music service. At the same time, all the talk would make a distinct contribution to the arts in America and, maybe, polish the reputation of National

Public Radio in the arts community. The better the program succeeded at one task, the more likely it would fail at the other.

For the first time in the development of a new NPR program, Boal turned to research, just as the task force said he should. He created sample programs to test on listeners. Six hundred sixty listeners gave their opinions in two communities, Ann Arbor and Atlanta. The verdict? As mixed as the program itself. Most listeners liked the *Performance Today* pilots, Boal reported, but did not perceive the program as "a dramatic breakthrough or unusually different show."[8] The talk features were problematic. "The same talk which functions as one of the positive draws of the program can apparently also be a negative to some listeners. We have," said Boal, "a delicate job of providing an unusual, informative feature of the show without drowning out the listener's interest in the music itself." Moreover, the research trashed the program's premise that had elicited NEA support: Listeners did not want a showcase for contemporary performance. The focus group report said:

> Listeners are fairly clear in telling us that they prefer more usual, standard, or classic classical music selections and will not react positively to using *Performance Today* as a venue for exploration of avant garde, new, or unusual selections.[9]

The *Performance Today* research proved prophetic, but it did not cause either Bennet or Boal to depart from their respective visions of the program. They would precede with the compromise in spite of the research—the task force had said producers should conduct research, it did not demand that they pay attention to the results—and the results were predictably disappointing to both.

Key members of the NPR board were more clearheaded. They saw the inherent contradictions in *Performance Today* as soon as Bennet proposed it. When research confirmed their doubts, they cautioned against going ahead with this hybrid.[10] Of course, Bennet had already secured the NEA money and was hard at work on other funding proposals. Moreover, for someone not especially interested in programming, Bennet was remarkably committed to this project. He was determined that cultural programming at NPR would not sink on his watch. The board allowed Bennet and Boal to proceed with *Performance Today* with the proviso that all funding come from outside sources. Once on the air, it sputtered, providing a useful service to some small stations but gaining little acceptance from larger more sophisticated classical music stations.

The key critic of *Performance Today*, Max Wycisk, manager of the public radio station in Denver, did not base his strong views about NPR's classical music project on gut instinct alone. More than any other, his station used research to design programming to please a target audience. With financial support from CPB, his station tried to discern the music preferences of people who like NPR news programming, which, Wycisk recognized, was the main reason listeners tuned to his station. Thinking along the same lines as the task force, Wycisk wanted to know how he could get those listeners to *Morning Edition* and *All Things Considered* to stay tuned to his station during the daytime, when many of them switched to music on commercial radio stations. He was not seeking new listeners so much as trying to get news listeners to spend a lot more time with his station. The Denver research found that no single type of music appealed to all those news listeners, but classical music provided the most promise. The research then sought to identify what classical music appealed most to NPR news listeners. Researcher George Bailey did not create a list of popular compositions or recommend music in traditional categories like Baroque or Romantic. Instead, he identified "sounds" that appealed to NPR news listeners based on tempo, density, and instrumentation. He called these sounds "modes" of classical music and the overall concept "modal music."

Wycisk's decision to program classical-music "modes" most appealing to NPR news listeners produced ambiguous results. Listening to the station did increase nicely, but music continued as the weakest programming on a strong station. Research proponents and detractors could both claim victory in this test, intensifying debate about the Denver approach and dividing the public radio community, just as the recommendations of the task force had. Applying research to the sacred repertoire of classical music seemed to violate all of public radio's traditional values. Music directors declared that they would never exclude "important" parts of the repertoire that fell outside the "modes" that appealed to public radio news listeners. Nonetheless, the music on many public stations gradually became "lighter" and "brighter" on the (partially erroneous) assumption that the Denver research had anointed it best-liked by listeners. Even those who rejected the Denver research most vociferously quietly gave more consideration to what they thought listeners wanted to hear and, more important, what would drive them away.

While the audience-building efforts helped improve the sound of many public stations and helped others define a market niche, the audience for public radio did not double in five years. All the program streamlining to extend listening time did not improve the average audience level as much as it promised. That result surprised me. Logically, it should have worked better than it did. I was less surprised by the failure of research and schedule streamlining to produce any new "hits" like *All Things Considered, Morning Edition*, or *A Prairie Home Companion*. Such major programs had proven essential in getting listeners to tune into public radio in the first place. Audience-building ideology hoped to keep those listeners from tuning out by surrounding the hits with consistent and relatively unobjectionable programming. Apparently, public radio listeners needed more positive reasons to stay tuned. Consistency was not enough. Public radio needed more hits, and research was probably not the best way to create them.

Bill Siemering, NPR's original philosopher and first program director, understood why the task force formula would not work, and his warning proved prophetic. While managing the public radio station in Philadelphia, Siemering attempted to strike a balance between the traditionalists and the "audience builders" in a paper he called, "Some Things to Consider about Audience Building."[11] Yes, he wanted to see audiences increase, and, of course, public radio needed to adapt to how people use radio. Public radio, he wrote, should not present the "aural equivalent of the *Congressional Record*," nor should it "require people to read from right to left." He cautioned the zealots, however, against emphasizing "the safe" and only aspiring "to minimize listeners tuning away." Cautious decision making underestimates public radio listeners, he said, and the other "bright, curious people we are trying to attract to public radio." He pointed out that public radio's most successful audience magnet, other than NPR news, was *A Prairie Home Companion*, a program that defied the audience-building formula on virtually every point. It was definitely unique and did not blend in with anything else on most public radio stations. It was eclectic within its own content. And Garrison Keillor broke the cardinal rule of audience flow by ending his program by saying "Good night, everyone" instead of urging his listeners to "stay tuned."

Siemering argued that strict adherence to the new audience-building orthodoxy would fail to attract listeners to public radio because simple formulas do not draw the kind of people who might listen to our service. Note that Siemering did not dispute "giving the audience what it wants."

He simply had a different perception from Mullally and the other audience-building activists of what their target audience wanted.[12] He saw public radio listeners as folks with eclectic tastes, who like "quality" in a variety of program types, who seek adventure and surprise. The audience-building task force saw public radio listeners as those who want comfort and predictability, just like most people. Siemering proved to have the better understanding of public radio listeners.

The task force's suggestions produced no memorable programming, certainly not *Performance Today*, the most direct progeny. NPR's now-bureaucratized structure produced no major successes outside of news. All the innovation in public radio during this period took place at individual stations and each of the programs was an idiosyncratic production built on a strong and creative personality. No focus group would have come up with any of these programs. The intuition of producers, program directors, and station managers generated programming that defined public radio outside of NPR news.

First and foremost of these idiosyncratic productions, of course, was Garrison Keillor's *A Prairie Home Companion*, a downright weird anachronism that, as Siemering pointed out, violated all the rules of audience-building and yet generated magic every Saturday night. The resources of Minnesota Public Radio and the gut instincts of its president, Bill Kling, made it possible, and the entire public radio community enjoyed the benefit of this nonscientific gamble.

Siemering himself played a key role in generating another idiosyncratic, personality-based program from his station in Philadelphia. Terry Gross created a national version of her local program *Fresh Air*. The veteran public radio program host began her career in public radio at Siemering's first station, WBFO in Buffalo. They resumed their partnership in Philadelphia. *Fresh Air*, like *All Things Considered*, was a direct descendent of Buffalo's *This Is Radio*, the free-wheeling "organic" program Siemering described, but only partially realized, before tackling NPR's mission statement and *ATC*. The Philadelphia version of *Fresh Air* mixed interviews, features, and performances and changed from day to day. Its unity emanated from the sensibility of its host, Terry Gross. Although *Fresh Air* and *ATC* had both evolved from the values and vision of Bill Siemering, they were quite different. *ATC* put news first, while *Fresh Air* emphasized the arts and popular culture, the interests of Gross and her staff.

Perhaps because of its common parentage with *All Things Consid-*

ered, *Fresh Air* was more like NPR news programs than were *A Prairie Home Companion* or the other personality-centered station-based programs that emerged about that time. When the task force told NPR to start *All Things Considered* a half hour earlier when more people were available to listen to the radio, news department head Robert Siegel said "no." He did not say "no" because he failed to understand why the task force made the recommendation nor did he take seriously the flimsy reason he offered for his "no"—that starting *ATC* at 4:30 would be more difficult and more costly because news events were still happening at 4:30, whereas they mostly stopped at the 5:00 close of the business day in Washington. He said "no" as leverage to get the NPR board and the stations to come up with a larger budget. If they did, he would agree to move up the start time of *All Things Considered*. Of course, getting such money was not in the cards. Most important, Mankiewicz's attitude toward those know-nothing provincial stations still pervaded the NPR news staff who questioned the credentials of these task force members telling the professionals at National Public Radio how and when to do their programs. In producing great journalism Siegal refused to pander to the whims of stations and the listeners they pretended to represent. Siegel, with Bennet's backing, was willing to compromise, however. Instead of starting *All Things Considered* a half hour earlier, NPR could distribute its close relative *Fresh Air* with Gross.

To go national, *Fresh Air* needed to focus its format and chop its length to an hour. Performance elements shrank to allow interviews and reviews about the arts and popular culture to fill most of the hour. "Cutaways" during the program that allowed stations to insert local announcements and do "forward promotion" of major *ATC* stories reflected the admonitions of the audience-building task force. Audience research confirmed that *Fresh Air* had lots of Philadelphia listeners and would probably attract lots of national listeners, but that research did not influence the program's content. *Fresh Air* got its content and its character, the old-fashioned way, from the values and instincts of Siemering, Gross, and their colleagues.

A decade later, Ira Glass created another idiosyncratic program. Glass had worked at NPR but exited when his unique style no longer seemed to fit into *Morning Edition* or *All Things Considered*. He found a sympathetic home at WBEZ in Chicago and the firm support of WBEZ's president, Torry Malatia. Their collaboration at a station prepared to take chances, as the bureaucratic NPR could not, produced

This American Life, stories of real people told by themselves and a cast of notable writers and producers. The program represents the ideas, the personality, and the sensibility of Ira Glass, as much as *Fresh Air* represents the ideas, the personality, and the sensibility of Terry Gross. *This American Life* fulfills the promises of the original NPR purposes to advance the art of radio and to tell stories of real people more consistently than most of the programming produced by NPR itself.

A similar scenario played out in Boston at WBUR in the mid-'80s, when two brothers appeared on a local car repair program and proved themselves more amusing than they were helpful in answering their callers' car-care questions. Tom and Ray Magliozzi turned occasional appearances into a regular program of their own and became Click and Clack, the Tappet Brothers. Nothing more scientific than the instincts of WBUR's program director and station manager backed the decision to air *Car Talk*. Nothing else on WBUR sounded quite like *Car Talk*, nor, in fact, did anyone else on public radio sound much like Tom and Ray. Loud, brash, and less than subtle in their humor, they represented the polar opposite of the intimate and melancholy Garrison Keillor or the controlled seriousness of NPR news. After WBUR's managers gambled on the show, audience numbers, pledge results, and anecdotes told them that they had struck gold, but research had not led them to the mother lode. A proven hit in Boston, *Car Talk* went through the same kind of tightening and focusing as *Fresh Air*, refining the program into a weekly hour suitable for national distribution. By the late '90s, *Car Talk* was the most-listened-to single hour on all of public radio.

I had a similar experience in Madison at about the same time the Car Guys were finding their formula in Boston. I wanted a showcase program for Wisconsin Public Radio with the impact of Garrison Keillor in Minnesota. I admired the quick wit of a guy named Michael Feldman who did a daily morning program on the little "community" radio station in Madison, WORT. By any objective standard, Feldman and Keillor had little in common. One was quick, nasal, edgy; the other, slow, mellifluous, soothing. One was urban, Jewish, a jazz/rock fan; the other, rural, Protestant, a country/gospel lover. One capitalized on spontaneous wit; the other wrote well-crafted humor. I enjoyed them both and was convinced other public radio listeners would, too.

Our first attempt to create a program for Feldman at Wisconsin Public Radio copied Keillor's format too closely. Its meticulous planning failed to capitalize on Feldman's unique strength, spontaneity. Our second attempt gave him two hours on Saturday morning in which to recreate the spontaneity and informality of his *The Breakfast Special* on WORT. This format did take advantage of Feldman's strength, and WHA had a local hit. Then we planned a more-structured national version of the local show. We turned it into a quiz show just to give our star a reason to talk with people in the studio and on the phone. We fully expected Feldman to regularly violate what little structure we imposed. He did, and public radio had another national personality public radio listeners embraced.

Research did not influence *Whad'Ya Know?* Wisconsin Public Radio did bring in some focus groups to react to tapes of the show, but Feldman ignored the comments. He dismissed positive reactions as obvious and negative ones as stupid. He was particularly dismissive of comments from public radio program directors, whom he judged, on the basis of what they put on the radio, if not on their actual personalities, as too stuffy to appreciate what he was trying to do. He would do what he thought was funny. Wisconsin Public Radio made little effort to control him, knowing that such effort was unlikely to have an effect and recognizing that he had great instincts for what appealed to public radio listeners.

Neither Feldman nor the Magliozzi brothers pretended that what they were doing served a great social purpose. Yes, a listener might get remedial help on something you "should have learned in school had you been paying attention," or pick up a little information about spark plugs or catalytic converters, but such enlightenment was purely inadvertent. These programs were entertainment, and they created a conundrum. These two programs—not to mention Keillor—defied conventional public radio wisdom in an era of establishing consistent formats and giving listeners only what they expected. Why were they successful on public radio, where the basic appeal was serious, in-depth treatment of news or perhaps classical music? Why would Feldman describing the contents of his daughter's diaper or the Magliozzi brothers joking about exhaust pipes on public radio not disappoint NPR news listeners? NPR thought it had found the answer when, in the new spirit of attention to audience, it conducted its first ever focus groups in five cities in 1986. The focus groups revealed that

> public radio listeners are a tolerant group. Listeners recognize that each listener's agenda is different and they appreciate public radio's efforts to offer eclectic programming elements for a diverse population. If a polka music show doesn't appeal to them personally, they know someone else

probably enjoys it. By accepting someone else's favorite programming, listeners enter into an implied agreement that their own programming preference will be adequately met.[13]

Participants expressed "gratitude for being treated as if they have a brain in their head." The researcher cautioned public radio not to underestimate this important dynamic, "which enhances listeners' sense of self respect."[14] These results gave more credence to Siemering's warning not to underestimate the audience than they did to the task force's warning simply to minimize tune-outs.

That tolerance for diversity contributed to listeners' affection for public radio. Such tolerance did not mean, however, that listeners actually tuned in to the polka programs. Listeners might respect diverse programming, but it probably caused them to listen to public radio less than they otherwise might. Public radio seemed to face the dilemma of keeping listeners listening longer with consistency or cementing their respect with diversity.

Another study resolved the dilemma. It found that the main distinction between those who contributed to public radio and those who did not boiled down to how much they listened.[15] Those who listened to public radio more than they listened to any commercial station were likely to contribute. Those who listened to a commercial station more were unlikely to contribute. A listener might respect public radio for doing a polka program, but that same polka program might send the listener to a commercial station, making that listener less likely to contribute to public radio. Appealing to the same listener for a long period of time produced more listener contributions than appealing to a variety of listeners for shorter periods of time. Apparently, the audience-building task force was right to insist on program consistency.

But maybe not. Yes, it might be important for people to listen a lot if they are to become contributors, but maybe such loyalty did not require the kind of consistency the task force advocated. Maybe the listener would listen more because of the variety of programs. That notion may have been counterintuitive, but the largest study of public radio listening to date, *Audience 88*, concluded that public radio did not need to present a consistent format.[16] Siemering was correct in advocating some program diversity. More important than a consistent format, the study concluded, was consistent appeal to an individual through his or her varying moods. A station could keep a listener tuned in by providing several types of programming that this particular listener wanted. If a station played to a listener's varied needs, that listener would become loyal and become a contributor.

Audience 88 demonstrated that the same people attracted to *All Things Considered* tended to like *A Prairie Home Companion*. Those who liked both programs tended to fall into a particular "psychographic group of highly educated individuals labeled "inner directed, societally conscious" in the marketing system known as *Values and Lifestyles*. Because of their education, societally conscious individuals did very well financially but valued material success less than the majority of prosperous well-educated Americans. The arts, ideas, and social issues such as the environment, education, and justice motivated the societally conscious individual. For some, commitment to the arts, ideas, and social issues put them in jobs that required education but were relatively low paying, like schoolteachers, social workers, librarians, artists—*and public radio producers*.

When public radio producers created programs that represented their personal values and interests, which is what they had traditionally done, they were creating programs that appealed to the people who shared their "values and lifestyles." The task force told public radio personnel to stop producing programs to please themselves and produce programs known to appeal to public radio's intended audience. *Audience 88* and its primary researcher, David Giovannoni, now delivered the happy, but not really surprising, news that the "societally conscious" core listeners drawn to public radio were pretty much the same kind of people who worked in public radio. Doing programs just because public radio producers liked them was not so wrong after all.

The underlying intelligence, wit, and humane values of Garrison, Terry, Michael, Tom, and Ray resonated with "societally conscious" personalities, both on public radio staffs and in the public radio audience. These entertainers shared something with one another—and with NPR news programs—that made sense to the "societally conscious." These programs gave NPR news listeners another reason to love public radio, another reason to tune to and pay for their public radio station. This discovery also presented a new dilemma for those in public radio. The audience-building movement told public radio to concentrate on a specific type of programming, which some in the business found limiting. Giovanonni now told public radio to concentrate on a specific type of listener, which some in the business found disturbing. The task force formula had the virtue of starting with program content and packaging it and scheduling it as effectively as possible for the convenience of any-

one interested in such programming. The task force called for programming consistency, which at least kept programming as its central
concern. On the other hand, *Audience 88* defined a particular type of
listener to whom public radio should attempt to appeal through a variety of programming that all appealed to that listener type. That the particular type of listeners happened to like the same type of programming
that public radio staff wanted to produce disguised, but did not negate,
the disturbing concept put forth by Giovannoni and his colleagues that
success for public radio meant having great appeal to a subset of the
population and none at all to the vast majority of the population. Whatever the pragmatic wisdom of this conclusion, it was far from what Lord
Reith, Lew Hill, educational radio, or Bill Siemering had in mind when
they enunciated their individual visions of public service radio.

CHAPTER 10

Talk of the Nation

While Frank Mankiewicz lifted NPR from obscurity, he had not made it a household name before his sudden departure in 1983. NPR's average weekly audience surpassed eight million,[1] not bad for an alternative medium, but not good for anything but an alternative medium. Over the next eight years, however, NPR gradually and steadily increased its presence. With the first Gulf War in 1991, it emerged as a minor national institution. NPR's much-noted coverage of that war told the nation that NPR had arrived. Out of that coverage came the daily call-in talk program *Talk of the Nation*, the title of which suggests what had happened to NPR and the public radio system as a whole in 1991.

NPR's journey from an obscure alternative to a real player in American journalism was steady but troubled. Its direction and troubles were most clear while Adam Clayton Powell III was its vice president of news. In 1987, Robert Siegel, who had run the news department since the departure of Frank Mankiewicz and Barbara Cohen in 1983, chose to leave management for the *ATC* hosting slot that Noah Adam had vacated. Bennet chose Powell to replace him.

Grandson of the towering Harlem minister and son of the flamboyant congressman, Adam Powell III was a scholarly appearing, somewhat diffident, light-skinned black man very different in style from his col-

---

Author's Note: I participated in the events in the early part of this chapter as chairman of the NPR board and in the events of the latter part as an opinionated station manager.

orful father. Affirmative action figured in the selection of Powell, but not decisively. His professional experience and job interviews impressed Bennet and the hiring committee so much that he would have gotten the job whatever his color. Powell had worked with Siegel and Jay Kernis at WRVR in New York during its days as a quasi-public radio news station in the '70s. He had served as news director of the Westinghouse all-news station in New York, WINS. He had headed CBS Radio News's national political coverage. He had owned radio stations and acted as a consultant to radio stations. Moreover, his critique of NPR's news operation impressed everyone. Without question, he was the guy NPR needed and Bennet wanted.

Either shy or aloof, Powell did not mix as easily with the news staff as had his predecessors. Powell was reserved, scholarly, and formal like Doug Bennet, and the two became close. Neither ever attained the personal popularity in the news department that Mankiewicz had enjoyed. More importantly, veteran news staff members who accepted the leadership of Mankiewicz, Cohen, and Siegel were inclined to question decisions made by a newsman schooled in the commercial perspective of CBS and Westinghouse, which asked listeners to "Give us twenty minutes and we'll give you the world." NPR prided itself on needing more than twenty minutes. Perhaps because of who Powell was or where he came from, or perhaps out of genuine principle, some staff began to rebel as Powell pushed NPR news farther along the path to quality, but essentially conventional, spot news that had taken root under Mankiewicz.[2]

Powell's most significant innovation in the news department was five-minute hourly newscasts identical in function and similar in style to the "news on the hour" services of CBS, ABC, and commercial AM radio in general.[3] The *National Journal* reported, "Under his direction, NPR has continued a gradual shift toward crisp, up-to-the-minute news coverage, sometimes at the expense of the offbeat, reflective stories that have set the public network apart from its commercial counterparts."[4] Those newscasts contributed to public radio's utility but not to its uniqueness.

Powell's newscasts were the next logical move down the road his predecessors had driven, but when proposed by an outsider from commercial broadcasting their implications for NPR's original mission were more obvious than they might otherwise have been. Even staff members associated with a hard-news philosophy began to ask questions. The struggle between NPR's role as an alternative versus its role as "the best" reached a dramatic climax when President Reagan traveled to

Moscow in 1988 to meet with President Gorbachev and NPR had to decide how many staff to send to cover this historic event.

When NPR first went on the air in the early 1970s, the decision would have been simple: none. As producer of NPR's only "news" program, I would have assumed that our listeners would watch the ceremonies on television and get initial news reports from television, commercial radio, newspapers, or from NPR quoting the Associated Press and Reuters. They would not hear anything from an NPR reporter at the scene. Instead, NPR listeners would have heard history professors, retired diplomats, print reporters in Moscow, foreign reporters in Washington, and perhaps some people in the streets providing explanation, background, and reaction to the events we reported only secondhand. To add that special *ATC* touch, we might have gone to a travel agent to discuss how an ordinary American might plan a trip to Moscow— how much it would cost, where to stay, where to eat, what to see. We might have talked to the owner of a Russian restaurant about the food the president would eat, or to a doctor about how the president could combat jet lag and get ready for tough negotiating. We might have called someone in Moscow to find out what jokes were making the rounds in the Soviet Union or played the current top tune on the Soviet hit parade. We would have talked about the trip, but we would not have sent a reporter on the trip. I would have argued that an NPR reporter could not add anything unique to the coverage hordes of other media reporters would provide. Besides, we would not have had the money to send someone to Moscow. NPR would have made its unique contribution by adding "sidebars" to the story others reported.

The NPR of Frank Mankiewicz would have felt obligated to send a reporter whether it had the money or not.

In 1988, NPR foreign editor John McChesney wanted to send three staff. Three were not enough for Adam Powell, who proposed sending ten staff members at a cost of about $70 thousand. Till then a symbol of NPR's "news" emphasis, McChesney now felt outrage and told the *Washington Post*, "I said this is largely ceremonial. . . . It's a picture story and we don't have to spend that much money." He charged Powell with bringing a "TV sensibility" to all of NPR's coverage, a sensibility that had "nothing to do with what NPR is about."[5] Powell fired him. A polarizing figure himself in the NPR newsroom, McChesney became an instant martyr and hero.

Powell kicked McChesney out. Others were squeezed out. Ira Glass, for example, resigned to freelance in Chicago. Glass had started at NPR when he was eighteen. After eleven years, his imaginative features had come to epitomize the network's alternative nature. Under Powell, he experienced declining demand for his work. "It's a natural part of the aging process," he told the *Washington Post*. "At the beginning of a program, people feel free to fool around. Nobody says no. Five years ago, somebody like me without a deep voice had an easier time getting on the air."[6]

Staff discontent contributed to Powell's resignation in early 1989, but that in no way meant the staff regarded him as totally wrong. Many probably felt he went too far in trying to compete with commercial media on their own terms, but most also endorsed an enlarged capacity for covering news as it happened, and they expressed anger at Bennet for not providing the funding necessary to implement this expansive and expensive philosophy.[7] Chasing breaking news aggressively did cost a lot more money than a more laid-back approach. When the NPR news department saw itself as a provider of news interpretation and analysis drawn from journalistic and academic resources outside the NPR staff and of the occasional offbeat feature, it could get by with a moderate budget. Even Powell's most vociferous detractors agreed with his basic premise that NPR had become a primary news gatherer in competition with CNN, ABC, and the *New York Times*. By that standard, its budget was woefully inadequate.

Powell's successor, NPR insider Bill Buzenberg, was more popular as a personality among the staff, but his journalistic priorities were as expensive as those of his predecessor. While Powell emphasized pouring resources into covering the big story that everyone else covered, Buzenberg emphasized original unique reporting. That emphasis required just as much money—maybe more, because it meant building and maintaining a large infrastructure of reporters across the country and bureaus around the world. It required specialist reporters in economics, in health, medicine, labor, even religion. Each of these resources would not produce stories every day, but they assured that NPR would provide informed coverage on a variety of issues and would have a jump on the "big" stories because NPR reporters were paying attention to them when they were still small stories.

A foreign correspondent himself, Buzenberg cared particularly about establishing bureaus throughout the world, some twenty of them. That put NPR in the same league as CNN and represented a far greater commitment to foreign news gathering than the commercial television networks, which pretty much dismantled their expensive foreign bureau systems to save money to pay the salaries of celebrity news anchors and do wall-to-wall coverage of the latest domestic circus.[8] Even more than his predecessors, Buzenberg pushed for the resources necessary to meet almost unlimited demands of an aggressive news organization.[9] Members of the news staff were as demanding as, or more than, Buzenberg. They expressed frustration at "the subsistence budget" of the news department. To do the kind of job that they thought they should do, they insisted that their department needed a lot more money: money for more travel, money for more staff, and money for more bureaus. Few on the staff understood that Bennet had done an exceptional job for them on the budget. During each budget cycle, Bennet worked skillfully to squeeze more money out of the stations than they wanted to give to support NPR news. The NPR news budget grew as fast as station revenue, but the news staff was not satisfied with the same percentage growth as the rest of the public radio system. They could make a strong case that NPR news was essential to public radio's appeal. In simple return on investment terms, NPR news, they said, deserved special treatment.[10]

Most public radio stations accepted the Powell and Buzenberg hopes for the NPR news department. But they were not so enthusiastic about paying for it out of their own pockets. The conflict came to the fore when the news staff asked the NPR board to enact special assessments on stations to pay for news reporting unaffordable in the department's budget. The staff's first request was for an extra million dollars to allow more extensive coverage of the 1988 presidential election. What bothered me, as chairman of the board, was that the staff did not propose to use that extra money for coverage that was particularly distinctive nor that added anything to the political debate.[11] Rather, Siegel and Powell laid out a menu of events that started with sending reporters to the Iowa caucuses and culminated in an election night extravaganza, exactly what the television networks and every other major media outlet would do.

The board turned down the requested special assessment, but, in an effort at conciliation, we encouraged Bennet to seek the money from foundations or corporate underwriters for this special purpose, a major break with the concept of stations paying for the level of programming they want. The board's compromise also highlighted a different problem: underwriting grants earmarked for specific news coverage. Richard Salant, former president of CBS News and a member of the NPR board, prickled at the idea. Salant was concerned about foundations and corporations buying coverage in their areas of special concern, even for something as straightforward as coverage of national presidential elections. For Salant, the best policy was Nancy Reagan's "Just say, 'No.'"[12] NPR had an uncomfortable number of underwriters who had given funds to cover topics in their areas of interest. The German Marshall Fund of the United States had long supported coverage of Europe. The Joyce Foundation of Chicago supported Midwest coverage. Other funders staked out science, the environment, health, and religion. In theory, the concept of earmarked funding probably bothered Bill Buzenberg, too, even though he emphatically denied that such funding in any way influenced coverage. When covering an issue or event, he insisted, NPR was scrupulous not to consider the views of those paying the bill. Few doubted his sincerity on that point. Less clear was the influence of earmarked funding on the decision to provide special coverage of a topic in the first place.[13] Buzenberg and Bennet insisted that such decisions were made by staff irrespective of potential funding. Bennet explained that the news staff first decided what topics it wished to cover, and only then did the underwriting staff seek funders to pay for the coverage. Most important, the coverage would happen with or without specific funding. To make coverage contingent on receiving a grant would hand editorial decisions over to funding agencies, which was as unacceptable to Buzenberg and Bennet as it was to Salant.

In a sense, NPR was saying one thing to Salant and the public and something slightly different to the funders. Few, if any, foundations have a mandate to support public radio. Most have specific missions, such as "world understanding" or "environmental education." To get money out of any such organization, NPR needed to relate its programming to the organization's mission. For example, if an organization's purpose were to promote world understanding, NPR would need to convince the organization that its grant would somehow promote world understanding. NPR had to tell potential funders that their commitment to NPR would further the funders' ends, yet it was assuring Salant that the contributions had no editorial impact at all. No wonder Salant worried about funders controlling NPR's news coverage. NPR could not have it both ways.

Salant wanted underwriting for general support only. He did not want it tied to specific content, no matter how loosely. Bennet said such nonspecific funding was very hard to come by, and NPR could not afford to reject specific grants and would continue to pursue them. Salant resigned from the board in protest.[14] He had advocated underwriting more like the commercial advertising that had supported his operation at CBS news. The commercial advertisers with whom he was familiar were not interested in promoting CBS's coverage of particular subjects. They simply wanted to sell their products to CBS News's viewers and listeners. They did not demand coverage of specific topics. Rather, they demanded large numbers of viewers and listeners, and that demand had its own deleterious effect on content. The advertisers' voracious need for large audiences led programs on commercial radio and television to pander and sensationalize.

As time went on, underwriting on public radio came closer and closer to what Salant had wanted, that is, selling the audience to underwriters rather than the content. That, in turn, suggested pursuing audiences as aggressively as commercial broadcasters did. Happily, the audience NPR attracted and the audience NPR underwriters hoped to reach wanted quality coverage of important issues. To draw in more listeners of this type, NPR had to maintain or increase quality rather than water it down.

The issue surfaced again with the Gulf War of 1991. Buzenberg wanted enough reporters and technicians to cover the Gulf conflict in a way that would allow NPR news to show its stuff just like CNN.[15] To cover the war as a primary news gathering organization, NPR needed a lot of money fast. Aware that the board was unlikely to pass a special assessment on to the stations and stung by Salant's criticism of earmarked special interest funding, Buzenberg asked stations to make voluntary contributions to the special coverage. Some did. Some did not.

Wisconsin Public Radio paid its reasonable share, but, as head of the organization, I made the decision to do so reluctantly. My reluctance was more philosophical than monetary, although the two were closely related. I wondered if it mattered whether NPR sent squadrons to cover the actual fighting. NPR had provided a critical public service when it provided blanket coverage of the policy debate before the war. It broadcast complete live coverage of the congressional debate leading to the resolution authorizing President Bush's action. That debate proved interesting and important, as members of Congress wrestled with ideas, with issues, with options about which there were legitimate and important disagreements. NPR's debate coverage came at a time when people still had an opportunity to react, to influence the decision and the course of history. In broadcasting the debate and explaining the issues, NPR provided a critical public service that in my opinion defined public radio. And, it provided that service without spending much money.

Once the decision to invade was made, however, I thought NPR's unique role was over. Battle coverage might contain drama and human emotion but would not enhance public knowledge of the issues. Inevitably, covering the Gulf War recalled for me NPR covering the Vietnam War twenty years earlier during its infancy. NPR had no reporters in Vietnam and never felt the need for any. Television had the pictures. Most of what was said in Saigon we did not believe anyway. Instead of the war, NPR covered the debate about the war taking place in Congress, on campuses, and in the streets, a very different approach than NPR proposed to take in covering the Gulf War in 1991.

In contrast to NPR's nonpresence in Vietnam, its contingent covering the Gulf War was the largest of any radio news organization in the world. NPR's staff provided feeds and facilities to other news organizations. It provided primary coverage not only in America, but provided the primary coverage for radio worldwide. In the eyes of the journalism profession, NPR had made the big time. To its credit, NPR did not cheerlead for "our side" to the extent that most commercial broadcasters did, nor did it totally ignore the muted dissent that persisted back home. Nonetheless, its coverage was remarkably unquestioning compared to the tone of discussions of the war on local public radio call-in shows, including those on Wisconsin Public Radio. Listeners commented on the difference. Siegel later told me that a contingent within the NPR staff was as disappointed in NPR's choice as many of our listeners were. Some staff, he charged, wanted NPR to act as the voice of antiwar dissent. Siegel said he and, presumably, Buzenberg were not going to let that happen. They did not. *Morning Edition*'s Bob Edwards commented later that some listeners "expected us to take an antiwar stand and felt betrayed when we didn't." Buzenberg, himself, felt NPR played it straight. Its coverage, he said, was "skeptical but balanced."[16] And it probably was. Most listeners seemed as impressed with NPR's efforts as Buzenberg was proud. Listenership jumped 14 percent during the war, and did not decline noticeably afterward.[17] NPR's coverage brought new listeners to the network and kept them.[18]

The Gulf War coverage certified that NPR had accomplished one of the most important goals its original board set out for it, providing the highest quality broadcast journalism. Perhaps unintentionally, it also helped realize other goals that board enunciated, goals that seemed to excite the passions of those founding board members more than did the journalistic ones. To establish itself as the primary radio—perhaps the primary broadcast—source for news of the Gulf War, Buzenberg needed a lot more station airtime to approximate the continuous coverage CNN provided, coverage on which that cable network had built its reputation. Yet he had little money to produce many more hours of news programming. His answer was the simple call-in talk format, in which a host and an expert guest or two discuss what is going on and take phone calls from listeners to make their own observations or to ask questions of the guest. In effect, they created a nationwide conversation about the war involving individuals with special knowledge and expertise and ordinary people wherever they might be. The format provided the flexibility to bring in reporters when there were new developments to report, while continuing an interesting discussion when there were none.

Buzenberg and the other creators of this call-in were most interested in maximizing their on air hours about the Gulf War. They may or may not have been aware that they were implementing parts of the NPR mission that had largely fallen by the wayside. They were giving voice to ordinary people, not in a highly edited and produced documentary format but in a free and open format in which listeners may make comments both wise and ignorant. They were approximating the *vox populi* that the most articulate members of NPR's founding board advocated. They were tapping in to the intellectual resources of the colleges and universities for background expertise, realizing yet another founding board goal. While definitely a holdover from old-fashioned educational radio, putting professors in this live spontaneous format modernized that historic function, forcing the experts to interact with one another and with listeners rather than merely lecture. The whole experience democratized the elitism of educational radio while retaining the expertise of those who spent their lives studying these issues. Like local call-in programs on a handful of public radio stations around the country,[19] *Talk of the Nation* raised the level of the call-in format above the mindless sloganeering and faked outrage of Rush Limbaugh and his dittohead callers. Call-in radio could be educational, informative, and community building if conducted with the intent to be educational, informative, and community building rather than merely entertaining.

When the Gulf War coverage ended, the call-in program did not. It continued as *Talk of the Nation*, two hours a day of talk radio with the public-radio difference—an articulate, but essentially neutral and fair-minded host, academic, journalistic, and other qualified experts, articulate spokespersons for divergent points of view, all interacting with one another and with listeners who more often than not have something to say that is worth hearing. Such a feedback loop from listeners demonstrated what had formerly been a hunch, that the fair-minded and intelligent approach of public radio attracted equally fair-minded and intelligent callers. Inviting those listeners into the conversation did not seriously lower the level of the discussion, but did offer opportunities for surprises, thoughtful questions, and a sense of community. *Talk of the Nation* put NPR's imprimatur and respectability on an approach to radio disdained by traditional educational broadcasters and traditional journalists, launching a wave of such programming at larger public radio stations across the country, a format now almost as essential to public radio as news and classical music.

CHAPTER 11

Marketplace

Public radio bit into the fruit of the tree of knowledge when it opened the cover of *Audience 88*. We had long known that the few listeners educational radio attracted were very well educated (and probably pretty well-off financially). When educational radio morphed into public radio, it reasserted educational radio's original goal to serve everyone or, as Siemering envisioned it, to create a meeting place for diverse people, educated or not, black or white, rich or poor, liberal or conservative—a place where all could feel welcome and comfortable. This happy dogma allowed public radio to move ahead with a sense of idealism and purpose, even as we suspected that the listeners we attracted were pretty much like us and like those who had previously listened to educational radio. We *suspected* that fact about our listeners, but we did not *know* it. Until we read *Audience 88*, we could hope our efforts to produce programming that had a less academic and more inclusive and egalitarian tone actually would attract a more diverse group of listeners.

Through the 1970s and early 1980s, the commercial rating services reported that the public radio audience grew, but they did not profile the listeners. Given the locations where public radio's audience was largest—Boston, Washington, the San Francisco Bay area, and university towns like Madison, Columbus, and Austin—one could assume public radio did best in communities with high education levels. For the most part,

---

Author's Note: I participated in these events as NPR board chairman during the period in which American Public Radio threatened to sue National Public Radio.

public radio staffers paid little attention to their audience's profile, but in their hearts most understood that public radio listening and education went hand-in-hand. From time to time, when they addressed public radio's elite demographics, staffers expressed some embarrassment and used anecdotes about listeners who were cross-country truckers or farmers in their barns to counter the impression that public radio was somehow elitist and added a vow to broaden our appeal in some vague way in the future.

Research guru David Giovannoni argued in the early 1980s that public radio should absolve itself of guilt over the nature of its audience. He declared that a well-educated audience was not an embarrassment. Rather, it signaled public radio's success! This declaration began the transition that his *Audience 88* project sealed later in the decade. Giovannoni argued that public radio sought to present intelligent programming, that intelligent programming appealed to intelligent people, and that, therefore, the surest sign of a program's intelligence is the degree to which it appeals to intelligent people. He said that definitions of quality proclaimed by producers were arbitrary. Musicians, for example, may think they recognize quality music, and journalists may think they understand quality journalism, but the final test of quality, he said, is not the producer's judgement but the verdict of intelligent listeners. According to Giovannoni, whatever programming an intelligent audience chose, was by definition, intelligent programming.

With that hypothesis he turned Lord Reith's and traditional educational broadcasters' theory of public-service broadcasting upside down. They had believed that they should decide what was good for the public, choose quality material, and elevate the audience. They were the professors; the listeners their students. They selected the curriculum. Giovannoni said public radio practitioners should follow, not lead, their audience. Their audience was capable of identifying quality programs. According to Giovannoni, broadcasters could use their creativity and knowledge to produce programs they *thought* were intelligent, but they could not *know* the programs were intelligent until intelligent people certified them as such by becoming enthusiastic listeners.

Having proposed this controversial hypothesis, Giovannoni "operationalized" his definition of intelligent people by equating them with highly educated people. That leap escalated the controversy. Even Siemering had argued that public radio would appeal to intelligent people, but he never equated intelligence with education. Giovannoni knew that intelligence and education were not synonymous, but he could quantify educational levels without administering IQ tests to listeners to measure intelligence—if, indeed, such tests really did measure intelligence. At minimum, he argued that it was fair to conclude that a program's strong appeal to highly educated people meant that it met the expectations of the most academically sophisticated people in the country, whatever their native intelligence. Giovannoni's definition of quality was too heretical to public radio practitioners to mention outside of public radio circles, but in their hearts, most probably accepted it. If they did not, they would have produced programming that appealed to a different demographic.

All of this controversy preceded *Audience* 88. That document told public radio practitioners that listeners' level of education alone did not predict loyalty to public radio. Passionate listeners were a minority of highly educated people classified as "inner directed" and "societally conscious" in their "Values and Lifestyles." The larger group of highly educated people, those the VALS system labeled "achievers," listened to public radio more than most Americans, but less often than the smaller group of highly educated people labeled "societally conscious." "Achievers" measured success by our society's general standard, accumulating wealth and spending it conspicuously. "Societally conscious" persons placed a higher value on nonmonetary achievements. They thought more about the common good.

Having learned that societally-conscious people loved public radio, public radio embraced the societally conscious. *Audience* 88 showed public radio that a majority of those in the societally-conscious psychographic did not yet listen and that it had lots of room to grow within the psychographic that already found it most appealing. Public radio saw that to build its listenership it could continue doing what it was doing and wait for other people with public-radio values to discover NPR and their local public radio station. Audience building demanded no great change. It meant doing what public radio would most comfortably have done anyway, but once public radio knew to whom it appealed, it was impossible not to keep that audience in mind as it made decisions. Even those put off by Giovannoni's argument that the quality of the audience measures the quality of the programming knew that a successful public radio program must resonate with inner-directed societally conscious listeners to succeed.

Audience 88 research findings help explain the evolution of another public radio mainstay, the program *Marketplace*, a "business" program distributed by the Minnesota-based network known first as American

Public Radio, then as Public Radio International. Bill Kling's Minnesota Public Radio came up with the concept of a public radio business program in the mid-1980s.[1] Public television had had success with such a program. Kling knew that public radio listeners tended to have higher than average incomes and might, therefore, have an interest in maximizing those incomes through knowledgeable investing. Kling knew, too, that financial services companies were anxious to deliver their messages to people with money. Moreover, the business people with whom Kling associated in Minnesota, those from whom he solicited financial support, and those he invited to serve the boards of Minnesota Public Radio and American Public Radio, were, not surprisingly, interested in business issues. No topic seems less congruent with Siemering's vision than "business," but Bill Kling and his network had a more "corporate" view of public broadcasting than Siemering or Mankiewicz or Bennet.

The Minnesota network made two attempts at creating a business program for public radio. Neither went well. Kling first contracted with a cable television business network. He asked that organization to translate its television reporting into a nightly half hour of business programming for radio. The program had not found its legs before its parent business-news organization folded. Kling turned next to a proven producer of economic news for radio, CBS News, to produce a daily public radio business show. If a business program in general marked a real departure from the initial values of public radio, a commercial radio network producing the program represented a total capitulation to alien values. I was not a fan of the idea. Others were not fans of the product. Not surprisingly, the CBS produced program sounded and felt "commercial" in a vague but unmistakable way. The announcing style said commercial radio. The information was stiff and impersonal, focusing on numbers, not on people or ideas. The tone lacked sensitivity and wit. Kling was about to learn the same lesson Frank Mankiewicz learned when he hired excellent commercial broadcasters to produce *Morning Edition*. Public radio loyalists did not like the result. Public radio program directors, who, *Audience 88* told us, closely resemble public radio listeners, did not like it either.

Audience 88 could have predicted the failure. In "values and lifestyles" terms, the business show aimed to serve well-educated "achievers." The core public radio listener, as we have seen, shares a high education level with these achievers, but not all of their values. Public radio's inner-directed societally conscious listeners put less importance on making money than they did on the other values that underpinned NPR programming.

The failure of the second program convinced APR leadership that public radio differs from commercial radio in more than its lack of commercials. Its third attempt came from within the public radio family, and people who understood and shared their listeners' values designed it. The network turned to Rick Lewis, a former *All Things Considered* producer then managing the public radio station in Long Beach, California. Long Beach is a long way from Wall Street and a peculiar choice as the locale of a national business program, but for public radio, a business show could not be a Wall Street show. To take charge of the project, Lewis and APR chose Jim Russell, another former producer of *ATC*.

Lewis and Russell created *Marketplace*, an unmistakably public radio program with a flair commercial producers could not capture nor even understand. The program proved that a show could sound "public radio" without duplicating the NPR news magazines. Its pace was faster and its tone less reverent than the NPR news magazines. It had some of the attitude and sense of audio Russell had brought to the early *ATC*. It nicely combined public affairs and human affairs, the terms Russell had used for the two facets that, ideally, would comprise *ATC*. It buried "the numbers" in the middle of the program instead of featuring them at the beginning. Russell knew public radio listeners. Of course, Russell's colleagues from the original staff of *ATC* would look down on business as subject worthy of consideration, but Russell described *Marketplace* as about more than just business. It was as much about the marketplace of ideas as about the daily ins and outs of the economic marketplace. It was more about people than it was about statistics. After all, the marketplaces of the old world involved social and political interactions as much as they did financial transactions. A program that viewed the marketplace so broadly put business in a public radio context.

Marketplace differed from the NPR news magazines in its funding structure. NPR's budget came largely from station payments with a small amount from corporate and foundation underwriting. *Marketplace* flipped that proportion. A major underwriting commitment from General Electric, the world's most successful corporate conglomerate, made the program possible. General Electric is the same corporation that funded Ronald Reagan's television appearances prior to his presidential candidacy and that sponsored the *McLaughlin Group* television shout show. One can only speculate about GE's motive for funding *Market-place*. Perhaps GE wished to encourage a program that treated business seriously on a radio system perceived as antibusiness or, at minimum, not a business. Perhaps GE hoped to build goodwill among people who might view the major defense and nuclear power corporation with suspicion. Or perhaps GE just wanted to sell light bulbs. In a most "un–pubic radio" fashion, the *Marketplace* theme music incorporated the GE jingle, "GE, we bring good things to life." And, if that wasn't disturbing enough for public radio listeners, APR accepted funding from Japanese interests to pay for *Marketplace*'s coverage of Japan's and Asia's economies.

Those who, like Kling, were intent on shifting the system from its reliance on tax support to private funding took particular pleasure in *Marketplace*'s success. Not only was it funded corporately at the national level, it attracted financially oriented underwriting at the local level. No program was easier to "sell" at premium prices than *Market-place*. In fact, this ability to pay for itself locally through underwriting virtually assured its widespread carriage on public radio stations.

APR's next step in business news provoked a reaction from NPR that placed competition over logic, not unlike Frank Mankiewicz's ill-advised decision to create the *NPR Plus* classical music service in response to Bill Kling's proposal for a twenty-four-hour-a-day classical music service in 1982. APR created nine-minute *Marketplace* segments for broadcast during the last ten minutes of each hour in NPR's *Morning Edition*. Recall that *Morning Edition* had been designed so stations could insert local material into the NPR program. NPR failed to anticipate competitors creating nine-minute programs that would neatly cover up segments of *Morning Edition* and take advantage of the large audience the NPR program attracted. The morning *Marketplace* segments quickly caught NPR's attention, particularly the attention of news vice president Bill Buzenberg. He complained that the casual listener might assume that these segments came from NPR and that NPR had no control over their quality. NPR responded by expanding its own business coverage and creating its own nine-minute business segment at exactly the time that APR fed the *Marketplace* segments. To make room, *Morning Edition* dumped the arts segment that had closed each hour, the pride of the program's original producer, Jay Kernis. NPR should have recognized the symbolism of dumping the daily arts segments for reports about the latest ups and downs of the Tokyo stock market, but its new president did not. In 1993, former phone company executive Delano Lewis became president of NPR. The board hired Lewis when Doug Bennet left to join the Clinton administration and gave Lewis orders to make NPR more like a business and to raise more of NPR's budget from underwriting and entrepreneurship and less from the NPR member stations.[2] Lewis understood his orders. From this point of view, dumping the daily arts segments for business news was a wise move. Underwriters lined up to fund this business segment as they had not for the arts segment. Businesses, particularly financial organizations, wanted an association with business reporting on public radio. Of course, NPR had never offered the arts segment for separate underwriting.

No one who had read *Audience* 88 should have been surprised when NPR's own research found that the inner-directed societally conscious psychographic at the core of public radio listenership put a low premium on these business segments. As a result, NPR backpedaled and dumped its morning business reports, opening the last ten minutes of *Morning Edition* to features on any topic, including business or the arts. It left in place, however, the special underwriting credits identifying funders for NPR business coverage, but without the business coverage itself, perhaps the best of both worlds.[3]

Public radio's newfound focus on business news reflected the interests of Bill Kling's Minnesota Public Radio, both in the sense that MPR initiated these efforts and in the sense that MPR has a different history from most public radio stations created by colleges and universities. National Public Radio grew out of those university-based stations with funding from the federal government and leadership from the Corporation for Public Broadcasting. Minnesota Public Radio is the creation of one person, Bill Kling, with mostly private money from the business and philanthropic elite of Minneapolis and St. Paul. MPR's financing depended on an enlightened Minnesota variety of socially responsible, even liberal, business leaders. MPR stands for private enterprise in a system built on governmental institutions.

Bill Kling disdained traditional institutional educational radio, but programmed his stations just as conservatively as those traditional educational stations. Kling sought a statewide network like that built by neighboring Wisconsin's state government before educational radio became public radio, and in many ways, his MPR would resemble Wisconsin's. He chose announcers for their fine, intimate, "FM" voices that had characterized Wisconsin's network. He gave Minnesota Public

Radio an on-air sound that mimicked his own voice: quiet, well modulated, reasonable, soothing. He made classical music and serious news his network's mainstays. Of course, he did not clutter his network with remnants of traditional farm and homemaker programs, college lectures, or school programs. With the exception of morning host Garrison Keillor, Kling's announcers were interchangeable, each suggesting an impeccable knowledge of and respect for their material, whether it was news or classical music. To some outsiders, it seemed a bit sterile, a bit haughty for the Midwest, but many in Minnesota came to cherish it.

Minnesota Public Radio began at St. John's University, a private Catholic institution in Collegeville, Minnesota. Kling managed the student radio station there. After graduating, he attended graduate school in Boston, home of the WGBH Educational Foundation, the country's leading public broadcast organization. It had close ties to Boston's educational and cultural elite and was supported by private wealth and business philanthropy more than by government. Kling returned to Minnesota after graduate school to build an institution for public radio much like what WGBH built for public television. Literally tall, dark, and handsome, Kling used his well-modulated voice and quiet, earnest style to ingratiate himself not only with the administrators at St. John's but with heads of other educational institutions and influential leaders throughout Minnesota. He commanded their support and convinced them to join the board of directors of the organization that became Minnesota Public Radio. He cut deals with private colleges and universities to "sponsor" regional stations throughout the state for which MPR— not the educational institution—would hold the license and exercise control.

Even though he ran a private enterprise, Kling took full advantage of federal and state government money that did not compromise his independence and total control. In fact, he often shaped the grant programs at the state and national level and then turned around and took full advantage of them. One such grant allowed him to move his headquarters from Collegeville in central Minnesota to a recycled building in downtown St. Paul.

Kling's aggressive approach did not endear him to his public radio colleagues in Minnesota. The University of Minnesota's old-line AM radio station in the Twin Cities, KUOM, was caught off guard when Kling built his first two stations in 1967, the same year President Johnson signed the Public Broadcasting Act. KSJR was on the St. John's campus in Collegeville, but Kling's second station was in a Twin Cities suburb, right in KUOM's backyard, on a frequency that by all logic should have gone to the university had it bothered to apply for it. Awakening to the threat after it was too late, the university decided to apply for its own FM license. Consulting engineers told KUOM that in the Twin Cities a high-power FM station was possible on only one educational frequency in the FM band, 91.7; Kling's KSJN at 91.1 was close enough to 91.7 to cause interference. The engineers offered a simple solution: KSJN could move over one channel to 90.9.[4] The university asked Kling to make the small shift in frequency. Kling declined. For three years they negotiated. The university promised to pay all costs involved. It then went to the Federal Communications Commission, which sided with Kling. The university might have pursued the matter in the courts, but by then Kling's radio stations and public relations effort had won many friends and the university gave up. Confined to part-time AM operation in an increasingly FM era, KUOM steadily declined, and the university ultimately gave it to students to play rock and roll. An educational-radio pioneer, second only to Wisconsin in the length and breadth of its heritage, KUOM fell victim to a new kind of public broadcasting entrepreneur. If it had been more dynamic and forward looking, the university could easily have claimed the Twin Cities frequency long before Kling came along. That the university had not taken advantage of the opportunity was all the more proof to Kling that public radio had little future if left to the initiative of educational institutions rather than the entrepreneurship of people like him. Thus, Kling launched his empire—and his unpopularity among more traditional public radio colleagues.

Nor was Kling popular at NPR. Don Quayle perceived him as a threat. Lee Frischknecht suffered public attacks on his presidency from Kling, who teamed with Bornstein to overthrow him. Frank Mankiewicz divided the world into friends and foes, and Kling was his worst foe. At the height of NPR's financial crisis, Mankiewicz publicly labeled Kling as Darth Vader. While milder in manner, Doug Bennet was no less a political fighter than Mankiewicz and resented Kling no less than his predecessor. Relations hit bottom when American Public Radio, still dominated by Kling, threatened to sue NPR under Federal antitrust laws if NPR continued to require stations to pay for its entire array of programs to use any, the central tenant of the 1985 Bennet–Mullally business plan.[5]

"Of all the laws I have considered breaking," I told a group of East

Coast station managers, "antitrust was never one of them." Yet, as chairman of the board of National Public Radio, I found myself meeting with antitrust lawyers after APR made its legal threats to force NPR to allow stations to buy just the programs they wanted without paying for the programs they did not want. Bennet feared—and NPR's critics believed—that a market system would support only two NPR offerings, *Morning Edition* and *All Things Considered*. No cultural program enjoyed much acceptance. A true marketplace might wipe out the entire cultural programming department. Understandably, Bennet wanted everything to survive.

APR would obviously benefit if NPR unbundled its program offerings. Unlike Bennet, I thought NPR could benefit as well. Forcing all stations to pay for all programming limited NPR's ability to offer new programs, since each addition raised the price of the total package for everyone even though the new programs might only interest some stations. NPR's reluctance to face stations' ire at a price hike translated into a reluctance to add new programs. Moreover, the single package approach discouraged multiple public stations in individual communities from differentiating themselves by buying different programs from NPR. Ultimately, I thought, what Kling proposed was probably in the interest of NPR as well as APR.[6] After two years of wrangling, enough public radio stations supported the National Public Radio board's vote to "unbundle" its program offerings and to create something closer to a free market in public radio programming. Of course, the NPR news programs had become so identified with public radio through their many years of protected status that stations had little choice but to buy them at whatever price NPR charged. Whatever money was left over might buy other programs from NPR or from American Public Radio, soon to change its name to Public Radio International.

What was bothersome about Kling's campaign to unbundle NPR programming was the heavy-handed, legalistic way he went about it. It seemed ludicrous that the authors of federal antitrust legislation designed to break up John D. Rockefeller's Standard Oil monopoly wanted their legislation to apply to a not-for-profit organization providing noncommercial radio programs to its member stations. Public radio was a public service, not a business. Bill Kling, of course, assumed it was both, and he enjoyed great success as a provider of public service and as a businessman.

MPR struck gold with tee-shirts and other paraphernalia related to its national hit, *A Prairie Home Companion*. It started marketing the items through a small catalogue mentioned on the air during *APHC* broadcasts. The small catalogue proved successful, so MPR turned it into *Wireless,* a large catalogue selling an array of items with appeal to a public radio demographic. Broadening its clientele beyond Garrison Keillor fans, MPR bought mailing lists and blanketed potential customers across the country with catalogues. The direct-mail retailing business became so profitable that it jeopardized MPR's not-for-profit tax status. Consequently, Kling created a holding company, the Minnesota Communications Group, with both for-profit and not-for-profit subsidiaries. Income from its Green Spring for-profit subsidiary helped finance its Minnesota Public Radio not-for-profit subsidiary. By the early '90s, Green Spring operated one of the largest catalogue businesses in the country and generated several million dollars a year in profit to support MPR.[7]

In 1998, Minnesota Communication Group sold its catalogue to the Dayton Hudson department store giant for over $100 million. Most of the proceeds went into an endowment for MPR, but Kling invested $10 million as capital for developing new activities, most notably on the Internet and in Los Angeles, where he bought a marginal college station and the LA-based *Marketplace* operation of Jim Russell. Kling poured in resources to make his West Coast operation as important to its community and the nation as his Minnesota home base. The demographics/psychographics of southern California were nowhere near as favorable for public radio as in the Twin Cities, but just on the basis of size alone the LA market included hundreds of thousands of potential public radio listeners. To keep up with Kling, National Public Radio, built a Los Angeles facility and relocated a significant portion of its staff to LA-LA Land, where superficial and materialistic values are the antitheses of those of Bill Siemering, of state universities of the Midwest, of power- and policy-obsessed Washington, DC, or of high-brow–cultured New York or Boston.

Of course, Kling and other top executives received several million dollars personally from the catalogue sale, "an appropriate return" for their contribution to this "unique experiment in social purpose capitalism."[8] In 1998, one could become a millionaire in public radio! Kling filled his colleagues in public radio with a combination of admiration, envy, and revulsion. They could not help but respect what he had built and, in many cases, tried to emulate what he had done. At the same time, many perceived his empire as selling out public radio's noncommercial values. MPR seemed as "corporate" as any insurance company and displayed the same bottom-line mentality of any other business. In reality, however, separating its for-profit business activities from its not-for-profit activities insulated Minnesota's public radio service from the marketplace more than any other public radio organization. Subsidized first by millions of dollars from its catalogue business and then by the $100 million endowment, Minnesota Public Radio enjoyed a far richer and more secure existence than any government or university funding source could provide.[9]

The business-generated endowment provided MPR a degree of independence from listener support and underwriting revenue and whatever corrupting influences they might imply. Listener support and underwriting did provide important amounts of revenue, however, and MPR paid as much attention to the size and demographics of its audience as anyone. It built a most sophisticated and effective machine for extracting listener and underwriting support.[10] Still, the subsidies provided by its for-profit enterprises ensured both a more generous and a more secure budget than found in other places. In a sense, except for the source of its funding, MPR came to resemble the fully-subsidized BBC and the fully-subsidized educational radio of old.

Ironically, therefore, Bill Kling came to symbolize entrepreneurial success as well as public radio's most traditional noncommercial values. His success in the marketplace of commerce provided a subsidy that insulated Minnesota Public Radio from the marketplace of public radio. When the MPR staff invited audience-building guru David Giovannoni to St. Paul, his presentation incited Kling to send a 1997 New Year's message to his staff and to select managers across the country. Kling's message questioned the appropriateness of Giovannoni's commitment to pleasing public radio listeners. Despairing of the trend he saw across the country, Kling reaffirmed his commitment to "quality" programming rather than popular programming. As surely as the BBC's Lord Reith, Kling defended imposing his own standards of quality over the public radio listeners' standard of quality. He said that fewer people might listen to programming he defined as quality, but that those who did listen would appreciate it more and would likely show their appreciation more through contributions. Unlike Giovannoni, Kling assumed that there was a difference between audience preferences and his view of "quality" programming.[11] Unlike most of his colleagues, Kling could afford to take the high road of paying less attention to audience definitions of quality than to his own definition. On the other hand, most others in public radio had come to understand that Kling's high road led to exactly the same place as the research and audience-centered low road, since public radio programmers—including Bill Kling—shared the same definition of quality as public radio listeners. The dichotomy between "audience" and "quality" had become a non-issue in practical terms, but that did not prevent the public radio community from debating it for many years to come.

PART THREE

Critics

CHAPTER 12

Critics on the Right

We have no reason to believe that Richard Nixon ever heard, or even heard of, public radio when he occupied the White House. Neither had most people. Only 2.2 million people in the entire country listened to public radio in 1971, the third year of Nixon's presidency and the first year of *All Things Considered*.[1] Nixon's staff never explained why the administration denied NPR space in the White House press room, but it is just as likely that they regarded the little network as too insignificant to occupy any coveted space in the executive mansion as that they regarded public radio as an "enemy."[2]

Richard Nixon, however, definitely believed that he had legitimate reasons for regarding public television as an enemy, an enemy he wanted to punish. Nixon hated the press in general and public television in particular. Public television's funding came from the Ford Foundation, headed by Kennedy/Johnson advisor and former Harvard dean McGeorge Bundy. Its leaders were educators, intellectuals, and blue-bloods congregated in Boston at WGBH Television. WGBH sat just down the road from Harvard and MIT. Nixon despised the Eastern liberal establishment, and he saw public television as its demon offspring. If Nixon loathed "the liberal media," he loathed public television most of all.

To justify his hatred, Nixon could point to public television's hiring of Robin McNeil and Sander Vanocur as its lead public affairs anchors. A Canadian, McNeil's work at Britain's BBC was very critical of the Vietnam War. Sander Vanocur, an NBC correspondent, was extremely close to the Kennedy family. As a questioner in one of the 1960 Kennedy/Nixon debates, Vanocur had lobbed a particularly loaded question at candidate Nixon. Even had he not been paranoid, Nixon would have had good reason to perceive public television as hostile to him and to the constituencies that elected him.

Conceived at the end of the Johnson administration but born in the Nixon administration, public television struggled for its first breaths with the hands of the president of the United States firmly around its throat. He might have killed it, but stunted it instead. In 1972, Nixon vetoed funding for the Corporation for Public Broadcasting and forced public television to reconstruct itself before he would reconsider.[3] Of course, the public affairs unit that hired Vanocur and McNeil had to go. So did the top leadership of the Corporation for Public Broadcasting. More importantly in the long term, public television restructured its network, PBS, to give the local public television stations rather than the centralized leadership at either CPB or PBS power over national programming. Most federal money would pass through CPB directly to local television stations rather than to producers of national programs such as the entity that hired McNeil and Vanocur. Recalling the Carnegie Commission recommendation to build the public television system on "the bedrock of localism," the new arrangement gave local stations control of the purse strings for national programming and the mandate to focus on local programming, especially educational or cultural.

A matching formula instituted under Nixon limited the level of federal support, assuring that CPB would never provide the primary source of money for public television. The formula made the federal appropriation just a supplement to nonfederal funding. Under the matching arrangement, the federal government would reward public broadcasting with, at most, one dollar of federal money for every three dollars of nonfederal money the system could raise. The federal government would provide a maximum 25 percent of public broadcasting's money. In reality, it would provide less.

Just as it had ridden in the wake of public television to get federal support, public radio rode in the wake of public television as Nixon dealt out punishment. Very underdeveloped compared to public television, public radio was in greater peril than public television from Nixon's onslaught just after its birth. The matching-funds concept would have drastically cut public radio's revenue because public radio had attracted far fewer nonfederal financial resources than had public television. Public radio existed as a national institution only because of federal money. Over the protests of public television, CPB limited the damage to public radio by essentially providing it with more money than it would "deserve" under a strict one-for-three matching formula. CPB would divert some of the money "earned" by public television under the matching formula to public radio. Coincidentally, NPR's first president, Don Quayle, was the vice president at CPB who made these allocations.

Public radio was lucky, too, that CPB continued to fund NPR directly rather than impose the "all money to the stations" dictum of the Nixon administration. After the 1983 financial crisis, public radio would adopt the television model, but in the crucial decade preceding that, National Public Radio had the opportunity to orchestrate its programs and fine-tune its sound. By the time public radio stations gained control of the money and could choose the programs to buy from NPR, they had to choose *All Things Considered* and *Morning Edition* because those programs had attained such a level of quality that their audiences demanded them.

Ironically, if the president or the president's men had actually listened to National Public Radio, they would have found the programming no more to their liking than that of PBS. With the possible exception of a few engineers, NPR's staff, to a person, disliked Nixon and hated the war he failed to end. While not consciously skewed, the program content undoubtedly reflected this antipathy. Following the "not just another microphone at the press conference" philosophy, the young NPR gave less emphasis to mainstream news widely covered elsewhere and more to alternative views less frequently covered. Emphasizing the debate about the war rather than the war itself, NPR probably provided more time to critics of the administration than mainstream media. NPR was a sympathetic haven for opposition views.

It was not just the war coverage that the administration would not have liked, however. NPR followed the lead of its hometown newspaper, the *Washington Post*, in tracking the slow unraveling of the scandal that became known as Watergate. The *Post* pursued the story during the 1972 election year, and NPR reported the *Post*'s findings. Other media did not pay anywhere near as much attention until after Nixon was safely inaugurated for his second term and the Congress and the legal system began their pursuit of the president. The Siemering philosophy of diversity and multiculturalism (before either word came into vogue) turned a sympathetic ear to covering the lives and opinions of minorities, few of whom regarded the Nixon administration as their friend. Contributions from campus-based member stations were likely to reflect the attitudes of the campuses at the time, pro–civil rights, antiwar, antiestablishment, and more open than most of the population—certainly more open than the Nixon administration—to sex, drugs, and rock and roll. Tied closely to those campuses, National Public Radio and its staff shared many of their attitudes. But as far as anyone can tell, Nixon never heard what was going on three blocks north of the White House at NPR headquarters,1625 Eye Street NW.

The Ford and Carter years gave public broadcasting a six-year respite from government criticism and retribution. Of course, after Nixon, public television provided fewer reasons for conservatives to take offense. Ronald Reagan's election as president in 1980 began a second round of attacks, but this time the attacks were more philosophical and financial than political. Reagan did not share Nixon's hatred of public television, he simply did not want the federal government paying for it. Nixon wanted to axe federal funding for public television to control its content; Reagan sought to reduce—ideally eliminate—federal funding for ideological reasons. Reagan's conservative faith in free markets excluded any role for a government-funded broadcasting alternative. To a true free-market conservative, public broadcasting could justify its existence only if it could convince enough private organizations or individuals to *voluntarily* pay for the service, the same test applied to any other business.

The historical context of public-service broadcasting made the conservative view perfectly understandable. The call for noncommercial alternative media began in the progressive movement, which explicitly rejected the wisdom of unregulated markets. Free markets, progressives said, do not necessarily provide everything the public needs, and particularly everything the community as a whole needs as opposed to the perceived needs of individuals. Free markets do not necessarily serve the public interest. The 1967 public broadcasting legislation crowned Lyndon Johnson's activist Great Society agenda. The Great Society assumed an interventionist government that sought and promoted "the public interest." It defined that "public interest" as removed from the marketplace. In fact, it defied and interfered with the free market. Under the rubric of the Great Society, government took responsibility for the health care of the elderly and the poor, care that the free market would likely limit. Similarly, it ensured that those who lacked economic resources have access to a good education. It decried discrimination by race, sex, and age even when the free market supported it. And the Great Society defied the free market in broadcasting by creating public broadcasting to provide what the marketplace did not.

Those who, like members of the Reagan administration, believe that what happens in the marketplace is always right found such a broadcasting system unnecessary, even dangerous. Philosophically, the Reagan administration could not support government-subsidized broadcasting. Politically, it settled for merely reducing federal support and encouraging public broadcasting to seek voluntary support elsewhere.

Reagan persuaded Congress to rescind—take back—20 percent of the federal appropriation for public broadcasting in the 1983 fiscal year. Since the federal appropriation accounted for only 20 percent of public broadcasting's total revenue, a 20 percent reduction would not prove fatal or even crippling, except for National Public Radio. NPR received nearly 100 percent of its budget from CPB and would sustain a full 20 percent cut. NPR's plight was unique in the public broadcasting system. All other parts of public broadcasting took much smaller cuts and easily replaced them by successfully chasing the carrot the Reagan administration dangled in front of them. The administration encouraged public broadcasters to seek private support, particularly underwriting or even advertising support. It authorized some stations to experiment with commercial advertising, an offer some major-market television stations with large audience bases accepted. Public radio did not chase that carrot, partly for philosophical reasons, partly because most stations—unlike the largest public television stations—were based in universities unaccustomed to thinking commercially, but mostly because public radio audiences were perceived as too small to generate much revenue from advertisers. Public radio did use more liberal guidelines on "underwriting," announcements that name and describe donors without asking listeners to actually patronize them. These guidelines allowed underwriters to provide more information than their name and address, thus making underwriting more commercially desirable and making flat-out advertising unnecessary.

The primary impact of the Reagan cuts on public radio stations, however, was not on underwriting revenue but on listener donations. Public radio stations anticipated a long-term reduction in federal support, the primary source of nonuniversity money for many of them. Stations that had previously not asked for listener support, or who had done so only half-heartedly, suddenly became serious about it. For example, Wisconsin Public Radio never asked listeners for money prior to 1979 and emphasized that contributions merely "supplemented" its core budget from the state, university, and federal governments. In 1982, however, WPR responded immediately to Reagan's rescission by proclaiming a "Seven Days in May" emergency fund-drive. That drive raised far more money than was necessary to cover the reductions and showed those of us in management that scores of listeners would send us money if only we asked effectively and plausibly.

In my opinion, listeners responded because they genuinely valued public radio and did not want to see it hurt but also because they wanted to protest against the Reagan philosophy. The administration was cutting many programs besides public broadcasting, some of them more important than public broadcasting. The type of person most likely to listen to, and identify with, public radio was deeply disturbed by Reagan's actions and contributed to public radio to object to them. Calling in a pledge to public radio was not only a way to preserve a valued service, it was a way to make a political statement. A listener might not be able to do much about cuts in food-stamp programs, but he or she could do something about cuts in public broadcasting by making a simple phone call. Some purists declined to give because they felt that the government should support public broadcasting and that calling in a pledge would give Reagan exactly what he wanted. Most, however, were more pragmatic.

Ultimately, public television's "experiment" with advertising ended. The free-marketeers in the administration, however, did win a victory in public radio. They stimulated public radio stations to far more aggressively raise money from listeners and underwriters. Again, National Public Radio was the exception. Its member stations jealously guarded the income from their local listeners and prohibited NPR from going directly to the stations' listeners for contributions. This restriction proved a real sore point for NPR staff members who were convinced, correctly, that their efforts were the primary reason listeners sent money to public radio stations. Nonetheless, NPR agreed that stations alone would collect listener money and might use it, in part, to pay for programming and other services from NPR. NPR was free to make its first serious effort to raise underwriting dollars, but the noncommercial sensibilities of its president during the latter Reagan years, Doug Bennet, and of most others at NPR inhibited efforts to tap what would eventually become a lucrative source of income for the network.

While the Reagan administration waged a philosophic attack on government-subsidized public broadcasting, other individuals renewed the old Nixon-like attacks on public broadcasting content, except now they targeted public radio's content as much as television's, a backhanded compliment to public radio's growth. An organization called

Accuracy in Media, run by reformed '60s radical David Horowitz, led a campaign to portray public radio and television as biased to the left. This view became accepted dogma among right-wing ideologues as more and more of them became aware of public radio's existence.

Those critics met with more sympathy from within NPR than some might have expected. NPR News vice president Robert Siegal asked rhetorically at the time if NPR's news coverage was "describing the America that elected Ronald Reagan?"[4] One must assume that he would not have raised the question if the answer were a clear "yes." NPR rightly dismissed *AIM* and Horowitz as paid mouthpieces of right-wing foundations and interests, but in 1986 an article in *The New Republic*, a respected mainstream publication, made the same accusation. Bennet and Siegal paid attention.

Fred Barnes wrote "All Things Distorted," in which he charged that NPR's news coverage was "palpably slanted."[5] While citing Cokie Roberts, Nina Totenberg, and Linda Wertheimer as "fine reporters," Barnes found their excellent work offset by "lengthy background pieces, cultural reports, interviews by anchors, and commentaries" in which "the left wing agenda dominates. NPR devotes lavish coverage to human rights abuses and other sins of the Nicaraguan *contras* while all but ignoring the abuses by the Sandinista regime. Dark stories about a resurgent ultra-right in America get high priority, as do pieces on radical feminism and homosexual rights." Barnes detected a pattern of bias in the way NPR "labeled" those whom it interviewed or quoted. Conservatives, he said, were dubbed "ultraconservatives"; liberals, "activists." A liberal organization was "a Washington think tank" or a "public interest organization"; a similar group leaning right, a "conservative think tank" or worse, a "right wing think tank."[6]

Barnes was particularly critical of NPR's Central American coverage, which he found consistently at odds with Reagan administration policies. He suggested that the receipt of special-foundation funding— the type of funding to which Richard Salant had objected—tainted NPR's Central American coverage. Barnes accused NPR of taking a similar antiadministration stance on the bombing of Libya. Popular as the attack may have been with the American public, "it was not popular with NPR. In the days before and after the attack, NPR was brimming with interviews and commentaries to the effect that a tough response to Muammar Qaddafi wouldn't work." He cited a particular piece in which a Massachusetts resident commented about the death of Qaddafi's little daughter in the bombing. "Maybe if I concentrate hard enough," the commentator said, "Nancy and Ronald Reagan in the privacy of their White House bedroom will see her just as the bomb strikes." Barnes said the piece implied that "Reagan is a baby killer" and typified NPR's bias.[7]

Bennet and news Vice President Robert Siegel issued a vigorous public response. But they also sent a private message to the NPR staff. It conceded that NPR was not beyond reproach. They could not dismiss *everything* Barnes said just because much of it was clearly wrong. For example, they said, NPR needed to make certain it did not unfairly label guests by their politics. Siegel reminded the news staff that NPR was committed to objectivity and balance, to professional journalism rather than alternative or advocacy journalism:

> We are not in politics. . . . We gather information. We verify it. We solicit interesting commentary on it. We have no "policy" on Central America, or Tax Reform, or South Africa sanctions. We . . . leave a lot of ourselves at the doorstep when we enter: Religious beliefs; political convictions; financial interests.[8]

Bennet, in turn, offered what would become his standard defense against charges of liberal bias at NPR. The world is a complicated and ambiguous place, he said. Those who want it simple and have already made up their minds about issues are often upset when the world is portrayed as complex and in conflict with their views. Bennet maintained that, while most objections to NPR came from the right, NPR's performance annoyed ideologues of all persuasions:

> Events aren't flat but have depth. Real issues aren't black and white, but full of ambiguities. When we are shallow, we betray our mission; when we are not, we can expect occasionally to irritate the orthodox of all stripes, but we can enjoy the rather strong defense of having contributed to the truth.[9]

Like Mankiewicz before him, Bennet did not believe NPR provided an alternative to other media in its ideology. He believed NPR provided an alternative through the depth and complexity of its reporting. The Harvard PhD and Hubert Humphrey speechwriter believed as strongly that NPR was politically neutral as those on the Reagan right believed it was not. As his board chairman, I heard Bennet explain that the "liberals" NPR appealed to were not necessarily political liberals, but people open to—eager for—new ideas, people seeking answers to questions and understanding of issues; in other words, the products of a "liberal" education. He argued that NPR news appealed to those seeking to augment their already above-average education, and that NPR news's depth and intelligence, not any political bias, attracted them.

While basically agreeing with him, as his board chairman I pointed to a nuance sometimes overlooked. When conservatives criticized NPR, they expressed no surprise at its orientation, seeing a liberal bias as part and parcel of what NPR was. When liberals criticized NPR, they often expressed surprise and disappointment that NPR failed to meet their expectations. Both conservatives and liberals, then, seemed to share the expectation that NPR normally looked at the world through a liberal filter. NPR layered journalistic values on top of academic values, both liberal in the sense that Bennet described liberal values, that is, an openness to—an eagerness for—new ideas and evidence, an effort to put aside ideology in favor of facts and an endless quest for new insights. Public radio reflected the values of a "liberal" education, which often translated into "liberal" positions on social issues such as abortion, gay rights, and feminism, although less predictably to "liberal" positions on economic or foreign policy matters.

NPR's defenders could also point to audience data that showed that as many public radio listeners described themselves as conservative as liberal. In the general population, however, more people described themselves as conservative than as liberal, which meant the public radio audience was disproportionately liberal compared with the population at large. Even more telling, however, many who called themselves conservatives were less loyal to public radio than their liberal counterparts. Conservatives might listen to public radio in reasonably high numbers, but they probably picked some other radio station as their favorite. Sometimes they just enjoyed the classical music or Garrison Keillor or Click and Clack. Those most loyal to public radio and those who listened most regularly to NPR news programs were indeed disproportionately liberal. Such generalizations do not prove that NPR programming tilted left, but they do suggest that liberals find the news NPR presents more to their liking than conservatives.

Of course, rabid conservatives had an alternative on the radio that rabid liberals did not. The rise of Rush Limbaugh and his imitators gave conservatives places on the radio dial to call their own and provided a stark contrast with NPR that only served to reinforce conservative perceptions of a left-wing bias at the public network. A clear left-wing equivalent to Limbaugh would have placed NPR in the fair-minded middle between the two extremes. Lacking a left-wing Limbaugh, public radio became his prime alternative, as left as talk radio gets. This perception may change with the arrival in 2004 of *Air America*.

Limbaugh and his fellow conservative talkers contributed to the triumph of conservative Republicans in the midterm congressional elections of 1994. These talk shows fanned the flames against the Clintons and their health-care proposal and embraced the innovative leader of the conservative movement, Newt Gingrich and his "Contract with America." Republicans saw their first congressional majority in forty years as an opportunity to dismantle Lyndon Johnson's Great Society and apply conservative principles wherever possible. Their "Contract with America" didn't mention public broadcasting, but the new Republican majority viewed it as part of the Great Society and as an excellent example of government involvement in a field best left to the private sector. Gingrich and his fellow Republicans did not like NPR's "liberal" bias, but they liked even less the "socialistic" ideology behind a government-funded broadcasting system. Gingrich put public broadcasting near the top of his party's agenda. He vowed to "zero it out" of the federal budget.

Public radio's reaction was surprisingly ambivalent. The act of Congress that Gingrich proposed to reverse had created our "industry," as practitioners had started calling it. Even more than public television, contemporary public radio was a creature of the federal government. Yet, many in public radio seemed rather anxious to, in the words of Frank Mankiewicz a dozen years earlier, "get off the federal fix" and used this crisis to push their individual agendas.

Those who advocated "audience building" used the threat of losing federal funds to promote more audience-building efforts, like streamlining schedules and "shooting the dogs," that is, getting rid of programs that didn't attract enough listeners. They thought the loss of federal funds would forever silence those who argued that audience building should not displace "mission." Public radio would have no choice but to build audience when the federal subsidy that made "mission" possible—indeed that made "mission" necessary—disappeared and forced it to compete in the marketplace.

Those interested in developing private support for public radio through memberships, underwriting, and business ventures thought Gingrich's threat made the future theirs. Public broadcasters threw additional resources into membership programs and underwriting sales staffs. Under its new president, former telephone executive Delano Lewis, NPR created more spots for underwriting in its major programs and began to sell underwriting on a frankly commercial basis, throwing off the inhibitions that had limited these activities under Doug Bennet and his predecessors. If all federal funds were lost, underwriters would become a main source of operating revenue, and public radio could best capitalize its assets by selling its upscale listeners to those advertisers who wanted to reach them.

Those at NPR, PRI, and individual stations interested in providing national programming to other stations could argue "economies of scale" in the looming years of reduced resources. Similar arguments about economies of scale justified attempts by large stations and networks to absorb smaller stations. Marginal, "subsidized" stations would not survive in the post-Newt world, they argued. Only "consolidations," in the name of efficiency, could "save" these stations. The Gingrich threat could transform the crass acquisitiveness of Bill Kling and some others (including me) into altruistic rescues.

Kling had created an organization of the largest and most entrepreneurial stations in the system. The organization, the Station Resources Group, had enjoyed great success influencing policy in Washington. It could have helped lead the fight against the Gingrich cuts but instead focused on ways to vastly improve private fund-raising activities and to promote consolidations of weak stations into strong stations. These large stations seemed to welcome the impending end of their subsidized economy. It would liberate them to pursue their destinies and their fortunes. Bill Kling had shown the way.

Anticipating drastically reduced funding on the "flight path to zero," the Corporation for Public Broadcasting developed a plan to more effectively use reduced federal appropriations.[10] It would stop subsidizing marginal stations and focus its resources on the strongest. As its test of strength, CPB would use success in attracting audiences and in attracting private support.[11] When the actual cuts in federal support for public broadcast turned out to be far less than a flight path to zero, the CPB stuck with its new criterion. Like so many other steps ostensibly taken in reaction to "zero out" fears, success in building audience and private support reflected directions many in public radio wanted to go anyway. In the previous decade, public radio had become increasingly "audience sensitive," and CPB simply translated that sensitivity into official policy. In the fifteen years since the election of Ronald Reagan, public radio leaders, at first out of necessity and later with considerable enthusiasm, embraced the entrepreneurial spirit the president had urged upon them.

National Public Radio hired Delano Lewis to bring a businesslike approach to NPR, to generate private money, and to tap into new technologies to generate new income for public radio. This businessman replaced Doug Bennet, the government bureaucrat—not a negative word in this context—who returned to the State Department with the election of Bill Clinton and later became president of Wesleyan University. Selecting Delano Lewis said a lot about how public radio anticipated its future direction.

Lewis's entrepreneurial efforts had not proved spectacularly successful by the time Newt Gingrich assumed power in 1995. Forced to contemplate the loss of federal money without a clear source of income to replace it, Lewis and his staff had to refocus their efforts. They would fight to keep the federal funds flowing for as long as possible. Lewis tapped into his experience as a Capitol Hill lobbyist for the phone company and his heavy involvement in Democratic politics to lead the fight against the Gingrich cuts. He was very effective.

Lewis took the position that no matter what happened in 1995, inevitably public broadcasting would lose all or most of its federal support in the next few years. That position was what the Republicans wanted to hear, and it made them more open to his plea to hold off the day of reckoning until public radio was better able to deal with it. As a fresh face in public broadcasting leadership and as a black businessman, Lewis had credibility among congressmen, even conservative Republican congressmen. He had more clout than the more familiar leaders of CPB and public television, who had somewhat worn out their welcome in the halls of Congress. Unlike Sandler and Burrows, who quietly sneaked public radio into the 1967 federal legislation that public television created, Lewis became an equal partner, perhaps a senior partner, with public television in the 1995 fight to preserve that same legislation. The Republicans could accept Lewis' sincerity when he agreed with them that, in the long run, federal funds were not the way to finance public broadcasting. Lewis, therefore, could and did argue effectively for a very gradual—perhaps imperceptible—"glide path" to financial independence or for, perhaps, an endowment to replace the annual appropriation.[12]

Ultimately, however, Lewis and his partners won the fight, not because of their credibility, prowess, or perseverance, but because, in a quarter century, public radio had raised battalions of listeners in every congressional district in the country.[13] Public radio had 20 million listeners armed with 20 million votes. Public radio listeners were the best-educated people in the country and, as a correlation, among the most affluent. They knew how to work the system, and they did. While many public broadcasting supporters valued other programs the Republicans proposed to cut, they felt that public broadcasting—especially public radio—touched them more personally and more directly than, for example, the National Endowment for the Arts or Aid for Families with Dependent Children.

Most joined the fight simply because they valued public radio, particularly NPR's news programs. Some of the more thoughtful fans of less popular programming—opera, for example—recognized that public radio's increasing reliance on listener contributions and other market-dependent income would jeopardize programming for narrow interests. These people understood that unchecked market forces would drive opera and other "important" programming from public radio prime time. They saw government funding as a check on those market forces and believed it warranted preservation, perhaps augmentation. Even those in the public radio family who saw private market-sensitive support as the long-term hope for public radio wanted to hang on to as much government support as possible. Hence they launched an unprecedented campaign to save federal money, even as public radio prepared to do without it.

Listeners and viewers overwhelmed Congress with pleas to save public broadcasting. More people wrote and called to defend Social Security, of course, but the federal budget bite of Social Security dwarfed the relatively tiny $300 million then appropriated for public broadcasting. While conservative legislators might dislike what they heard on public radio and disliked even more the very idea of government-subsidized broadcasting, they ultimately concluded that any savings from eliminating federal funds for public radio and television was not worth the political price they would pay in the voting booth with incensed listeners and viewers. For true ideologues, those who hated the very idea of public broadcasting, Gingrich had fought the good fight, but he was not prepared to fight to the death.[14] Rather than "zero out" public broadcasting, Congress phased in a reduction of about 25 percent over several years. At the end of the reduction period, the Republicans quietly allowed CPB's appropriation to slip up to and beyond previous levels. By the end of the decade, the federal subsidy for public broadcasting reached the highest amount in history and no one dared talk about dropping it.

During the threatening times, however, listeners made unprecedented contributions. Gingrich may not have eliminated government support, but he did contribute to the "privatization" of public broadcasting by provoking an influx of private money.[15] Believing that federal money might disappear, public broadcasting set out on the road to self-sufficiency, a journey it did not abandon when the threat abated. Stations continued to implement their strategies for building audiences and private support. They made particular efforts to solicit major philanthropic gifts. However, they did not implement most of the painful plans they had devised to economize. When money from listeners poured in and Gingrich retreated, they set aside proposals to combine operations and reduce costs. Instead, they moved ahead with their more pleasant remedies to attract more listeners and more private income.

Ironically, when Newt Gingrich tried and failed to end federal support for public broadcasting, he probably did more to ensure the long-run success of public radio than any political leader since Lyndon Johnson. If that were not enough, he then promoted another piece of legislation that virtually assured a long, successful life for public radio. Republicans, with the cooperation of Bill Clinton, enacted the Communications Act of 1996 removing nearly all restrictions on the operations of commercial radio broadcasters. Public service had become increasingly invisible on commercial radio over two decades, but the 1996 act removed any pretext that commercial radio existed for any reason other than to make as much money as possible.

Profit, of course, is the difference between revenues and costs. Any combination of higher revenues or lower costs can increase profits. In the radio world of the late 1990s, in which the audiences are splintered among many stations, lowering costs is easier than raising income. After 1996, stations and station-group owners gobbled one another up. At the local level, a single owner might have as many as eight radio stations. This consolidation makes possible a reduction in management, sales, and technical staffs and an ability to program the stations to complement rather than to compete with one another. Even stations reluctant to consolidate had little choice if groups of their competitors did. Nationally, corporations bought out stations to the point that one station owner, Clear Channel Communication, owned well over a thousand stations across the country.

Needless to say, a corporation owning that many stations could not possibly have much commitment to—or understanding of—any of the communities it served. The conglomerate owners created formulas to plug into their stations, often programming them centrally by satellite. Purchasing more than a thousand stations in the course of just three or four years meant corporations like Clear Channel incurred huge debts. Income from advertising on those stations had to go first to servicing the debt, cutting deeply into resources for investing in local programming and services. At most stations, news and public affairs disappeared in favor of nonstop streams of cheap-to-produce music. These changes reduced commercial stations to shoestring operations. Only public radio stations, unconcerned about the bottom line, were willing to devote the resources necessary for meaningful news and public affair programming, locally or nationally.

Begun as the low-budget alternatives to mainstream commercial radio, public radio stations now spend far more money on programming than most commercial stations. The poor cousins became the standard for the most basic community service, not the alternative. As commercial radio ruthlessly cut costs, public radio steadily increased spending, attracting more and more listeners and generating more and more income from listeners and the underwriters who wanted to reach them. At the beginning of the twenty-first century, only public radio provided anything approaching meaningful radio journalism.

Conceived as "alternatives," *Morning Edition* and *All Things Considered* are the second and third most listened-to radio programs in the United States. Only Rush Limbaugh attracts more listeners. His success, in contrast to the "institutional" success of public radio, is personal—and he, unlike NPR, cannot live forever. More people now start their day with *Morning Edition* than with any other radio or television program, commercial or noncommercial. In communities with the right demographics, public radio ranks right up there with the most successful commercial stations in audience share, and even in places with demographics less hospitable to public radio, stations maintain respectable audience levels relative to commercial stations. The critics from the right never managed to kill public radio, end its federal funding, nor fundamentally change its programming. In some respects, their ire boomeranged. By reducing the federal proportion of public broadcasting's funding, they lost much of their influence over its content. They also scared public radio into embracing success as a service supported by its listeners, both financially and politically.

Ironically, Newt Gingrich helped ensure the long term prosperity of a public radio system funded by both government and listeners. He also insured that public radio would continue to serve listeners with values antithetical to his own, the contemporary equivalents of turn-of-the-twentieth-century progressives. These modern progressives "own" public radio because they pay for much of it directly and exercise political influence to protect it politically.

CHAPTER 13

Critics on the Left

U nlike critics on the right, critics on the left usually embrace public radio in theory, while expressing disappointment with public
radio's performance. Critics on the left often remain loyal listeners and
generous contributors; indeed, many of them volunteer for their public
radio stations, and more than a few work in public radio. They have exceptionally high expectations for public radio. They often know its history and philosophy, or at least the parts of its history and philosophy
with which they identify. Whether consciously or not, their criticisms
grow directly out of the purposes that Bill Siemering set for National
Public Radio at its beginning. These critics on the left complain that
public radio has not lived up to its promise. More precisely, they complain that public radio has failed to live up to one or more of the *many*
promises it and its predecessors, educational and community radio,
made over the years.

All these critics may not share political views that are strictly "left"
in terms of social, economic, or national security issues. Indeed, a minority of them are quite conservative in some or all of these areas, but
all of them criticize public radio from the left, because they all assume
the economic market system fails to provide everything that society and
its citizens need. All of them envision noncommercial radio as a stark
alternative to market-driven commercial media, and all of them see the
differences between noncommercial and commercial radio diminishing.
Fundamentally, all object to the corrupting influences of the economic
marketplace on a medium that they envision above such corruption. It
does not matter to them whether the marketplace influences come in

the form of encroaching corporate underwriting or of an unhealthy concern with pleasing listeners.

Frustrated Progressives

People who are most like the anticorporate progressive reformers of a century ago are the most frustrated with what they hear on public radio. Turn-of-the-twentieth-century progressives saw large business enterprises stifling potential competitors, corrupting government, and using the media of the day to manipulate and exploit a gullible public for their own selfish ends. Their twenty-first-century equivalents fear the encroachment of contemporary corporations and a corporate mentality on the mass media in general. They particularly fear this encroachment on public radio. The titles *Public Television for Sale: Media, the Market, and the Public Sphere,*[1] by William Hoynes, and *Made Possible by . . . The Death of Public Broadcasting in America,*[2] by James Ledbetter, suggest the nature of their indictments of noncommercial broadcasting, both television and radio.

These critics indict the corporate media for ignoring big business's indiscretions and the plight of those that the economic system treats poorly. They also indict the corporate media for blaming character flaws or "cultures of poverty" for problems that they see inherent in the economic system itself. They argue that corporate media never seriously question a capitalist economic system or consumption as a way of life and that public broadcasting's increasing dependence on corporate funds stifles its willingness to ask those questions. Edward Herman and Robert McChesney have written prolifically from this point of view.[3] McChesney and those who think like him see public radio as an uncorrupted, noncorporate bastion of independence that will increasingly succumb to the market forces that corrupt commercial media as corporate money replaces government money in its financing.

In fact, the left-of-center organization Fairness and Accuracy in Reporting has stated that the range of opinions on public radio differs little from that on commercial media. In a review of public radio, it concluded that the public medium's reporting differed from commercial media's in depth and detail, but not in its fundamental point of view: "NPR stories focus on the same Washington-centered events and personalities as commercial media."[4] It noted that the people NPR is likely to interview are the same people likely to appear on Ted Koppel's *Nightline*, another intelligent, but hardly radical, news program.

The progressive critics want to solve the creeping corporatism in public radio with more tax support for public broadcasting. Tax support, they argue, would insulate public broadcasting from the marketplace, much as Britain's television license fee frees the BBC from the marketplace. While such government support could indeed insulate public broadcasting from commercial money-grubbing, it is naive to assume that it would shift the political center of public radio to the left. Founded on academic principles intertwined with the ideals of journalistic professionalism, public radio was never any further from the political mainstream than other academic and journalistic institutions. As National Public Radio became a minor national institution, it was swimming in the middle of the mainstream, and more generous government support will not push it to the left. Why these critics see government support as a solution is somewhat mystifying, since they also believe that corporations control government. A grandstanding congressman is just as likely as a corporate giant to lash out at public broadcasting when it drifts outside the mainstream. Government is a dubious source of funding for an institution designed to question the unquestioned. In fact, any monied funder—government, corporations, foundations, or wealthy individuals—that public radio must depend upon will affect its willingness to question. Public radio is as unlikely as a dog to bite the hand that feeds it.

Modern progressives' frustration goes back to the legislation that created public broadcasting in 1967. That legislation specifically codified "fairness and balance" as the principles guiding public broadcasting journalism. Those principles are the same ones that supposedly guide commercial media. No wonder the modern progressive critics do not see enough difference between public and commercial radio.

While modern progressives express legitimate concerns, public radio does treat seriously and respectfully a broader range of ideas than do commercial media, even if it swims in the same center of the stream. It does ask questions and explores answers with reasonable skepticism. With its roots in academia, public radio more easily rejects simple answers and demands evidence than media which lack that academic heritage. Public radio cannot present the positions of the left as doctrine, but it will not present the positions of the center or the right as doctrine either.

Frustrated Pacifists

For similar reasons, public radio disappoints those in the Lewis Hill's Pacifica tradition. Corporate media seldom question America's role in the world and its investment in the military. Corporate media do not take seriously President Eisenhower's warning about the power of the "military-industrial complex." Pacifica people take that warning very seriously, and find public radio disappointing when it does not. They want NPR to take an antiwar stance, and it will not. NPR's enthusiastic and relatively unquestioning coverage of the 1991 Gulf War is an example of such disappointment. However, NPR's mainstream thinking about foreign affairs existed long before that conflict.

During the Reagan administration, news director Robert Siegel responded to State Department complaints about NPR's coverage of Nicaragua by inviting the complaining officials to lunch with the news staff. In explanation, Siegel said, "I thought it was pretty important for us to get off the self-righteous kick that anyone from the State Department is a crank and that one could safely ignore all their criticism. I don't believe that."[5] The magazine *Mother Jones* reported that Siegel expressed agreement with the State Department about the unfairness of a report that ended with the sound of relatives throwing dirt into the graves of Sandinistas killed by Contras. "It was," Siegel said, "a piece of almost entirely emotional content. It wasn't a policy piece or a strategy piece, or a state-of-the-struggle-for-Nicaragua piece."[6] It was, however, the kind of real-people piece envisioned in the Siemering purpose statement and the observations of the founding board members of NPR.

The producer of that report on the Sandinistas, Gary Covino, told *Mother Jones* that Siegel "sent the message, spoken or unspoken, that this was not the kind of stuff NPR should be doing concerning this area of the world. And people picked up on it and began to censor themselves." The article said Siegel sent the same message when he blackballed freelance reporter Paul McIsaac because of his coverage of America's invasion of the small Caribbean island of Granada during the Reagan years. McIsaac had scored a journalistic coup for NPR as one of a handful of reporters who successfully evaded the American Naval blockade of the invasion site. *Mother Jones* said McIsaac produced a "vivid and personal account of what he found from the moment he set foot on the island after the invasion." Siegel heard it differently and described the report as "dead wrong." He felt the piece gave "the impression that this was an utterly unwelcome intervention and that there was wanton brutality." Siegel told the *Mother Jones* reporter, "How one covered a U.S. intervention . . . was a very important test of our integrity." This remark led the reporter to deduce that Siegel was more worried than necessary about NPR's image in Washington.[7] Siegel responded to *Mother Jones's* criticisms by saying, "I have never been terribly concerned about left-wing magazines painting NPR as turning right. It is not something that really hurt terribly."[8]

Public radio, like any institution that is government- or corporate-funded, will never swim far from midstream. It will never assuage the Pacifica listener by taking an ideological position against war and American intervention in the world. It can and does ask the difficult questions, seek the facts, and explore the issues that might counter American foreign policy. It behaves with journalistic and academic professionalism. The Pacifica listener can expect no more from what is now a mainstream institution.

Frustrated Curators

From the days of Lord Reith at the BBC and from the beginning of American educational radio, quality took precedence over popularity in determining program schedules. Initially, these institutions pursued quality programming to educate and lift the standards of a mass population. In the Third Programme and in pre-1967 American FM educational radio, airing quality programs, rather than the impact they might have on listeners, became the goal. To those in this curator tradition, the greatest threat to quality programming was public tastes. Reith and his followers on both sides of the Atlantic wanted radio free of corporate and government influence. Reith won that freedom by financing the BBC through mandatory license fees. But even more important to Reith and his followers than freedom from business and government was freedom from *popular* influence. Curators believed that the public could not recognize quality as they could and that their role was to select and air it whether or not anyone else listened or cared.

The curatorial role dominated the latter days of educational radio. When public radio rejected the belief in quality for its own sake, the curators dissented and have continued to dissent. Indeed, the essential difference between the last years of educational radio and public radio was accepting that radio programming exists for listeners rather than for its own sake. Most public radio practitioners see their medium as a form of mass communication, and mass communication takes place only if programs reach a mass, or at least a significant, audience. Nonetheless, a declining number of critics still pine for the "quality" of yesterday. These critics fear that, in their quests for larger audiences, those who make decisions in public radio will exchange quality for popularity. They charge that marketplace values cause public radio to maximize listeners so that it can maximize its income from listener contributions and underwriters wanting to reach as many people as possible. Public broadcasters counter that they seek larger audiences to communicate quality to more people, a goal of little interest to the curators.

Curator-like listeners often accuse public radio of "dumbing down" its programming—the most mortal of sins—when a station proposes to drop live broadcasts of the Metropolitan Opera, or reduce hours of classical music, or substitute a magazine or call-in format for a lecture or documentary series. Public radio must uphold standards, they cry, even if public broadcasters demonstrate how few actually listen to the Met, the classical music, or the lecture. Statistics carry little weight with curators, who implicitly regard few listeners as a sure sign of quality and many listeners as a sure sign of debasement. "Public radio is becoming no different from commercial radio!" shriek these critics, demonstrating that they do not listen to much commercial radio.

In fact, this conflict exists more in the mind of the combatants than in reality. The listeners to whom public radio appeals *want* quality. They constitute only a relatively small slice of the population, 15 percent, but that slice comes to public radio for its quality. High standards, taste, intelligence, and understatement make public radio special. Public radio's success in building an audience depends on retaining, even enhancing those attributes.

Frustrated Mass Educators

Public radio critics who could wear the label "mass educators" make the flip side of the curator's complaint. How, they ask, can public radio ignore the other 85 percent of the population, who need education and uplift? The curators, who condemn public radio for chasing after audiences, forget that Lord Reith himself was a mass educator. Granted, he prized high-quality programs, but he also prized exposing a mass audience to them. He believed that only if listeners had no choice could the

BBC maintain the highest standards for the largest possible audience; they could listen to the best or they could listen to nothing. Hence, he insisted that the BBC have a monopoly. American educational broadcasters tried to accomplish Reith's goal without the monopoly. Frustrated, many of them went from espousing mass education to valuing quality for its own sake, from being mass educators to being curators. Mass educators who remained loyal to the Reithian tradition would never condemn public radio for seeking more listeners, assuming quality program content, but condemn it for providing its quality content only to the 15 percent minority that already wants it. Even though reaching more than that percentage, given the realities of niche radio and human nature, is impossible—Reith was right, those who do not want to listen will not—the criticism persists that public radio serves too narrow a slice of the population to justify public support or to accomplish its most noble purpose.

Ironically, those highly educated societally conscious listeners, the 15 percent, to whom public radio most appeals are likely to endorse public radio's most noble purpose. They are, after all, "societally conscious" and likely to worry about serving the 85 percent majority that public radio largely ignores. True to their ideology, such educated liberals feel guilty about ignoring the less advantaged. They worry about the poor, the minorities, the less educated. They ask if tax-supported public radio should not serve them, too? Or, perhaps, should it serve them *instead*?

NPR President Doug Bennet epitomized the mass educators' guilt. The former Hubert Humphrey speechwriter and international development expert expressed that guilt in a "draft" proposal that he floated in the spring of the year of *Audience 88*. His proposal called for public radio to aim at a radically different audience. Bennet wanted to target the poor and disadvantaged. He would retain the "lifeline" NPR already provided for people with "good educations, comfortable incomes, and a strong sense of social responsibility."[9] But he proposed "creating another 'lifeline' for listeners at the other end of the social spectrum—people who were acutely disadvantaged and whose needs were not being met adequately by either commercial or noncommercial radio." He called on NPR to discover whether radio can "help offset the disadvantages of illiteracy, help empower and motivate, and foster individuals' knowledge, dignity, and sense of worth."[10]

He acknowledged that to hit this target NPR would need to sign up additional member stations and develop totally new program concepts. He also acknowledged that these targeted listeners were not potential contributors. For funding, he proposed that "the new service should attract support from foundations and service agencies frustrated by being unable to communicate with their disadvantaged clientele."[11]

In an earlier time, Bennet's proposal might have found traction, but, in 1988, it stuck in the mud. Few in public radio believed he could be serious. Public radio had just reconciled itself to less dependence on government subsidies, identified its audience, and acknowledged the marketplace. We were enjoying some success at coaxing money from our listeners but had a long way to go. The last thing we needed in 1988 was some quixotic quest to save the world with programming we did not know how to produce to air on stations not currently part of the network for audiences we did not understand using money we did not have. Everyone with whom Bennet discussed his proposal, including me as his board chairman, told him to forget it. We needed to focus on a service for the societally conscious not a service that was itself more societally conscious.

Frustrated Populists

Bennet's proposal suggested a streak of paternalism worthy of Lord Reith. He proposed to do something *for* the less educated, the less wealthy, the less privileged. That paternalism contradicted the participatory democratic philosophy of Bill Siemering and National Public Radio's founding board. Siemering and the founding board echoed the grassroots philosophy of Lewis Hill of the Pacifica Foundation more than that of the educational radio from which they came. Just as public radio failed to "educate" 85 percent of the population, prompting Bennet's guilt and his proposal, it also failed to realize the populist philosophy of Siemering and the founding board. As "expert" journalists took more and more control of NPR programs, the voices of the people in the street became quieter and quieter. NPR's failure to become the *vox populi* its founders envisioned generated yet another criticism from the "left." These populist critics reject elitism of any type, including educational and journalistic elitism. They see public radio as too authoritarian.[12] They want radio of the people, by the people, and for the people.

Siemering and the founding board members of National Public Radio did describe public radio as a democratic instrument, as much a broadcast forum as an authoritative source of information. As board chairman Bernard Mayes put it in 1970, "The BBC is as authoritarian in its outlook as our own commercial radio is exploitive. NPR will have the lucky chance to make the invention available, at last, to the public."[13] He wanted to give voice to ordinary people and to create a place for honest discussion of issues political and issues personal, a place to foster understanding among groups. Board member Karl Schmidt saw "a true *vox populi*" as "the cornerstone of program policy."[14] It is ironic that Mayes, who came to public radio from the top-down BBC, and Schmidt, who spent his entire career at the ultimate university-based educational radio service, WHA, expressed such democratic hopes. The statements of each repudiated his own professional history and each might have reflected the excitement of the moment more than genuine conviction.

Promises by the NPR board, however sincerely made, proved difficult to implement. The opinions of ordinary people were antithetical to the authoritative analyses of faculty and other experts and to the philosophy of educational radio and Reithian radio. The opinions of ordinary people were equally antithetical to the authoritative analyses of professional journalists, who increasingly dominated National Public Radio. Public radio leadership at the local and national level nodded in agreement at the democratic purposes enunciated for NPR, but could not bring themselves to actually let listeners onto the air in a regular forum. Madison's Karl Schmidt is a case in point. He touted a *vox populi*, yet he had no inclination to listen to call-in programming on public radio and found more to dislike than to like about it when he did.

Don Quayle and his engineering staff vetoed Siemering's plan for a national call-in program in the earliest days of NPR. NPR carried the Canadian national call-in show *Cross Country Checkup* from time to time, but nothing of its own. As it turns out, I plunged NPR into the call-in format without planning to do so and without seeking permission. Like Bill Buzenberg twenty years later, I needed to fill a lot of time and had few resources to fill it. I took the plunge the day Richard Nixon resigned in August, 1974. Of course, I realized that this major story demanded special programming, but NPR—which the Nixon administration had been starving—did not have the journalistic prowess to provide continuous coverage. This pragmatic problem produced a philosophic solution. Harkening back to the founding board's vision, I decided to give citizens the opportunity to talk about what they were feeling as much as what they were thinking. For hours, we broadcast calls from listeners across the country. The result genuinely moved me. Public radio listeners proved themselves thoughtful and articulate. Some sympathized with the president, but most did not. Some were angry, but most were sad. Even those elated to see Nixon fall muted their glee to reflect the seriousness of the events. We gave expression to a genuine sense of national community. To use Bill Siemering's phrase, *This Was Radio*—public radio. The NPR board chairman called to say how proud he was of National Public Radio that day. So was I. It would take almost twenty years before such programming aired regularly on public radio, and even in its contemporary form, experts and reporters play a more important role in public-radio talk shows than do ordinary listeners. Deep down, public-radio professionals trust the public less than its populist critics do.

Frustrated Community Builders

One could not help but notice the day Nixon resigned that most of the callers sounded white and well educated. That fact, still true, is central to the frustration of those community builders who believed in the founding board's call for communication across walls of race, region, religion, and social class. The board spoke of diverse people talking *and listening* to one another, of lowering barriers and raising understanding. A naive hope, perhaps, but a powerful one in public radio's early days.

Over the years, various groups, like feminists, Hispanics, blacks, gays, and the blind have misinterpreted and subverted the hope of the community builders. They cited NPR's founders' words to demand programming *by, for, and about* their groups rather than programming to foster understanding *between* their groups. Pacifica radio and many other community stations bowed to the demand and provided each group its hour or two a week on the air in the name of free speech and free access. The community builders who wrote or believed in the real meaning of those words find such *by, for, and about* programming frustrating.

Public radio tended to resist *by, for, and about* demands because a schedule of such programs, each aimed at a different audience, simply will not work in radio. To effectively reach an audience, any radio station must consistently address that audience. Trying to serve many different audiences means not serving any of them well. The cardinal rule of radio programming is that a station must focus consistently on the one type of programming that appeals to a particular type of listener. Following that rule became more and more important as public radio turned increasingly to its most loyal listeners for support. With more than fifty stations on the dial in most places, almost any listener will find one that tries to please him or her all of the time. Only a rather special person would tune to another station that pleases him or her only some of the time.

NPR's resistance to *by, for, and about* programs, however, was as philosophical as it was practical. Like the community builders, it really does adhere to Siemering and his contemporaries' goal of bringing groups together. Very different motives drove public radio and the identity groups who demanded access. NPR sought intercommunity communication, while they sought intracommunity consciousness. Even if NPR has never achieved a level of intercommunity communication that would make the community builders happy, it has not abandoned the goal.

NPR has made a consistent effort to embrace diversity. NPR interviews a variety of people for its magazine programs and produces features about multifarious people and groups. Even the Fairness and Accuracy in Reporting report that criticized public radio for its mainstream politics acknowledged that it did a better job than most media in including the voices of a broad spectrum of the public. It fell short of what FAIR—or Bill Siemering, for that matter—would have liked, but it was more inclusive than most media.[15]

NPR has always tried to hire a diverse staff. At its beginning in 1969, National Public Radio made a conscious decision to include a variety of people on its programming staff. For example, about half of public-radio professionals were women, a disproportionate number were gay, and a disproportionate number were minorities.

In addition, NPR does attract minority listeners. Listening to public radio among *educated* minorities is just as high as it is among educated whites. If public radio divides the nation, it is by education level, not by race, gender, handicap, or sexual preference.

However, even with its efforts to resist *by, for, and about* programs, to hire a diverse staff, and to attract minority listeners, public radio cannot argue that it brings widely diverse people together to listen to one another and to better understand one another.

One public radio idealist tried to bring diverse people together. The results proved the difficulty of the task. Dr. Wally Smith made his effort at community building as public radio embraced the societally-conscious listeners that *Audience 88* identified as its natural audience. Smith, an ordained minister and manager of KUSC in Los Angeles, belligerently defied orthodoxy. At the time, his was the most listened-to public radio station in the country. He had built his success following the cardinal rule of radio: target a specific audience with specific programming. Smith targeted classical music listeners. He jettisoned almost all other programs and placed all bets on classical music with such success that he helped drive his commercial classical music competitor out of the format.[16]

Enjoying a monopoly on classical music in the nation's second largest radio market, Reverend Smith suffered a crisis of conscience and began to ponder questions: How did KUSC's classical music service differ from that of the commercial station it had displaced? Did public radio not have a mission beyond piping classical melodies into the stereo systems of upscale Angelenos? Did public radio not have a commitment to the poor and disadvantaged as well as to the wealthy and privileged? Did the University of Southern California not have an obligation to its mostly minority neighbors in south central Los Angeles? And, what was the future? As Asians, Mexicans, and other immigrant groups burgeoned in southern California, could public radio continue as an Anglo service? Did KUSC have a future if classical music turned off young people of all races and backgrounds? Smith concluded that he had to serve immigrants, minorities, women, and youth—with classical music! Smith decided to introduce diversity into classical music. KUSC would tailor its announcing style to the young. It would feature Latin or Asian performers and play works by women composers.

The results were predictable. Like devotees of any other music genre, classical listeners wanted to hear the music they liked and not what Smith thought would please somebody else. These offended listeners were as fervent about their preferences as Smith was about his social mission. Listeners complained angrily to the radio station. Alumni and university donors objected to the University of Southern California administration. KUSC alienated a significant chunk of its audience; its pledge drives reflected the alienation. If it did attract any of the listeners it targeted, their praise was faint and their financial contributions meager. The university ended Smith's pursuit of "mission," and, under new management, KUSC refocused on traditional classical music for traditional classical-music listeners. In Los Angeles, as in the nation, public radio could not ignore the realities of radio—even of public radio—as a medium that must please a specific audience. Idealistic community builders will remain forever frustrated.

Conclusion:
The Ideas Network

Although public radio has evolved beyond recognition from its origins, in fundamental ways it has not changed at all.

Public radio's combined budget now totals well in excess of a half a billion dollars a year. The stations that incorporated National Public Radio in 1970 had minuscule subsistence budgets. Today, National Public Radio supports the largest news gathering organization in American radio and among the largest of any news organization in the world. In 1967, when President Johnson signed the Public Broadcasting Act, most educational stations did little or no news, and in 1971, National Public Radio emphasized "alternative" or "sidebar" news. NPR's *Morning Edition* now reaches more people than any other morning show on radio or television. Today public radio produces two of the three highest-rated programs in all of radio. In 1967, educational radio had barely measurable audiences. In scale, professionalism, and impact, public radio bears little resemblance to the educational radio stations of just thirty-five years ago.

The characteristics of public radio's audience has not changed, however. Public radio appeals to the same highly educated, societally conscious listeners to whom educational radio appealed thirty-five years ago. Public radio just reaches many, many more of them. Public radio's professionalism and consistency have cemented the loyalty of its many listeners in a way that was impossible for the fewer, unreliable, and marginally operative educational radio stations of thirty-five years ago. Even so, public radio's loyal listeners differ little from the listeners of decades past. In other words, the basic appeal of the programs on educational and then on public radio has remained remarkably stable through the decades.

The ideals of higher education have lent that stability. Educational institutions gave the nation public radio. They pioneered its technology, provided its first practitioners, and shared their own mission to improve society. Moreover, these educational institutions gave public radio its listeners, their graduates. Institutions of higher education indelibly formed the values and attitudes of both public radio and its listeners. Many of today's public radio stations are less directly tied to the educational institutions that once owned and fully supported them, but they continue to reflect those institutions and to appeal to their graduates. Those graduates/listeners have taken over primary responsibility for supporting public radio financially and politically.

These graduate/listeners respond most enthusiastically to NPR's major news programs. In-depth news programs, however, fulfill only one of public radio's original purposes. These authoritative news programs are critical to the mission, but not sufficient. In Wisconsin, we offer those programs along with the other stalwart of public radio, classical music, but I felt a need in my last years as head of Wisconsin Public Radio to do more. I created a second network for call-in talk programming. I named it *The Ideas Network*. I wanted that network to combine what I regarded as historically the most important and viable visions for public radio. It would combine authoritative guests in the tradition of educational radio, a wide range of opinions characteristic of the Pacifica stations, and public participation in the democratic egalitarian spirit of the *National Public Radio Purposes*. It summed up for me much of what public radio was all about.

The Ideas Network's missing ingredient was diversity among its callers and listeners. It simply could not live up to that public radio purpose (I certainly would have liked it to), but a single radio station, public or not, on a radio dial brimming with other stations, can only appeal to one kind of listener. *The Ideas Network* welcomes listeners and callers of all types and attracts some unexpected calls from time to time, but its community of listeners remains, by and large, a like-minded community.

I put no music on *The Ideas Network*. I did recognize music's importance in the history of public radio and its importance to many current public radio listeners, but I do not believe music provides a future for public radio. With satellite broadcasting, Internet radio, and Internet file sharing, all types of music are now widely available to anyone at any time. Since public radio does not compose the music it presents, the music it presents will be the same music available elsewhere. Classical and other music, once the main audience draw for educational/ public radio, now occupies a secondary role. In the future music will have little, if any, role.

My pessimism about the future of music on public radio does not extend to the future of public radio itself. Having the second and third most-popular programs on radio and the largest audience of any program in radio's morning "prime time," public radio will have to fend off commercial broadcasters who want a piece, if not all, of its audience. The XM Satellite Radio service obviously had that strategy in mind when it snapped up Bob Edwards to host a national morning radio program to compete with NPR. Whatever the fate of the Edwards endeavor, commercial broadcasting will not cut seriously into public radio's audience.

The National Public Radio news programming, public radio's primary draw, costs millions of dollars to produce. Commercial radio cannot afford that level of investment and, at the same time, maximize profits. The secret of profitability in the fragmented radio marketplace among debt-ridden conglomerate terrestrial and satellite broadcasters is keeping costs low. Quality public radio programming does not come cheap. Commercial organizations cannot duplicate it profitably. If the economics do not work for commercial broadcasters at the national level, they certainly do not work at the local level, where the number of potential listeners and, consequently, the potential advertising is limited. Producing quality local programming presents public radio with its greatest opportunity. Not only are public radio stations prepared to pay more for local programming than commercial broadcasters, they can implement the populist philosophy of participatory democracy more effectively at the local level than National Public Radio can at the nation level.

Beyond the economics, however, as Frank Mankiewicz discovered when he hired top commercial broadcasters to create *Morning Edition*, and as Bill Kling discovered when he hired CBS news to produce the forerunner of *Marketplace*, even the smartest commercial broadcasters cannot quite understand public radio listeners. Their societally conscious values differ too dramatically from the achiever values of commercial broadcasters. Being noncommercial and not-for-profit translates as having integrity and being sincere to public radio listeners. In the intimate medium of radio, integrity and sincerity are hard to fake.

Notes

Introduction

1. The letter says: "Public radio has a significant role in American life today because it stands for something, for significant values, and sensibilities that resonate with our listeners. Public radio is a place of honesty, intelligence, integrity, and respect for the listener. We take the time to get the story right and to tell it in depth. We laugh with people, not at them. . . . We celebrate the culture and traditions from many communities.

"This character to our service is no accident. It reflects the character of people like Jack Mitchell. Jack has lived these values throughout his public radio career, which has spanned the entirety of public radio's modern era. Jack shaped both important institutions and important principles that give our field its distinctive character, mission, and role in American life."

Chapter 1: The Progressives

1. Steve Carney, "NPR Changes Key Host," *Los Angeles Times*, March 24, 2004.

2. W. H. Murray, "An Endowed Press," *The Arena*, October 1890; Brooke Fisher, "The Newspaper Industry," *The Atlantic Monthly*, 1902; James Rogers, *The American Newspaper* (Chicago: The University of Chicago Press, 1909); Hamilton Holt, "Commercialism and Journalism" (The Barbara Weinstock Lectures on the Morals of Trade, Boston, 1909); Will Irwin, "The Power of the Press," "The Editor and the News," "The New Era," *Colliers* 46 (1911); Hamilton Holt, "The Possibility of a University Newspaper," *The Independent*, 1912; E. E. Slosson, "The Possibility of a University Newspaper," *The Independent*, 1912.

3. Hamilton Holt, "Can Commercial Journalism Make Good, or Must We Look for the Endowed Newspaper?" *Bulletin of the University of Wisconsin, General Series No. 386* (1913).

4. Ibid.

5. George Dunlop, "Can Commercial Journalism Make Good, or Must We Look for the Public Newspaper?" *Bulletin of the University of Wisconsin, General Series No. 386* (1913).

6. Ibid.

7. The Newspaper Conference took place in Music Hall on the University of Wisconsin campus. Across the lawn from that building stands Science Hall, in which faculty and students were experimenting with wireless telephony equipment, experiments from which WHA radio would shortly emerge. On those hot August days, were the windows open in Music Hall and Science Hall? Did the oratory from Music Hall reach the ears of the physicists and students working in Science Hall? I like that image, although I have no evidence whatsoever that the link between calls for noncommercial media and the birth of noncommercial radio was ever that direct. The coincidence of time and place, however, does suggest the atmosphere in which educational radio was born.

8. Walter Lippmann, *Public Opinion* (New York: Harcourt, Brace and Company, 1922).

9. Ibid.

10. These labels came into use in the landmark presidential election of 1912, when Theodore Roosevelt, the Progressive (Bull Moose) Party candidate called his program the New Nationalism, while Woodrow Wilson, the Democratic candidate, called his the New Freedom. Republican William Howard Taft represented a more mainstream brand of Republicanism, while Eugene Debs mounted a serious campaign for the Socialist Party.

11. John Dewey, *The Public and Its Problems* (New York: H. Holt and Company, 1927).

Chapter 2: Pioneers

1. Lippmann, *Public Opinion*.

2. John Birt, "Lecture marking the 75th anniversary of the BBC," 1998, personal files.

3. Ibid.

4. I spent almost a year at the BBC radio headquarters in London in 1969–70, working on its public affairs programs and studying its operations. It was there that I came to understand the Reithian philosophy and the attempt to realize it in a contemporary, competitive media environment.

5. Stanley Penn, "History of the Development of Radio Broadcasting at the University of Wisconsin" (PhD diss., University of Wisconsin, 1959).

6. I was public-affairs director of the University of Wisconsin radio station, WHA, for a little over one year in 1968 and 1969. At that time, WHA was the

largest and most influential noncommercial radio operation in the nation. It epitomized the university extension vision of educational radio. From 1976 until 1997 I headed WHA's successor organization, Wisconsin Public Radio.

7. Herbert Hoover, *American Individualism* (Garden City, NY: Doubleday, Page and Company, 1922).

8. Robert McChesney, *Telecommunications, Mass Media, and Democracy: The Battle for the Control of U.S. Broadcasting, 1928–1935* (New York: Oxford University Press, 1993).

9. The reformers supported an amendment to the communications legislation named for its sponsor, Senator Robert Wagner of New York. The amendment to set aside 25 percent of radio channels for noncommercial uses was never rejected *per se*. It was tabled for further study and remained on the table indefinitely.

10. Professor E. L. Eubanks testified on behalf of the University of Wisconsin and other university broadcasters. He emphasized not university courses nor agricultural information but the critical role of noncommercial radio as a venue for political debate and discussion; Penn, "History of the Development."

11. McChesney, *Telecommunications*.

12. Hill committed suicide in 1957.

13. Ralph Engelman, *Public Radio and Television in America: A Political History* (Thousand Oaks, CA: Sage Publications, 1996).

14. Ibid.

15. Ibid.

16. Matthew Lasar, "Pacifica Radio's Crisis of Containment," in Michael McCauley et al., eds., *Public Broadcasting in the Public Interest* (Armonk, NY: M. E. Sharpe, 2003).

17. Pacifica featured some conservatives. Caspar Weinberger, the future secretary of defense in the Reagan administration, presented conservative commentary. The John Birch Society, a rabidly anticommunist organization, had a regular program.

18. Lasar, "Pacifica Radio's Crisis."

19. When the BBC killed the Third Programme in 1970, the defenders of that elite service invoked the name of Reith. They erroneously described the Third Programme as the epitome of his philosophy. In fact, Reith would probably have applauded the reform, which created four program streams based on genre—popular music, middle-of-the-road music, classical music, and talk—and sprinkled Third Programme material into each of them, particularly the classical and talk services. Each of the four formats appealed to an audience and each could be laced with unexpected material that might uplift, inform and educate. Reith did not seek a cultural ghetto, the essential nature of the Third Programme. He was an evangelist rather than a curator.

20. I worked at one of the largest university station of this type, WUOM at the University of Michigan in Ann Arbor, from 1964 until 1967.

Chapter 3: Public *Radio*

1. Carnegie Commission on Educational Television, *Public Television: A Program for Action* (New York: Harper & Row, 1967).
2. Ibid.
3. Ibid.
4. Ibid.
5. Ibid.
6. Ibid.
7. Ibid.
8. Jerrold Sandler, interview by Burt Harrison (Transcript, National Public Broadcasting Archives [NPBA], 1978).
9. Dean Costen Papers, NPBA.
10. Sandler interview.
11. Costen Papers.
12. Sandler interview.
13. Jack Burke, interview by Burt Harrison (Transcript, NPBA, 1978).
14. Sandler interview.
15. Jack W. Burke, "Memo to Board of Directors of National Educational Radio," April 20, 1967, *E. G. Burrows Papers,* NPBA.
16. Ibid.
17. Ibid.
18. Herman W. Land Associates, *The Hidden Medium: Educational Radio, A Status Report* (New York: The National Association of Educational Broadcasters, 1967).
19. Ibid.
20. Ibid.
21. Ibid.
22. Ibid.
23. Ibid.
24. U.S. Congress, Senate, Committee on Commerce, subcommittee on communications, *Hearings, The Public Television Act of 1967*, 90th Cong., 1st sess., 1967.
25. Burke interview.
26. Sandler interview.

Chapter 4: Purposes

1. Hartford Gunn, "A Model for a National Public Radio System," duplicated proposal, 1968, personal files.
2. Ibid.
3. Samuel Holt, *Report. The Public Radio Study* (Washington, DC: Corporation for Public Broadcasting, 1969).
4. Joseph Brady Kirkish, "National Public Radio, 1970 to 1974" (PhD diss., University of Michigan, 1980).

5. Holt, *Public Radio Study.*

6. Holt, *Public Radio Study.*

7. William Siemering, "WBFO and the Genesis of Public Radio. Remembrance," undated, personal files.

8. Ibid.

9. Ibid.

10. William Siemering, "Proposal for Radio Production Grant," June 10, 1970, personal files.

11. Ibid.

12. Karl Schmidt, "Programming and Program Policy (Memorandum to NPR Board and Staff)," September 15, 1970, personal files.

13. Joe Gwathmey, "National Public Radio Network (Memo to NPR Planning Board)," January 14, 1970, personal files.

14. Bernard Mayes, "National Public Radio—Some Preliminary Considerations (For the NPR Planning Board)," January 12, 1970, personal files.

15. William Siemering, *National Public Radio Purposes* (Washington, DC: National Public Radio, 1970).

16. Ibid.

17. Ibid.

18. Ibid.

19. Kirkish, *National Public Radio.*

Chapter 5: *All Things Considered*

1. Siemering, *National Public Radio Purposes.*

2. Gwathmey, "Network"; Mayes, "Preliminary Considerations."

3. William Siemering, "Implementation of Goals," (Washington, DC: National Public Radio, 1970).

4. Ibid.

5. Ibid.

6. Ibid.

7. Ibid.

8. Ibid.

9. Ibid.

10. Kirkish, *National Public Radio.*

11. William Siemering, "Present and Future of *All Things Considered*," memo to staff, June 16, 1971, personal files.

12. Kirkish, *National Public Radio.*

13. Stamberg's choice also proved easy on the budget, since we paid our "star" for only twenty hours a week at a rate that said pocket money for the spouse of a fully employed male. For that, we considered ourselves very forward looking, which, at the time, I suppose we were.

Chapter 6: All Things Reconsidered

1. Zelnick was indeed anti-Nixon, but far from a liberal. One did not need to be a liberal to recognize Nixon's actions as a threat to the liberties of all Americans. A former Marine and specialist in military matters, Zelnick subsequently covered the Pentagon for ABC News, but left to write a scathing biography of Democratic presidential candidate Al Gore. He then became dean of the Journalism School at Boston University.

2. As with Zelnick, Totenberg was, and remains, among the least-liberal members of the NPR staff. Her goals are not political. Instead she thrives on breaking a "big story" and the notoriety that comes with it. She told *The American Lawyer,* "I think people would be surprised at just how unliberal I really am. . . . On a lot of issues that liberals consider an article of faith, I frankly don't agree with them. On law and order issues, for example, I really am more of a cop." Gay Jervey, "Diva Nina," *The American Lawyer,* November 1993.

3. "Supreme Embarrassment," *Newsweek,* May 9, 1977.

4. John Elson, "When Reporters Make News," *Time,* October 28, 1991.

5. Jervey, "Diva Nina."

6. Richard Holwill went on to join the Heritage Foundation, a conservative think tank, and then moved into important positions in the Reagan administration.

7. Lee Frischknecht, "An Assessment of Internal Communication/Organization and Actions Required to Move toward Fulfillment of the Mission," *Frischknecht Papers* (College Park, MD: NPBA, 1976).

8. Demoralized, I left NPR reluctantly about six months after Zelnick. Ron Bornstein, an acquaintance from my days in Michigan and Wisconsin, convinced me that Frischknecht would not remain NPR president much longer. New management would soon replace him and all those associated with him, including me. Bornstein persuaded me to return to Wisconsin as manager of his radio operation. I made the move in October 1976.

9. Bornstein left management of WHA to me, while he devoted most of his time to the reforms at NPR. We talked weekly, however, about the situation in Washington. Much of this narrative derives from those conversations.

10. National Public Radio, Board Minutes, July 11, 1977.

11. Ron Wolf, "The Rise, Fall, and Rescuing of National Public Radio," *Philadelphia Inquirer,* August 14, 1983.

12. Steven Weisman, "Carter, in a Radio Call-in, Stresses Need for More Energy Conservation," *New York Times,* October 14, 1979.

13. Frank Mankiewicz, Executive office papers, box one, NPBA.

14. William Gildea, "Live from the Senate Chamber, It's. . . ." *The Washington Post,* April 4, 1978.

15. National Public Radio, "Drama on Public Radio: The Next Step," application, 1979, personal files.

16. "*Star Wars* On the Air," *Time,* April 13, 1981.

17. Robert Lindsay, "Will *Star Wars* Lure Younger Listeners to Radio?" *New York Times*, March 8, 1981.

18. Judson Klinger, "Here Comes Star Wars Again," *Playboy*, March 1981.

19. Those who knew her at NPR never characterized Cokie Roberts as radical. Boggs family members were southern Democrats. A staunch Catholic, Roberts is not the type of social radical that conservatives assumed dominated NPR.

Chapter 7: *Morning Edition*

1. This is the same Sam Holt who conducted the insightful *Public Radio Study* for the Corporation for Public Broadcasting in 1968, which told public radio not to be embarrassed if its audience was demographically narrow, as long as it was satisfied. Mankiewicz named Holt programming vice president when he took over the NPR presidency.

2. The Cohens were friends with Watergate reporter Carl Bernstein and his wife Nora Ephron. When Ephron wrote a thinly disguised autobiographical novel called *Heartburn* (New York: Alfred A. Knopf, 1983) about the breakup of her marriage to Bernstein, those in the know said Richard and Barbara Cohen were the real-life prototypes for two key characters.

3. David Giovannoni, "The State of Public Radio Programming in FY 1984," duplicated report, 1983, personal files.

4. Ibid.

5. Ibid.

6. Ibid.

7. Ibid.

8. Most stations remained part of university structures. Many of their managers saw NPR as a cooperative effort that allowed stations to fulfill their missions better than if they operated independently. Election of NPR board members by those managers reflects this view of station control. From Washington's perspective, station control meant shackling NPR, preventing it from realizing its full potential. From the station perspective, station control meant keeping NPR on track, meeting the needs of the stations, and adhering to the traditional mission of educational radio or the somewhat less-traditional mission of Bill Siemering.

9. Brooke Gladstone, "NPR Board Report," *Current*, August 20, 1982.

10. Minnesota Public Radio, "*Classicsat*, An Answer to the Challenge," brochure, 1982.

11. Jack Mitchell, contemporaneous notes during the 1983 crisis, personal files.

12. Ibid.

13. Jacqueline Trescott, "NPR Said to Use Withheld Taxes for Daily Operations," *Washington Post*, June 15, 1983; "NPR Auditors Warn of Fiscal Collapse," *Washington Post*, June 16, 1983; "NPR Financial Mismanagement Decried," June 18, 1983, *Washington Post*.

Chapter 8: *Weekend Edition*

1. Mitchell, contemporaneous notes.

2. Jacqueline Trescott, "NPR Loan Held up as Talks Hit Snag," *Washington Post*, July 15, 1983; "NPR's Drive to Survive," *Washington Post*, July 16, 1983.

3. Ronald Bornstein, personal interview with author, 1998.

4. Sally Bedell Smith, "Fate of Public Radio Could Be Decided Today," *New York Times*, July 28, 1983; "Loan Is Approved for Public Radio," *New York Times*, July 29, 1983.

5. Bornstein interview.

6. Coopers and Lybrand, "National Public Radio Consolidated Financial Statements as of September 30, 1983," duplicated report (Washington, DC: Coopers and Lybrand, 1983).

7. National Public Radio, "Five Year Business Plan," duplicated proposal, February 6, 1985, personal files.

8. I rejoined the board of directors of National Public Radio not long after Bennet arrived. I firmly supported the Mullally–Bennet taxation plan. The next year, Mullally left the board, and I replaced him as chairman for the next three years. In that role, I worked very closely with Bennet and came to respect him highly.

9. The business plan assumed a unity of purpose among stations and NPR, but also put NPR at the mercy of the stations financially. The arrangement broke down over a period of years, essentially because NPR's aspirations exceeded what the stations were willing to pay. After about three years, NPR "unbundled" its program service, providing stations some choice in what they purchased. After Bennet's departure, a new board and new president agreed to hold down station costs in exchange for NPR's freedom to aggressively seek independent funding from underwriters, foundations, and wealthy individuals.

10. Just as he set up American Public Radio to distribute programming independently of NPR, Kling instigated creation of a new organization to represent the interests of the larger public radio organizations, those least dependent on NPR. The Station Resources Group (SRG), as he called it, became Bennet's constant irritant. For leadership, the SRG found an exceptionally talented husband and wife team, Tom Thomas and Terry Clifford, who often proved themselves more effective than NPR in lobbying for the interests of their members (and, they would argue, the long term interests of public radio as a whole).

11. Dusty Saunders, "Seems Like Old Times on *Weekend Edition*," *Washington Times*, May 8, 1987.

12. Bruce Porter, "Has Success Spoiled NPR?" *Columbia Journalism Review*, October 1990.

13. Lawrence Zuckerman, "Has Success Spoiled NPR?" *Mother Jones*, June/July 1987.

14. Marc Fisher, "Soul of a News Machine," *Washington Post Magazine*, October 22, 1989.

15. Nicols Fox, "NPR Grows Up," *Washington Journalism Review* (September 1991).

Chapter 9: *Performance Today*

1. Giovannoni, "State of Public Radio Programming."
2. Ibid.
3. Corporation for Public Broadcasting, "Public Radio Member/Subscriber Support, 1970–1985," duplicated report (Washington, DC: Corporation for Public Broadcasting, 1986).
4. I was chairman of the board of NPR and the individual who formally appointed the task force. I participated in its discussions and championed its recommendations.
5. National Public Radio, "Audience-Building Task Force Report" (Washington, DC: National Public Radio, July 1986).
6. Ibid.
7. Ibid.
8. National Public Radio, "*Performance Today* Listener Reaction to Pilot," duplicated report, 1986, personal files.
9. Ibid.
10. Jack Mitchell, "Performance Today," memo to Doug Bennet, March 10, 1986, personal files.
11. William Siemering, "Some things to Consider about Audience Building," duplicated paper, August 29, 1986, personal files.
12. Ibid.
13. Lauer, Lalley, and Associates, "Summary Report on Focus Groups on Public Radio Listeners, Prepared for National Public Radio," December 1986 (Washington, DC: Lauer, Lalley, and Associates).
14. Ibid.
15. David Giovannoni, "Public Radio Listeners: Supporters and Non-Supporters," duplicated report, Washington, DC: Corporation for Public Broadcasting, 1985.
16. Tom Thomas and Terry Clifford, *Audience 88, Issues and Implications* (Washington, DC: Corporation for Public Broadcasting, 1988).

Chapter 10: *Talk of the Nation*

1. Giovannoni, "State of Public Radio Programming."
2. Jack Robertiello, "Trouble on the Second Floor," *Current*, April 20, 1988; Fisher, "Soul," and Porter, "Success."
3. Carol Matlack, "Adding a Harder Edge to Public Radio's News," *National Journal* (December 2, 1989).
4. Ibid.

5. Fisher, "Soul."

6. Ibid.

7. Porter, "Success."

8. Bill Buzenberg, "An Open Letter to All Member Stations," January 30, 1997, Washington, DC: National Public Radio.

9. Fox, "NPR Grows Up."

10. Porter, "Success."

11. Jack Mitchell, "NPR Political Coverage," memo to Doug Bennet, November 2, 1987, personal files.

12. Porter, "Success."

13. Fox, "NPR Grows Up."

14. Porter, "Success."

15. "SDX Hat Trick for National Public Radio," *Quill*, July, 1992.

16. Fox, "NPR Grows Up."

17. Ibid.

18. NPR noted a similar surge in listenership just after the events of September 11, 2001, giving rise to a widely held theory within public radio that major news events drive up listenership for NPR just as they do for cable news organizations. In contrast to cable news viewers, however, those extra listeners seem to stay with public radio after the crisis passes.

19. A few public radio stations had pioneered this approach to radio. It grew most naturally out of the state land-grant colleges of the Midwest. The University of Illinois, Ohio State University, and Michigan State University were among the first to institute the call-in approach. "Second" public radio stations in some major markets instituted this approach for parts of the day, differentiating themselves from the "first" public station in the market, which often paired NPR news with classical music. WAMU in Washington, KCRW in Los Angeles, and WBUR are examples. My own Wisconsin Public Radio took the concept to its logical extreme in 1990 by creating an entire second network built on the call-in format to complement our more traditional network built on news and classical music.

Chapter 11: *Marketplace*

1. Nicols Fox, "Public Radio's Air Wars," *Columbia Journalism Review* (January 1992).

2. My term on the NPR board ended in 1988. I was subsequently elected for another six years beginning in 1993. Delano Lewis became president before I returned to the board, and his first board meeting as president coincided with my first meeting as a returning board member. Most board members were content to see Bennet return to the State Department after Clinton's election, freeing them to hire a businessman who would concentrate on raising money for NPR through grants, underwriting, and entrepreneurship, thus relieving pressure on station budgets and the limitations on NPR growth that went with them.

3. In late 2004, NPR reinstituted the "business news" segment of *Morning Edition*, but with a very "public radio" approach. The new segment contained no market information. Instead it provided "human interest" features about the economy.

4. AMPERS (Association of Minnesota Public and Educational Radio Stations), "Policy on State Non-Commercial Radio Development," *Mankiewicz papers* (College Park, MD: NPBA, 1977).

5. Al Hulsen, Letter to NPR President Doug Bennet regarding anti-trust, January 7, 1987, personal files.

6. Jack Mitchell, Letter to Al Hulsen regarding anti-trust, January 20, 1987, personal files.

7. Aaron Kahn, "MPR Is Successful Raising Money; Its For-profit Sister is Even Better," *St. Paul Pioneer Press*, February 26, 1995.

8. Minnesota Public Radio, "Friends and Supporters of MPR," letter to MPR membership from board chairs of Minnesota Communications Group and its two subsidiaries, March 19, 1998.

9. In 2004, National Public Radio gained a similar level of autonomy from its member stations and the economic marketplace when the widow of McDonald's founder Ray Kroc left $250 million to NPR in her will. NPR placed the money in an endowment, similar to that of MPR, but considerably larger.

10. Kahn, "MPR successful."

11. William Kling, "New Year/Old Thoughts," January 2, 1997, open letter to MPR staff and public radio station managers (St. Paul: Minnesota Public Radio).

Chapter 12: Critics on the Right

1. Corporation for Public Broadcasting, "Radio Listening Estimates to Qualifying Corporation for Public Broadcasting Stations," 1973, duplicated report.

2. NPR finally got access to the White House the week Nixon resigned. Without asking White House permission, we simply called the telephone company and ordered a broadcast line from the White House to NPR. We figured that the White House press office would be too preoccupied to object, and we were right. Since the White House had not credentialed any NPR reporters, we hired a freelance reporter with White House credentials from the Canadian Broadcasting Corporation to broadcast on our newly installed broadcast line. The Ford administration quickly granted NPR the credentials and White House access the Nixon administration had denied us for three years.

3. John Witherspoon and Roselle Kovitz, *A History of Public Broadcasting* (Washington, DC: Current Publishing Company, 2000).

4. Zuckerman, "Success."

5. Fred Barnes, "All Things Distorted," *New Republic*, October 27, 1986.

6. Ibid.

7. Ibid.

8. Robert Siegel, "Fred Barnes' Piece on NPR," memo to news staff, October 9, 1986, personal files.

9. Douglas Bennet, "Barnes' piece," duplicated memo to NPR staff, October 10, 1986, personal files.

10. Corporation for Public Broadcasting, "Public Radio Issues and Policies Task Force Interim Report" (Washington, DC: Corporation for Public Broadcasting, 1995).

11. Ibid.

12. Elizabeth Rathbun, "Congress Keeps up Threat to Public Broadcasting," *Broadcasting and Cable*, January 23, 1995, and "Public Broadcasters Look Elsewhere for Funds," *Broadcasting and Cable*, February 27, 1995.

13. Kim McAvoy, "Public Broadcasters Go on Offense," *Broadcasting and Cable*, December 19, 1995.

14. Paul Farhi, "Big Bird Taken off Death Row?" *Washington Post*, July 13, 1995.

15. Corporation for Public Broadcasting, "Public Broadcasting Revenue by Major Source," www.cpb.org.

Chapter 13: Critics on the Left

1. William Hoynes, *Public Television for Sale: Media, the Market, and the Public Sphere* (Boulder CO: Westview Press, 1994).

2. James Ledbetter, *Made Possible By . . . The Death of Public Broadcasting in the United States* (New York: Verso, 1997).

3. Edward Herman and Robert McChesney. *The Global Media: The New Missionaries of Corporate Capitalism* (New York: Cassell, 1997).

4. Engelman, *Public Radio and Television.*

5. Zuckerman, "Success."

6. Ibid.

7. Ibid.

8. Ibid.

9. Douglas Bennet, "Draft Proposal for a New Public Radio Service," June 6, 1988, personal files.

10. Ibid.

11. Ibid.

12. Engelman, *Public Radio and Television.*

13. Mayes, "Preliminary Considerations."

14. Schmidt, "Programming."

15. Engelman, *Public Radio and Television.*

16. John Horn, "KUSC Signals Its Graduation," *Los Angeles Times*, October 8, 1985.

Bibliography

Books

Avery, Robert K., ed. *Public Service Broadcasting in a MultiChannel Environment: The History and Survival of An Ideal*. White Plains, NY: Longman, 1993.

Balas, Glenda. *Recovering a Public Vision for Public Television*. Lanham, MD: Rowman & Littlefield Publishers, 2003.

Blakely, Robert J. *The People's Instrument: A Philosophy of Programming for Public Television*. Washington, DC: Public Affairs Press, 1971.

———. *To Serve the Public Interest: Educational Broadcasting in the United States*. Syracuse, NY: Syracuse University Press, 1979.

Burke, J. E. *An Historical-analytical Study of the Legislative and Political Origins of the Public Broadcasting Act of 1967*. New York: Arno Press, 1979.

Calhoun, Craig, ed. *Habermas and the Public Sphere*. Cambridge, MA: MIT Press, 1993.

Carnegie Commission on Educational Television. *Public Television: A Program for Action*. New York: Harper & Row, 1967.

Carnegie Commission of the Future of Public Broadcasting. *A Public Trust*. New York: Bantam, 1979.

Collins, Mary. *National Public Radio, The Cast of Characters*. Washington, DC: Seven Locks Press, 1993.

Dewey, John. *The Public and Its Problems*. New York: H. Holt and Company, 1927.

Engelman, Ralph. *Public Radio and Television in America: A Political History*. Thousand Oaks, CA: Sage Publications, 1996.

Ephron, Nora. *Heartburn*. New York: Alfred A. Knopf, 1983.

Ford Foundation. *Ford Foundation Activities in Noncommercial Broadcasting, 1951–1976*. New York: The Foundation, 1976.

Garrels, Ann. *Naked in Baghdad: The Iraq War as Seen by NPR's Ann Garrels*. Farrar, Straus, and Giroux, 2003.

Gross, Terry. *All I did was ask: Conversations with Writers, Actors, Musicians, and Artists*. New York: Hyperion, 2004.

Herman, Edward, and Robert McChesney. *The Global Media: The New Missionaries of Corporate Capitalism*. New York: Cassell, 1997.

Herman W. Land Associates. *The Hidden Medium: Educational Radio, A Status Report*. New York: National Association of Educational Broadcasters, 1967.

Hoover, Herbert. *American Individualism*. New York: Doubleday, Page and Company, 1922.

Horowitz, David, and Laurence Jarvik. *Public Broadcasting and the Public Trust*. Los Angeles: Center for the Study of Popular Culture, 1995.

Hoynes, William. *Public Television for Sale: Media, the Market, and the Public Sphere*. Boulder CO: Westview Press, 1994.

Jarvik, Laurence. *PBS: Behind the Screen*. Rocklin, CA: Forum, 1997.

Lasar, Matthew. *Pacifica Radio: The Rise of an Alternative Network*. Philadelphia: Temple University Press, 2000.

Ledbetter, James. *Made Possible By . . . The Death of Public Broadcasting in the United States*. New York: Verso, 1997.

Lewis, Peter, and Jerry Booth. *The Invisible Medium: Public, Commercial, and Community Radio*. Washington, DC: Howard University Press, 1990.

Lippmann, Walter. *Public Opinion*. New York: Harcourt, Brace and Company, 1922.

Looker, Thomas. *Sound and the Story: NPR and the Art of Radio*. Boston: Houghton Mifflin Company, 1995.

Macy, John W. *To Irrigate a Wasteland*. Berkeley: University of California Press, 1974.

McCauley, Michael, Eric Peterson, B. Lee Artz, and DeeDee Halleck, eds. *Public Broadcasting in the Public Interest*. Armonk, NY: M. E. Sharpe, 2003.

McChesney, Robert W. *Telecommunications, Mass Media and Democracy: The Battle for the Control of U.S. Broadcasting, 1928–1935*. New York: Oxford University Press, 1993.

———. *Rich Media, Poor Democracy: Communication Politics in Dubious Times*. Urbana: University of Illinois Press, 1999.

McKinney, Eleanor, ed. *The Exacting Ear*. New York: Pantheon Books, 1966.

Milam, Lorenzo. *The Original Sex and Broadcasting*. San Diego: Mho & Mho Works, 1988.

Noam, Eli, and Jens Walterman, eds. *Public Television in America*. Gütersloh, Germany: Bertelsmann Foundation Publishers, 1998.

Rogers, James. *The American Newspaper*. Chicago: The University of Chicago Press, 1909.

Stamberg, Susan. *Talk. NPR's Susan Stamberg Considers All Things*. New York: Perigee Books, 1994.

Starr, Jerold M. *Air Wars: The Fight to Reclaim Public Broadcasting*. Boston: Beacon Press, 2000.

Stone, David M. *Nixon and the Politics of Public Television*. New York: Garland Publishing, 1985.

Streeter, Thomas. *Selling the Air: A Critique of the Policy of Commercial Broadcasting in the United States.* Chicago: University of Chicago Press, 1996.

Tracey, Michael. *The Decline and Fall of Public Service Broadcasting.* New York: Oxford University Press, 1998.

Wertheimer, Linda, ed. *Listening to America: Twenty-five Years in the Life of a Nation, as Heard on National Public Radio.* Boston: Houghton Mifflin, 1995.

Witherspoon, John, and Roselle Kovitz. *A History of Public Broadcasting.* Washington, DC: Current Publishing Company, 2000.

Journals, Dissertations

Croteau, K., W. Hoynes, and K. Carragee. "The Political Diversity of Public Television: Polysemy, the Public Sphere, and the Conservative Critique of PBS." *Journalism and Mass Communication Monographs* (1996).

Dunlop, George. "Can Commercial Journalism Make Good, or Must We Look for the Public Newspaper." *Bulletin of the University of Wisconsin, General Series No. 386* (1913).

Fox, Nicols. "NPR Grows Up." *Washington Journalism Review* (September 1991).

———. "Public Radio's Air Wars." *Columbia Journalism Review* (January 1992).

Haney, James. "A History of the Merger of National Public Radio and the Association of Public Radio Stations." PhD diss., University of Iowa, 1981.

Holt, Hamilton. "Can Commercial Journalism Make Good, or Must We Look for the Endowed Newspaper?" *Bulletin of the University of Wisconsin, General Series No. 386* (1913).

Kirkish, Joseph Brady. "National Public Radio, 1970 to 1974." PhD diss., University of Michigan, 1980.

Matlack, Carol. "Adding a Harder Edge to Public Radio's News." *National Journal* (December 2, 1989).

McCauley, Michael. "From the Margins to the Mainstream." PhD diss., University of Wisconsin–Madison, 1997.

Mitchell, Jack. "Britain Debates Broadcasting in the Seventies." *Journal of Educational Broadcasting* (June 1970).

Penn, Stanley. "History of the Development of Radio Broadcasting at the University of Wisconsin." PhD diss., University of Wisconsin, 1959.

Porter, Bruce. "Has Success Spoiled NPR?" *Columbia Journalism Review* (October 1990).

"SDX Hat Trick for National Public Radio." *Quill*, July 1992.

Stavitisky, A. G. "The Changing Conception of Localism in U.S. Public Radio." *Journal of Broadcasting and Electronic Media* 38 (1994).

———. "Guys with Suits and Charts: Audience Research in U.S. Public Radio." *Journal of Broadcasting and Electronic Media* 39 (1995).

Stavitisky, A. G., and T. W. Gleason. "Alternative Things Considered: A Comparison of National Public Radio and Pacficia Radio News Coverage." *Journalism Quarterly* 71 (1994).

Press Accounts

Adelson, Andrea. "The Business of National Public Radio." *New York Times*, April 5, 1999.

Barnes, Fred. "All Things Distorted." *The New Republic*, October 27, 1986.

Beek, James. "Satellite Radio Network Debut." *Forecast Magazine*, August 1980.

Brady, Frank. "*Star Wars* Was a Stunning Experience." *Fantastic Magazine*, March 1981.

Carney, Steve. "NPR Changes Key Host." *Los Angeles Times*, March 24, 2004.

Elson, John, and S. S. Gregory. "When Reporters Make News." *Time*, October 28, 1991.

Farhi, Paul. "Big Bird Taken off Death Row?" *Washington Post*, July 13, 1995.

Fisher, Brooke. "The Newspaper Industry." *The Atlantic Monthly*, 1902.

Fisher, Marc. "Soul of a News Machine." *Washington Post Magazine*, October 22, 1989.

Gildea, William. "Live from the Senate Chamber, It's. . . ." *Washington Post*, April 4, 1978.

Gladstone, Brooke. "NPR Board Report." *Current*, August 20, 1982.

———. "Uneasy NPR Board Edges out Chairman Jones." *Current*, June 21, 1983.

———. "Even More Distress Signals from NPR." *In These Times*, June 29, 1983.

———. "NPR Drive to Survive Draws $2.1 Million in 3 Days." *Current*, August 9, 1983.

Holt, Hamilton. "The Possibility of a University Newspaper." *The Independent*, 1912.

Horn, John. "KUSC Signals Its Graduation." *Los Angeles Times*, October 8, 1985.

Ingrassia, Lawrence. "Live from St. Paul, Here's *A Prairie Home Companion*." *Wall Street Journal*, January 21, 1981.

Irwin, Will. "The Power of the Press," "The Editor and the News," and "The New Era." *Colliers* 46, 1911.

Jervey, Gay. "Diva Nina." *The American Lawyer* (November 1993).

Kahn, Aron. "MPR Is Successful Raising Money; Its For-profit Sister Is even Better." *St. Paul Pioneer Press*, February 26, 1995.

Klinger, Judson. "Here Comes Star Wars Again." *Playboy*, March 1981.

Lewis, Anthony. "Nightmare Brought to Life." *New York Times*, April 23, 1981.

Lewis, Dennis. "NPR 'Sticks' Promises to Chill Your Spine." *Washington Times*, October 27, 1982.

Lindsay, Robert. "Will Star Wars Lure Younger Listeners to Radio?" *New York Times*, March 8, 1981.

McAvoy, Kim. "Public Broadcasters Go on Offense." *Broadcasting and Cable*, December 19, 1995.

Murray, W. H. "An Endowed Press." *The Arena*, October 1890.

"New Cycle for Adam Powell." *Broadcasting and Cable*, January 22, 1990.

"NPR Stations Approve CPB Loan Agreement." *Broadcasting and Cable*, July 24, 1983.

Peterson, Iver. "Rivalry Grows at Low End of Dial." *New York Times*, March 2, 1998.

Rathbun, Elizabeth. "Congress Keeps up Threat to Public Broadcasting." *Broadcasting and Cable*, January 23, 1995.

———. "Public Broadcasters Look Elsewhere for Funds." *Broadcasting and Cable*, February 27, 1995.

———. "Delano Eugene Lewis, President/Chief Executive Officer of National Public Radio." *Broadcasting and Cable*, March 20, 1995.

"Report on CPB Board." *Broadcasting and Cable*, June 27, 1983.

Robertiello, Jack. "Trouble on the Second Floor." *Current*, April 20, 1988.

Saunders, Dusty. "Seems Like Old Times on *Weekend Edition*." *Washington Times*, May 8, 1987.

Slosson, E. E. "The Possibility of a University Newspaper." *The Independent*, 1912.

Smith, Sally Bedell. "Fate of Public Radio Could Be Decided Today." *New York Times*, July 28, 1983.

———. "Loan Is Approved for Public Radio." *New York Times*, July 29, 1983.

"*Star Wars* On the Air." *Time*, April 13, 1981.

"Supreme Embarrassment." *Newsweek*, May 9, 1977.

Trescott, Jacqueline. "NPR Said to Use Withheld Taxes for Daily Operations." *Washington Post,* June 15, 1983.

———. "NPR Auditors Warn of Fiscal Collapse." *Washington Post*, June 16, 1983.

———. "NPR Financial Mismanagement Decried." *Washington Post*, June 18, 1983.

———. "NPR Loan Held up as Talks Hit Snag." *Washington Post*, July 15, 1983.

———. "NPR's Drive to Survive." *Washington Post*, July 16, 1983.

Vick, Karl. "Newspaper Brings Woe to Wobegon." *Minneapolis Star*, January 29, 1981.

Weisman, Steven. "Carter, in a Radio Call-in, Stresses Need for More Energy Conservation." *New York Times*, October 14, 1979.

Wolf, Ron. "The Rise, Fall, and Rescuing of National Public Radio." *Philadelphia Inquirer*, August 14, 1983.

Zuckerman, Laurence. "Has Success Spoiled NPR?" *Mother Jones*, June/July 1987.

Pamphlets, Memos, and Similar Sources

Association of Minnesota Public and Educational Radio Stations. "Policy on State Non-Commercial Radio Development." *Mankiewicz Papers*. College Park, MD: National Public Broadcasting Archives (NPBA), 1977.

Association of Public Radio Stations and National Public Radio. *Public Radio: The Next Step*. Pamphlet. Washington, DC: APRS and NPR, 1977.

Bennet, Douglas. "NPR Financial Status and Debt Retirement." Duplicated report. Washington, DC: National Public Radio, 1984.

———. "Questions and Answers on NEA Grant." Draft memo. April 7, 1986. Personal files.

———. "Barnes' Piece." Duplicated memo to NPR news staff. October 10, 1986. Washington, DC: National Public Radio.

———. "Draft Proposal for a New Public Radio Service." Duplicated report. June 6, 1988. Personal files.

Birt, John. "Lecture Marking the 75th Anniversary of the BBC." 1998. Personal files.

Burke, Jack W. "Memo to Board of Directors of National Educational Radio." April 20, 1967. *E. G. Burrows Papers*. College Park, MD: NPBA.

———. Interview by Burt Harrison. Transcript. College Park, MD: NPBA, 1978.

Burrows, E. G. Papers. College Park, MD: NPBA.

Buzenberg, Bill. "An Open Letter to All Member Stations." January 30, 1997. Washington, DC: National Public Radio.

Cambridge Associates, Inc. "American Public Radio Toward a Market-Oriented Strategy." Duplicated report. Cambridge, MA: Cambridge Associates, 1987.

Cohen, Barbara. "NPR Plus News and Information Programming." Duplicated report. November 19, 1982. Washington, DC: National Public Radio.

Coopers and Lybrand. "National Public Radio Consolidated Financial Statements as of September 30, 1983." Duplicated report. Washington, DC: Coopers and Lyband, 1983.

Corporation for Public Broadcasting. "Public Radio and Its Subscribers in the Washington, D.C., area." Duplicated report. Washington, DC: Corporation for Public Broadcasting, 1972.

———. "Radio Listening Estimates to Qualifying Corporation for Public Broadcasting Stations." Duplicated report. Washington, DC: Corporation for Public Broadcasting, 1973.

———. "Public Radio Member/Subscriber Support, 1970–1985." Duplicated report. Washington, DC: Corporation for Public Broadcasting, 1986.

———. "Public Radio Issues and Policies Task Force Interim Report." Duplicated report. Washington, DC: Corporation for Public Broadcasting, 1995.

———. "Public Broadcasting Revenue by Major Source." Corporation for Public Broadcasting Website, www.cpb.org, 2000.

Costen, Dean. Papers. College Park, MD: NPBA.

Estell, Richard. "Comments from Dick Estell (to the National Public Radio Planning Board)." Duplicated memo. January 9, 1970. Personal files.

Frischknecht, Lee. "An Assessment of Internal Communication/Organization and Actions Required to Move toward Fulfillment of the Mission." Duplicated report. *Frischknecht Papers*. College Park, MD: NPBA, 1976.

———. Papers. College Park, MD: NPBA.

Giovannoni, David. "The State of Public Radio Programming in FY 1984." Duplicated report. Personal files, 1983.

———. "Public Radio Listeners: Supporters and Non-Supporters." Duplicated report. Washington, DC: Corporation for Public Broadcasting, 1985.

Gunn, Hartford. "A Model for a National Public Radio System." Duplicated proposal. Personal files, 1968.

Gwathmey, Joe. "National Public Radio Network (Memo to NPR Planning Board)." January 14, 1970. Personal files.

Harris, Louis, and Associates. "The Listening of Public Radio." Washington, DC: Corporation for Public Broadcasting, 1971.

Hirschman, Ruth. "The News at NPR." Message sent to all NPR member stations. May 17, 1983. Personal files.

Holt, Hamilton. "Commercialism and Journalism." The Barbara Weinstock Lectures on the Morals of Trade, Boston, 1909.

Holt, Samuel. *Report. The Public Radio Study*. Washington, DC: Corporation for Public Broadcasting, 1969.

———. "Islands in the stream." Duplicated paper. Washington, DC: National Public Radio, 1986.

Hulsen, Al. Letter to NPR President Doug Bennet regarding antitrust. January 7, 1987. Personal files.

Kling, William. "New Year/Old Thoughts." Open letter to MPR staff and public radio station managers. January 2, 1997. St. Paul: Minnesota Public Radio.

Lauer, Lalley, and Associates. "Summary Report on Focus Groups on Public Radio Listeners, Prepared for National Public Radio." December 1986. Washington, DC: Lauer, Lalley, and Associates.

Mankiewicz, Frank. Executive Office Papers, Box One. College Park, MD: NPBA.

Mayes, Bernard. "National Public Radio—Some Preliminary Considerations (for the NPR Planning Board)." Memo. January 12, 1970. Personal files.

Metropoulos, Effie. "Peak Listening Hours." Duplicated report. December 5, 1986. Washington, DC: National Public Radio.

Minnesota Public Radio. "*Classicsat*, An Answer to the Challenge." Brochure. 1982.

———. "Friends and Supporters of MPR." Letter to MPR membership from board chairs of Minnesota Communications Group and its two subsidiaries. March 19, 1998. St. Paul: Minnesota Public Radio.

Mitchell, Jack W. Contemporaneous notes during 1983 crisis. Personal files.

———. "Performance Today." Memo to Doug Bennet. March 10, 1986. Personal files.

———. Letter to Al Hulsen regarding antitrust. January 20, 1987. Personal files.

———. "Bundling." Memo to Doug Bennet. March 19, 1987. Personal files.

———. "NPR political coverage." Memo to Doug Bennet. November 2, 1987. Personal files.

National Public Radio. Board Minutes. July 11, 1977.

———. "Drama on Public Radio: The Next Step." Application. 1979. Personal files.

———. "Five Year Business Plan." Duplicated proposal. February 6, 1985. Washington, DC: National Public Radio.

————. Resolution to adopt NPR business plan. May 22, 1985. Personal files.

————. *"Performance Today* Listener Reaction to Pilot." Duplicated report. 1986. Personal files.

————. *Audience-Building Task Force Report.* Washington, DC: National Public Radio, July 1986.

————. "New Study Shows that NPR Has Become Primary News Source for Headlines and Breaking News." Press release on NPR Web site, www.npr.org. September 24, 1999.

Sandler, Jerrold. Interview by Burt Harrison. Transcript. NPBA, 1978.

Schmidt, Karl. "Programming and Program Policy (Memorandum to NPR Board and Staff)." September 15, 1970. Personal files.

Siegel, Robert. "News Priorities." Memo to programming committee. July 9, 1986. Personal files.

————. "Fred Barnes' Piece on NPR." Memo to News and Information Staff. October 9, 1986. Personal files.

Siemering, William. "WBFO and the Genesis of Public Radio. A remembrance." Undated. Personal files.

————. "Proposal for a Satellite Radio Studio." 1968. Personal files.

————. *National Public Radio Purposes.* Washington, DC: National Public Radio, 1970.

————. *Implementation of Goals.* Washington, DC: National Public Radio, 1970.

————. "Proposal for Radio Production Grant (for *This Is Radio*)." June 10, 1970. Personal files.

————. "Present and Future of *All Things Considered.*" Memo to staff. June 16, 1971. Personal files.

————. "Future Program Development." Memo to staff. October 1972. Personal files.

————. Memo to staff members (upon his resignation). December 11, 1972. Personal files.

————. "Some Things to Consider about Audience Building." Duplicated paper. August 29, 1986. Personal files.

Thomas, Tom, and Terry Clifford. *The Public Radio Program Marketplace.* Washington, DC: Corporation for Public Broadcasting, September 1985.

————. *Audience 88, Issues and Implications.* Washington, DC: Corporation for Public Broadcasting, December 1988.

U.S. Congress. Senate. Committee on Commerce, subcommittee on communications. *Hearings, The Public Television Act of 1967.* 90th Cong., 1st sess., April 11, 1967.

Wirth, Timothy. Letter to the CPB President Robben Fleming. May 22, 1979. *Mankiewicz papers.* NPBA.

Wycisk, Max. "Performance Today." Memo to Jack Mitchell on March 14, 1986. Personal files.

Zelnick, Robert. "To All Concerned. Open Memo to NPR Staff and Stations." May 9, 1976. *Frischknecht papers.* NPBA.

Index

ABC, 136, 138

Accuracy in Media, 167

Adams, Noah, 116, 135

Adler, Margot, 116

Albee, Edward, 89

All Things Considered: author as producer, 68–73, 75–78, 80–81; beginning, 59, 62, 65–68; during Bennet presidency, 115–116, 123, 128–129, 133, 163, 175; during Mankiewicz presidency, 90, 93, 98; and *Morning Edition*, 94, 96, 98–102

"All Things Distorted," 167

American Civil Liberties Union and Lewis Hill, 20–21

American Individualism, 15

American Public Radio, 87, 104–105, 110; and anti-trust, 153–154; and business show, 147, 149–150

Association of Public Radio Stations, 82

Audience: educational radio demographics, 3, 39, 45; public radio demographics, 145–146, 169, 173, 183, 189–190; size, 100–101, 119–120, 135, 142, 145, 173; values, 3, 66, 73, 133, 168–169, 189–190

Audience 88, 132–134, 145–148, 151, 183, 187

Audience building, 119–122, 127, 170; task force, 122–129, 132–134

Audience research, 125–133

Bailey, George, 101, 126

Barnes, Fred, 167–168

Bennet, Douglas: and American Public Radio, 153–154; and audience building, 120; background, 111–112; and business plan, 112–113; and critics, 151, 168–169; and news, 116–117, 135–136, 138–140, 166; and *Performance Today*, 119, 123–125; and service to poor, 171–172, 183–184

Boal, Dean, 124–125

Bornstein, Ronald: and *Earplay*, 89; and 1983 crisis, 106–111, 113; and 1977 merger of NPR and APRS, 81–84

British Broadcasting Corporation: founding philosophy, 13–14, 16, 18–19, 181, 183; Home Service, 24; Light Service, 24–25; as model for Americans, 28, 31–32, 54–55, 63, 71, 120; Third Programme, 24–26, 28

Bundy, McGeorge, 161

About the Author

JACK W. MITCHELL was the first producer of *All Things Considered* and served three times as Chair of the NPR board of directors. He is now a Professor in the School of Journalism and Mass Communication at the University of Illinois, where he teaches courses in public broadcasting, broadcast journalism, and mass media and society.